THE Horticulture GARDENER'S GUIDES
Planting with trees

Andrew & Rosamond McIndoe

HORTICULTURE
BOOKS

A HORTICULTURE BOOK
Copyright © David & Charles Limited 2007

Horticulture is an F+W Publications Inc. company
4700 East Galbraith Road
Cincinnati, OH 45236

First published in the US in 2007

Text copyright © Andrew McIndoe and Rosamond McIndoe 2007

Andrew McIndoe and Rosamond McIndoe have asserted their rights to be
identified as authors of this work in accordance with the Copyright, Designs
and Patents Act, 1988.

ISBN-13: 978-1-55870-811-2
ISBN-10: 1-55870-811-1

Printed in Singapore by KHL Printing Co Pte Ltd
for Horticulture Publications, Boston, Massachusetts

Visit our website at www.hortmag.com

**Produced for David & Charles by
OutHouse Publishing**
Winchester Hampshire SO22 5DS

Series Consultant Andrew McIndoe

For OutHouse Publishing:
Series Editor Sue Gordon
Art Editor Robin Whitecross
Editor Polly Boyd
Design Assistant Caroline Wollen
Proofreader Lesley Riley
Indexer June Wilkins

For David & Charles:
Commissioning Editor Mic Cady
Editorial Assistant Emily Rae
Designer Sarah Clark
Production Controller Beverley Richardson

American edition by Creative Plus Publishing Ltd.,
2nd Floor, 151 High Street, Billericay, Essex CM12 9AB, United Kingdom.

Previous page (left to right): *Acer platanoides* Princeton Gold ('Prigo'), *Pinus wallichiana*, *Acer pseudoplatanus* f. *variegatum* 'Leopoldii'

Above (left to right): *Sorbus* 'Sunshine', *Acer rufinerve*, *Eucalyptus parvifolia*, *Betula szechuanica*, *Prunus* 'Pandora', *Magnolia* × *soulangeana* 'Rustica Rubra'

ORNAMENTAL PLANT OR PERNICIOUS WEED?

In certain circumstances ornamental garden plants can be undesirable when introduced into natural habitats, either because they compete with native flora, or because they act as hosts to fungi, bacteria, and insect pests. Plants that are popular in one part of the world may be considered undesirable in another. Horticulturists have learned to be wary of the effect that cultivated plants may have on native habitats and, as a rule, any plant likely to be a problem in a particular area if it escapes from cultivation is restricted and therefore is not offered for sale.

Contents

Introduction

Trees are among the oldest and largest living things on our planet. They have played a vital role throughout man's evolution, providing fuel, food, building materials, weapons, paper, and an enormous number of other essentials.

Trees are so much a part of the structure of our world that they often go unnoticed. Despite their size and presence, their diversity and beauty goes unappreciated. In a garden, the lifespan of a tree often exceeds that of the gardener, and certainly the planting that surrounds it, yet little attention is paid to the value of its contribution. Meanwhile smaller plants are praised and admired for their blooms, their compact habit, and maybe their foliage.

All gardens, however small, need trees. Not just a token tree in the lawn, but trees used as part of the planting scheme, to complement the other plants and to contribute essential height. Mature trees are sometimes seen as a disadvantage in a garden, especially a small one. But if the right plants are chosen to grow around them, they present no problem.

When we moved from a small garden to a much larger one—an empty plot surrounded by mature oaks—we suddenly had space for more trees. Cautiously we started encroaching into the central space with about six favorite trees. Our greatest problem was deciding where to position them and what their impact would be immediately, in ten years, in 30 years, and beyond our lifetime. Timescale is such an important factor and we, like most other gardeners, are gardening for today but with a thought for the future.

The number of trees in our garden has increased over the past five years to more than 30, and we have plans for more. Some will undoubtedly have to be removed in the future to give others the space to develop. We believe that trees should be treated like other, smaller garden plants—they need not necessarily be permanent items that should be preserved regardless of their state of health or what they contribute to the planting.

No garden stands still. It grows and develops, and the trees are very much a part of that evolution. They can add to the garden in so many ways—with their diverse shapes and silhouettes, with beautiful foliage, colorful flowers, or interesting bark. And at the same time they provide a habitat for wildlife.

However, as with any other garden plant, a tree should be selected not only for its features but also for its ability to thrive in the chosen situation. We hope that this book on English-style tree planting will help gardeners select trees as part of their planting scheme and that it will encourage them to plant more trees.

Andrew & Rosamond McIndoe

WHAT IS A TREE?

A tree is a woody plant with a single stem arising from ground level that divides into a number of branches at a height of 3 ft. (1 m) or more. This distinguishes it from a shrub, which has multiple stems arising from the ground. The definition of tree or shrub has nothing to do with size—there can be large shrubs and small trees. In broader terms, any plant with a stem and a head can be used to fulfil the role of a tree in a garden design.

A standard tree has 6 ft. (2 m) of clear stem from ground level to the base of the head. A feathered tree, on the other hand, has a definite single stem rising from the ground but has light side branches, often to ground level.

Availability

Some of the trees mentioned are new and others are traditional British varieties, which, if you can find them, will give authenticity to your design. These sources will help you create a traditional, English-style planting:
Ecolage, 2623 West Sale Road, Lake Charles, Louisiana 70605, tel (toll free) (866) 562 8088
Forest Research Nursery, University of Idaho, PO Box 441137, Moscow, Idaho 83843, tel (208) 885 3888

USDA hardiness zones

Most species listed in this book thrive in temperate areas (around Zone 7), and the seasonal changes described apply to these areas. With the exception of annuals, zones are given next to each species name, and cultivars are suitable for the same zones unless otherwise stated. Remember that a plant's site can also affect its hardiness.

Zone	Avg. annual min. recorded temp.	Zone	Avg. annual min. recorded temp.
1	Below -50oF	7	0oF to 10oF
2	-50oF to -40oF	8	10oF to 20oF
3	-40oF to -30oF	9	20oF to 30oF
4	-30oF to -20oF	10	30oF to 40oF
5	-20oF to -10oF	11	Above 40oF
6	-10oF to 0oF		

To find your zone, see the USDA zone map on the back flap of this book.

LEFT: Springtime at West Green House, Hampshire, in England.

INTRODUCING TREES

Gardens need trees. They provide essential vertical structure, and are the highest points around which the rest of the planting is assembled. As trees are the most dominant living features in our landscape, selecting the right ones and using them to their best advantage can be a daunting prospect. However, if a little thought is put into their selection and cultivation, they will become key focal points in the garden picture, giving pleasure for many years to come.

RIGHT: *Quercus rubra*.

Trees through the ages

Trees have been cultivated since antiquity, for their fruit and their ornamental qualities. Topiary, the art of trimming and training trees and shrubs, was born in ancient Rome and has since been in vogue at several points over the centuries, while the Landscape Movement of the 1700s introduced the naturalistic use of trees on a grand scale. For the last 150 years gardeners have enjoyed an ever-growing range of trees, from those introduced by Victorian plant hunters to compact forms specially bred for the small modern plot.

Above: The olive, *Olea europaea*. Above right: A trimmed *Carpinus betulus*, hornbeam, dominates a knot garden composed of box, yew, and berberis.

The earliest known tree to be cultivated is the date palm, *Phoenix dactylifera*, which has been grown for over 6,000 years. Not only does it produce fruit but it has attractive architectural leaves and a tall, stately single stem; pillars in ancient Egyptian temples were modeled on palm trees.

Ancient Mediterranean civilizations were dependent on the olive, *Olea europaea*, for its oil, extracted by pressing the ripe fruits. Olive oil continues to be the foundation of the Mediterranean diet today. Olive trees are remarkably long-lived: it is believed that some of the trees alive today are so ancient they were in existence at the time of Christ.

The Romans, as their empire spread, took fruit and nut trees with them to colonies across Europe, North Africa, and western Asia. They introduced the walnut (*Juglans*) and sweet chestnut (*Castanea*) into the British Isles.

THE ORNAMENTAL USE OF TREES

Egyptian tomb paintings dating from 2,500 BC depict some of the earliest cultivated gardens, with trees, flowers, and water used in formal rectangular designs. We also know that dwarf trees were grown in pots in China some 4,000 years ago—the birth of the art of bonsai. In Japan, where the Chinese style of gardening was adopted in the 6th and 7th centuries, trained dwarf trees were used with rocks, gravel, mosses, and ferns to create miniature landscapes that echoed the natural world.

THE TREE OF LIFE

Since earliest times, civilizations throughout the world have believed trees to be powerful and significant; the Tree of Life is an important symbol in many religions. Ancient peoples believed the tree represented Mother Earth, providing food, shelter, and protection for all. In the Bible, the Tree of Life stands at the center of the Garden of Eden, connecting heaven and earth.

For centuries, in times of prosperity, trimmed and trained woody plants formed the basis of European garden design. In the 16th century, the wealthy began to use hedges to enclose areas alongside their houses where ornamental flowers and herbs were grown for the enjoyment of the occupants of the house and their visitors. The Italian Renaissance had seen the birth of formal gardens, with patterns created by low hedges of trimmed evergreens, usually boxwood, and this style of gardening was soon adopted by the French in the parterre and the English in the knot garden. The Dutch, too, created formal gardens, often including flower bulbs, such as tulips and auriculas. In all cases, any trees were formally trimmed and trained, usually as standards and often in containers.

In the 17th century, both the French and the English used deciduous trees formally, in grand avenues, often leading up to the house. These were affluent times, the golden age of topiary. Trimmed and trained evergreen plants were popularized by Mollet, gardener to James I of England (James VI of Scotland), who often used them in conjunction with avenues of deciduous trees.

LANDSCAPE GARDEN TO SUBURBIA

The 18th century saw a move away from formality to more naturalistic gardens, influenced greatly by British landscape gardener Lancelot 'Capability' Brown (1716–83). A pupil of architect and landscape gardener William Kent (1685–1748), Capability Brown is best known for ambitious schemes that included diverting rivers, forming lakes, re-contouring great tracts of land and, perhaps most importantly, transplanting mature trees. Examples of his work can be seen at Blenheim Palace, Oxfordshire, and at Prior Park in Bath, Somerset. Trees were to be the dominant feature in the landscape garden for many years to come.

The Victorian era saw the beginning of the main influx of new plant introductions into our gardens. Wealthy garden owners and some nurseries sponsored plant hunters to travel to remote regions of the world in search of the unknown, the rare, and the unusual. Although much was found in a relatively short period of time, new discoveries were jealously guarded by the gardening aristocracy, so the wider availability of new woody plants was in many cases

Hillier Nurseries in England, in the 1950s, supplying a growing demand for plants for smaller, suburban gardens.

delayed. Also, some newly introduced trees and shrubs took years—even generations—to reveal their potential, especially if they were brought back as seed. *Magnolia campbellii*, for example, takes 15 years or more to flower, as does *Davidia involucrata*, the handkerchief tree. Plant introductions continued apace into the 20th century, and it is surprising to learn how recently some of our popular trees and shrubs arrived in the West. For example, *Acer griseum*, the paper-bark maple, was brought to the West by Ernest Wilson in 1901, and *Metasequoia glyptostroboides*, the dawn redwood, was introduced in 1948.

In the 20th century, rapid population increases and the spread of the suburbs meant that gardens became smaller and more numerous. As a result, there was a growing demand for different types of plants, particularly for small, compact trees that would not outgrow their position in gardens or amenity plantings. Hybridists and nursery workers continue to work hard at selecting more compact forms of species and raising hybrids to fulfill these needs.

Why have trees in the garden?

There are many compelling reasons to plant trees. Not only are they highly ornamental, they form an essential part of the garden's long-term framework and their size and structure influence all the other elements in the garden. They also provide shelter, shade, and privacy. Trees create a vital link between the garden and the natural landscape, and they benefit the environment in many different ways.

A pleasing landscape has interest at all levels. In the lowest layer of the planting, below eye-level, are dwarf shrubs, ground-cover plants, herbaceous perennials, and bulbs. This is the level at which we tend to focus most of our efforts, frequently changing, rearranging, and adding color to the display. In the middle layer, at eye-level, shrubs, taller perennials, and climbers steal the show; this is the most prominent part of the picture. Above eye-level, trees come into their own. They provide essential height and a three-dimensional element. Without trees, gardens seem flat and uninteresting, and they also appear smaller.

Although the highest layer of planting belongs to the trees, they are not content with this alone. They also steal attention in the lower layers: some display interesting bark, and deciduous trees cover the plants and ground beneath with a colorful deluge of leaves in fall and, in some cases, a delicate shower of flower petals in spring.

Many trees are productive as well as ornamental, producing seeds and fruits for consumption by wildlife and man. Trees grown specifically for their fruit, such as apples, pears, plums, and cherries, can fulfill a decorative function in the garden in the same way as trees grown specifically as ornamentals. Most fruit trees have attractive

Liquidambar styraciflua, sweet gum, is an impressive structural tree, spectacular in fall.

spring blossom, and a well-grown specimen in full fruit is a wonderful sight—as long as the birds don't get there first. Fruit trees do require a little more attention than most ornamentals and few have good autumn foliage color.

Some ornamental trees, such as crab apples (*Malus*) and sorbus, produce edible fruits that can be used for making preserves. Walnuts (*Juglans*) are wonderful majestic trees for large gardens, and mulberries (*Morus*) and medlars (*Mespilus*) have a fascinating historical heritage; they have been cultivated in our gardens for centuries.

SHELTER AND SHADE

The size and habit of a tree has a direct influence on the amount of sunlight that reaches plants under its canopy or within its shadow. The extent of the shade may vary with the direction of the sun, the time of day, and the season of the year. Also, the area of shade will usually become larger as the tree grows and matures. Shade should not be seen as a disadvantage—in shade, foliage normally appears richer in color and more defined, and there are many lovely plants that resent direct sunlight; even those that enjoy full

The spreading branches of *Cercidiphyllum japonicum* create dappled shade and in fall cover the ground with a fragrant carpet of fallen leaves.

sun can appear pale and bleached in the glaring light of midsummer sun. Always select plants that are suitable for the conditions.

The dappled shade found at the edge of the canopy of a deciduous tree provides the ideal conditions for growing a wide range of plants, including woodland subjects. Some trees, such as birch (*Betula*) and alder (*Alnus*), have an open leaf canopy and provide dappled shade right up to the trunk of the tree. This means that they do not steal planting space—an important consideration in a smaller garden.

SHADE FOR COMFORT

When planning a garden, it is important to consider the pleasure and comfort of those using the space, as well as its aesthetic appearance. Some shade is necessary in any garden. Whether eating *al fresco* or reading a book on a hot summer's day, most people prefer to sit in the shade for comfort as well as for health reasons. The natural shade provided by a tree or a vine-clad arbor is cooler and more attractive than the shade of a parasol or gazebo. A strategically positioned tree that casts shade upon an area that is used when the sun is at its strongest is ideal. Trees with large leaves, such as *Acer platanoides* 'Drummondii', cast heavier shade than those with small leaves, such as *Acer negundo* 'Elegans'.

SHELTERED GARDENS

Many great gardens could never have been established without the planting of substantial shelter belts of trees that afford protection to the more delicate plants. Gardens such as Tresco Abbey (above), on the Scilly Isles, and Logan Botanic Garden, in Galloway, Scotland, can cultivate tender and subtropical subjects. This is not only because of their proximity to the sea warmed by the Gulf Stream, but also because of the shelter provided by belts of pines (*Pinus*) and evergreen oaks, for example *Quercus ilex*.

At The Garden House, in Buckland Monachorum, Devon, in England, birches and other native trees provide a natural link between the garden and the landscape that surrounds it.

Trees can also provide invaluable shelter for other plants, as well as for people enjoying the garden. Deciduous species and some conifers can be planted to filter the prevailing wind, reducing its physical impact and the effect of wind chill. Some trees, such as pines (*Pinus*) and evergreen oaks (*Quercus*), are particularly resistant to wind, even when it is salt-laden, making them suitable for coastal gardens.

A well-positioned tree will shelter the patio from a prevailing wind, making it a more comfortable place on which to sit in sunny but windy weather. In a large garden on a cold, exposed site, trees planted along the boundaries facing the prevailing wind will have a dramatic effect on the success of plants in the garden, and will influence what can be grown there.

PRIVACY AND SCREENING

One of the great benefits of trees is that they can screen the garden from the outside world and provide privacy. Indeed, the need for seclusion is often the most common stimulus for planting a tree in a small garden. Before planting a tree for privacy, remember to take into account all the prime factors, such as the amount of shade cast by the tree, its ultimate size, the amount of space required, and the proximity of buildings (see page 15).

CREATING DRIER CONDITIONS

In warm weather, a deciduous tree, particularly a large, mature specimen, loses a large amount of water through its leaves, especially in windy weather. This moisture needs to be replaced from the soil. On particularly wet sites, you can take advantage of this by planting thirsty trees such as willows (*Salix*) to help drain the soil of water and provide drier conditions for other plants.

Some plants, especially certain bulbs, corms, and tubers, thrive in the dry conditions around the roots of deciduous trees. They take advantage of the additional light and water available in late winter and early spring to produce leaves and flowers. Once the leaf canopy robs them of light and water, they retreat beneath the surface and lie dormant until the following spring. (See pages 42–43.)

To most gardeners looking for an effective screen, a solid evergreen tree that will block out as much of the offending view as possible in the minimum amount of time might seem to be the obvious choice. However, a well-positioned, attractive deciduous tree will often do the job more efficiently. It will attract the eye and, by allowing light to pass through its branches, it will draw attention away from the object to be screened. By its very nature, the natural, irregular framework and outline of a tree contrasts with and overpowers the regular, angular lines of a man-made building or structure.

A LINK TO THE LANDSCAPE

In a rural situation, garden trees form a link with the surrounding landscape; they both bring the countryside into the garden and extend the garden beyond its boundaries. Just as a garden should fit the property to which it is attached, so it should be in keeping with its surroundings. The trees selected must sit comfortably in the rural landscape (see pages 100–103).

In an urban situation, trees may provide the upper layer of the entire visible landscape or may be part of a connecting layer of tree canopy that eventually links with the countryside many gardens away. In a town garden, it is often possible to 'borrow' the trees of neighboring gardens as part of the overall design.

ENVIRONMENTAL BENEFITS

Even a single garden tree can provide a valuable habitat for wildlife, attracting animals, birds, and insects. Birds use trees for shelter, roosting, and nesting, and as a natural larder. Trees that produce berries and fruit, such as sorbus, cotoneaster, and crab apples (*Malus*), are particularly appreciated by birds. In turn, a tree equipped with a hanging bird feeder and a nesting box can provide an endless source of pleasure for the garden owner, particularly when it is visible from the windows of the house.

Trees also play a crucial role in maintaining wildlife corridors through our towns and cities—they are the aerial masts that enable migrating wildlife populations to locate the green oases within built-up areas, and they act

A mature *Acer griseum* fits into a small garden, providing privacy and screening and enhancing the urban environment.

as look-out towers and landing platforms. Where enough trees are planted in gardens, the impact that expanding urbanization has on some wildlife populations will be significantly reduced.

Another very good reason for including trees in a garden is to improve air quality, a particularly important factor in urban environments. Plants take carbon dioxide from the air and water from the soil and convert them into starch for growth and development. In doing so, they discard oxygen, which is then used in the respiration process of all living things.

In urban areas, plants play a vital part in replenishing the oxygen in the atmosphere depleted by traffic and industry. As no plants are better equipped to do this than trees, it is essential that we include them in our gardens wherever possible.

Trees in garden design

There are a number of different ways to include trees in the garden. Most frequently they have been used as specimens, positioned to stand alone in a lawn. However, now we that have become more adventurous with garden design and the range of plants has broadened, trees are increasingly combined with other plants and are used in a variety of situations. Because trees live longer than most other garden plants, you need to consider timescale when making design decisions.

Carpinus betulus, hornbeam, trained as a 'hedge on legs' provides height in the foreground and windows through to the garden beyond.

Small trees can be used to provide height in mixed borders containing shrubs, herbaceous perennials, and roses. Many can be grown in containers or in very confined spaces, especially if they are trimmed and trained to introduce a degree of formality (see pages 86–93). Trees can also be used as effective screens, to provide shelter, and to create divisions between properties. A barrier of trees, sometimes referred to as a 'hedge on legs', can create essential screening but still allows room for interesting plants to be grown in the ground beneath, an area that a traditional hedge would completely fill.

TREES AS SPECIMENS

The positioning of a tree that is to be planted as a specimen in a lawn is critical (see opposite). Without the softening effect of planting surrounding it, the tree will be a dominant focal point from the moment it is planted. As it grows bigger, it will become even more prominent, so it is important to select a tree that will remain in proportion to the size both of the lawn and of the garden as a whole.

TREES WITH OTHER TREES

When planting more than one tree, or planting a tree alongside existing trees, consider the ultimate height and spread of each of the trees concerned. Some trees work well planted in groups, especially in informal situations, such as a paddock. This is often how the silver birch, *Betula pendula*, and the wild cherry, *Prunus avium*, grow in nature, so they are ideal choices for this purpose in a country garden. However, most trees need plenty of space to develop their potential, so bear this in mind when making plans. The lifespan of the trees involved may be significant: Trees can often be planted in close proximity if one is to be removed before the other matures. This practice is used in amenity plantings and forestry situations, and is a form of thinning.

CONSIDER TIMESCALE

Most trees are planted for their effect in the shorter term rather than for future generations. We have probably all seen examples of mistakes made in the past: a monkey puzzle, *Araucaria araucana*, planted in the front garden of a 19th century villa and probably now far too large and towering awkwardly above the house; housing developments full of decapitated and butchered specimens of *Cedrus atlantica* Glauca Group planted in the 1980s, parkland trees confined to postage-stamp gardens. However, although no gardener wants to plant a subject that will be a problem in the future,

Magnolia × soulangeana in a tiny city garden screens the street from the house and supports a *Clematis montana*, which flowers after the magnolia.

or a potential threat to his own or neighboring properties, a tree does need to fulfill its role in a realistic timescale. A very slow-growing subject may well be the right choice for a small space in the long term, but if it takes 30 years to make a significant impact, and the gardener is going to live there for only ten years, then the tree has not done its job.

TREES NEAR BUILDINGS

There is always concern about the impact of trees on buildings—the threat of a tree falling onto a property and the damage its roots may do to foundations and drains. This should not be ignored, but it is important to note that not all trees pose a threat; also, much depends on the age and health of the tree and the type of soil it is growing in.

If you wish to plant trees near a building, choose subjects with compact root systems, such as birch (*Betula*), sorbus, hornbeam (*Carpinus*), and magnolia; these rarely cause problems. Willows (*Salix*), however, tend to seek out water, so their roots are liable to invade drains if planted close by. If an existing tree is a concern, seek expert advice from a reputable tree surgeon or advisor.

POSITIONING IS VITAL

The strategic positioning of a tree can have a dramatic effect on the perspective of the garden and on the orientation of its layout.

A tree or a group of trees can be used as a focal point, an exclamation mark to draw the eye. Trees planted in the foreground increase the perspective, while those in the distance give a sense of scale. So, in a small garden, a large tree in the foreground and a small tree at the end of the garden will make the garden seem longer.

Where more than one specimen tree is to be planted in an area of grass, the relationship of one tree to another will be critical to the effect. This relationship may change according to where you are in the garden. Use tall bamboo canes to mark the proposed planting stations, and view these from various angles, including the windows of the house. Consider what the trees will look like as they grow and what they might obscure.

Height and shape

Our ability to judge the height and spread of anything above head height is limited, so it is not surprising that we have difficulty gauging the size of trees. Because some trees are such large, dominant structures, we are often fearful of planting them. However, the ultimate size of a tree is rarely a cause for concern for the gardener who planted it. The lifespan of a tree varies from roughly 25 to more than 300 years, so its ultimate size may not be reached for several generations.

The height and spread that a tree will achieve depends on the growing conditions, as well as the vigor and habit of the particular variety in question. Like all plants, most trees grow best on a well-drained but adequately moist, fertile soil. On shallow alkaline and sandy soil that is lacking in nutrients, and when the tree's roots are confined in a container or a raised bed, growth will be restricted and the tree will not reach its full potential.

The habit and shape of trees also vary according to the species and, often, with age. A tree that is narrow and compact when young may become broader as the tree gets older. For example, *Carpinus betulus* 'Fastigiata' can be very narrow and upright as a young specimen but makes a broad tree with upright branches when mature.

Weeping trees and those with a compact, upright habit make a striking contrast to the majority in the tree canopy. They need careful positioning if they are to fulfill their potential and their role in the garden. A tree of upright habit can be planted to rise out of surrounding shrubs and perennials, or can perhaps be positioned as a statement at the end of a border. To be seen at its best, a weeping tree usually needs either to stand alone or to hang its branches above a carpet of low ground-cover plants.

Aesculus indica matures into a large round-headed tree, often becoming more oval-headed with age. This tree would have been planted long before the house was built.

TREE NAMES

Just as a tree's name may indicate its place of origin, habitat, color, or size, so it sometimes describes its habit. For example:

pendulus means weeping—as in *Cotoneaster* 'Hybridus Pendulus' (**1**)

fastigiata means upright, fastigiate— as in *Taxus baccata* 'Fastigiata' (**2**)

columnare means columnar—as in *Acer platanoides* 'Columnare'

ULTIMATE HEIGHTS OF TREES

In this book, trees are classified as:

Dwarf—ultimate height less than 10 ft. (3 m)

The height is usually attained quite quickly, because the plants are top-worked (grafted onto a stock 6 ft./2 m or so high). Examples include: *Acer palmatum* var. *dissectum* 'Crimson Queen', *Cotoneaster* 'Hybridus Pendulus', *Salix caprea* 'Kilmarnock'.

Small—ultimate height 15–30 ft. (5–10 m)

Could reach the height of an average two-story house in 20 years or so. Most trees recommended for small gardens fall into this category; some will only get as tall as the upstairs windows. Examples include: *Malus floribunda*, *Pyrus salicifolia* 'Pendula', *Sorbus* 'Joseph Rock'.

Medium-sized—ultimate height 30–60 ft. (10–20 m)

Growing higher than the average house, but this does not mean the tree is unsuitable for the average garden if it has a slight habit and light canopy. Many birches fall into this category. Examples include: *Acer platanoides* 'Crimson King', *Betula utilis* var. *jacquemontii*, *Robinia pseudoacacia* 'Frisia'.

Large—ultimate height over 60 ft. (20 m)

These are potentially big trees for large gardens, parks, and open spaces. Some, such as oak (*Quercus*) and beech (*Fagus*), are fairly slow-growing. Others, such as ailanthus, are quite fast. Most are long-lived subjects and do not reach their potential in the gardener's lifetime. Examples include: *Cedrus deodara*, *Fagus sylvatica*, *Quercus robur*.

TREE SHAPES

The trees in this book are classified into the following shapes. This is only a guide to the potential habit of a tree; trees vary from one to another, and growing conditions, surrounding plants, and climate may affect the growth of individual specimens.

Round-headed

Branches form a rounded canopy, which may become more spreading with age. Examples include: *Crataegus* × *laevigata* 'Paul's Scarlet', *Acer platanoides* (**1**).

Spreading

Branches form a canopy that is wider than it is high. Examples include: *Malus floribunda*, *Prunus* 'Shirotae' (**2**).

Conical

Branches form a conical head. This can be narrow, as in *Pyrus calleryana* 'Chanticleer', or broad, as in *Carpinus betulus* (**3**).

Broadly columnar to oval

Branches form a broad column or oval above the trunk; this may be because the branches grow outward and curve upward, as with the oak *Quercus frainetto* 'Hungarian Crown' (**4**), or the tree may form layers of branches radiating from a central stem, as with the monkey puzzle, *Araucaria araucana*.

Columnar or fastigiate

Branches may form a narrow column on top of a short trunk, or the tree may be grown with ascending branches from ground level, so there is no obvious single stem originating from ground level. Examples include: *Prunus* 'Amanogawa', *Quercus robur* f. *fastigiata*, *Prunus* 'Rancho' (**5**).

Weeping

Branches weep from the crown of the tree. This may be a result of grafting a prostrate plant on top of a stem, as in *Salix caprea* 'Kilmarnock', or it may be the tree's natural habit, as is the case with *Salix* × *pendulina* var. *elegantissima* (**6**).

Speaking botanically

Latin plant names can be daunting to both the novice and the experienced gardener. However, a little knowledge of botanical Latin helps gardeners to understand the characteristics of the plants they are growing. Most importantly, botanical names avoid confusion. While common names of plants vary from place to place, Latin names are used internationally and ensure accurate identification.

PLANT CLASSIFICATION

FAMILIES All flowering plants are classified into families. Each family contains a number of genera that share similar characteristics. These genera can include plants of all types—woody and herbaceous—and the characteristics they share can be subtle or obvious. For example, hawthorn (*Crataegus*, above) and cotoneaster, which are not the same genus, are both members of the rose family, Rosaceae. They appear quite different at first inspection, but close examination will reveal similarities, in this case in the structure of the flowers and the fruits.

GENUS The first part of the botanical name, the generic name, always starts with a capital letter and is always a noun. In some cases, it is derived from a name found in another language, for example *Tsuga* and *Catalpa*.

Generic names often commemorate people, perhaps the person who introduced the plant to cultivation or discovered it. For example, *Davidia involucrata*, the handkerchief tree (above), was discovered by the French missionary Père David (although it was introduced to the West later, by Ernest Wilson).

SPECIES The specific name, or epithet, follows the genus name and always starts in lower case. As a Latin adjective, it normally takes the gender of the generic name, so its ending agrees with the noun. However, there are always exceptions; in fact, there are more exceptions with trees than other plants. The Latin word for tree, *arbor*, is feminine, so a tree's specific name normally has a feminine ending, even if the genus appears masculine. For instance, the white poplar is *Populus alba* rather than *Populus albus*, as might be expected.

The specific name may indicate where the plant comes from. For example, *Acer japonicum* tells us that the tree comes from Japan. Alternatively, the name may give a clue

BOTANICAL NAMES

A botanical name consists of the generic name followed by the specific name. Both can convey information about the plant: its place of origin, size, habit, color, and a host of other characteristics. The generic or specific name may relate to the person who discovered or introduced it. As most plant hunters usually worked in a particular country or region, the name alone may give the gardener a clue as to where the plant originates. For example, Ernest Wilson is well known for plant-collecting in China, therefore plants that bear his name, such as *Magnolia wilsonii*, are usually of Chinese origin.

Classification and naming of plants is ongoing. Often new evidence comes to light that results in the reclassification and therefore renaming of a plant. If an old name is well known, it is often shown after the new name.

to its natural habitat, for example *Acer campestre*, meaning 'of fields', indicates that this is not a tree from the forest but one of more open habitats. Often the specific name describes features of the plant, such as size, habit, leaf shape, or flower color. For example, *Magnolia grandiflora* tells us the plant has large flowers. As with the generic name, the specific epithet often commemorates a botanist, plant collector, or famous horticulturist, for example *Trachycarpus fortunei* (opposite, top right) is named after the plant hunter Robert Fortune, who introduced the Chinese windmill palm to England in 1849.

SPECIES AND HYBRIDS   Species are collected from the wild, while hybrids usually originate in gardens or nurseries. Over the years, gardeners have cross-pollinated species and, in some cases, genera. Where a hybrid has originated from a cross between two species, the new

hybrid epithet is preceded by a multiplication sign, for example *Populus* × *jackii* 'Aurora'. Both species and hybrids can show much variation between individuals when they are propagated by seed. However, this is not always the case: Distinct and recognizable forms, classified as subdivisions of a species that occur in the wild, are known either as subspecies (ssp.), varietas (var.), or forma (f.), for example, *Betula utilis* var. *jacquemontii* (left).

CULTIVARS   A cultivar is a distinct, selected form of a species, a clone that has been maintained by vegetative methods of propagation only, such as cuttings or grafting (never seed). So all offspring are identical to the original and all originate from the one specific plant. The cultivar name always begins with a capital letter and is written

within single quotation marks. It follows the specific name—as in *Gleditsia triacanthos* 'Sunburst'. In the garden, the terms cultivar, form, selection, and variety may be used interchangeably.

GROUPS   Groups are used to classify a collection of individuals that are very similar but are impossible to identify individually from a botanical point of view. These individuals are often raised from seed but show relatively little variation in their characteristics, as in *Fagus sylvatica* Atropurpurea Group (left).

SPECIFIC NAMES RELATING TO OTHER TREES
Many trees have specific names that liken them to other trees.

Quercus ilex: oak with leaves like a holly (*Ilex*)
Quercus castaneifolia: oak with leaves like a chestnut (*Castanea*)
Acer carpinifolium (above):
maple with leaves like a hornbeam (*Carpinus*)
Pyrus salicifolia: pear with leaves like a willow (*Salix*)

Buying trees

Trees are sold in a number of different ways. Traditionally, they were grown in the field and lifted, with bare roots, during the dormant season for immediate transplanting into gardens and landscape schemes. However, some types of trees do not respond well to this treatment and are more successfully transplanted with less disturbance to the roots. Hence the advent of rootballed and container-grown specimens.

BARE-ROOT TREES

Normally, only deciduous trees are offered bare-root. These are lifted during the dormant season, when fairly young, and are transplanted during the same fall and winter. The roots are usually protected by a loose plastic bag, to prevent desiccation and frost damage. It is often surprising how lifeless the tree appears when it arrives, and how little root there is. Secure staking and tying is essential for establishment (see page 22), and watering is critical, particularly if a dry spring follows planting.

Trees should only be bought in this form from a reputable specialist nursery. They must have been regularly transplanted, or undercut, during their time in the nursery to encourage a compact root system and to prevent the early formation of strong tap roots that will be cut off during transplanting. Some trees transplant successfully in this way even as large specimens, for example *Acer platanoides*, *Acer campestre*, *Alnus cordata*, *Crataegus laevigata*, *Prunus avium*, and many others.

BALLED AND BURLAPPED TREES

Balled and burlapped (B&B) trees are also lifted from the field in the dormant season. However, the roots are cut out with a ball of soil that is kept intact using burlap and sometimes a wire cage. This keeps the young fibrous roots in contact with soil and minimizes disturbance.

A young half-standard *Fagus sylvatica* 'Atropurpurea'. The lower branches could still be removed to raise the crown and make a standard tree.

TERMS DESCRIBING YOUNG TREES

There are a number of terms used to describe young trees.

A **maiden tree** is a young plant, usually only one year old, with a single stem and no branches. This term is often used for fruit trees.

A **feathered tree** has side branches down the main stem, often to ground level. Young container-grown trees are often sold in this form. It is up to the gardener to remove the branches to whatever level is desired.

A **standard tree** has at least 6 ft. (2 m) of clear stem below the first branches. Heavy standards and extra-heavy standards refer to standard trees of greater stem girth.

A **half standard tree** has only 3 ft. (1 m) or so of clear stem below the branches. Fruit trees are often grown in this form to make picking easier.

A **multi-stemmed tree** has two or more main stems from ground level, with the intention that the tree will continue to develop with these stems. Birches and other trees grown for their bark are often grown in this form.

Lifting in this way may be done by hand using a spade or, particularly in the case of larger specimens, by machines. These are heavy to handle and care is needed not to break the rootball or the tree.

The ball and burlap method is always used for evergreen trees, such as *Magnolia grandiflora* and *Quercus ilex*, and for conifers. Some deciduous trees are best transplanted in this way, too, as the failure rate is high when they are transplanted bare root. These include the walnut *Juglans regia*, *Liquidambar styraciflua*, and most birches, apart from young specimens of *Betula pendula*.

CONTAINER-GROWN TREES

Container-grown specimens have the advantage that they can be transplanted at any time of the year. However, fall, winter, and early spring is still the best time to plant as the tree has time to establish before the foliage is fully developed in summer. A typical garden-center stock tree will be grown in a 2.5–4 gallon pot and will be 8–10 ft. (2.5–3 m) tall. This may seem small, but container trees of this size are easy to handle and quick to establish.

Larger trees for instant impact: standard *Betula utilis* var. *jacquemontii*.

Young container-grown, feathered *Robinia pseudoacacia* 'Frisia', suitable for further training in the garden.

WHAT SIZE OF TREE TO BUY

Tree size is normally measured not in height but in girth. The circumference of the main stem is measured in inches, at a height of 3 ft. (1 m) above the ground; this gives an indication of the age and maturity of the tree. Often, more than one size is offered for sale. Usually one size up means one year older. For example, a tree described as 4–5 in. will be a year older than one described as 3–4 in. Ease of planting and transportation is a major consideration in deciding what size of tree to buy.

BUYING TIME

Whether you opt for a field-grown or a container-grown tree, planting a larger specimen is a way of buying time. When instant results are needed, the investment may well be worthwhile, providing the tree is given the right treatment in terms of planting and aftercare. If time is not of the essence, a smaller specimen is often the better choice. It is easier to handle and plant, and usually suffers less of a check when transplanted than a more mature specimen.

Container-grown trees virtually guarantee success. For this reason they have become popular with commercial landscapers: The risk of failure and the expense of replacement are minimized.

Larger container trees are available in pots 8–20 gallons in volume. These probably cost three or four times as much, but give instant impact and are still manageable in terms of transport and planting. Much larger specimens are grown in containers holding anything up to 500 gallons of compost; these are normally for commercial landscape projects and require specialized handling equipment.

Planting and tree care

Bare-root and balled and burlapped (B&B) trees are planted in late fall, winter, and early spring, when the plants are not in leaf. Container-grown trees can be planted at any time. However, particular attention must be paid to watering if the trees are planted during the summer. Care early in life reaps rewards, in terms of speed of establishment as well as shape and development. Once established, most trees require relatively little regular care.

SOIL PREPARATION

Thorough soil preparation is vital, whatever the condition of the garden soil. Dig out a hole much larger than the roots of the tree: at least 1 ft. (30 cm) bigger in diameter than the rootball and 1 ft. (30 cm) deeper. Break up the soil at the bottom and sides of the hole thoroughly, using a fork. Mix in good garden compost or well-rotted manure and a generous sprinkling of a general slow-release fertilizer.

STAKING

Secure staking is essential: If the tree rocks from side to side in the ground, any new roots will be broken as they start to develop. Container-grown and balled and burlapped (B&B) trees are normally supported with an angled stake, or two short stakes, one each side of the rootball, plus a cross-member (a goal post construction) to avoid damage to the roots. Bare-root trees are normally supported with one stout upright stake next to the trunk (see right). Hold the tree in the planting hole to help judge the position of the stake, or stakes, and check that the planting depth is correct. Then drive in the stakes. It is easier if the tree is removed from the planting pit during this operation. Once the stakes are secure, replace the tree, and fix the tree ties.

Staking a bare-root tree: (1) Dig a hole wide and deep enough to accommodate the tree root with room to spare. (2) Put the tree and its stake in the hole in order to check the position of the stake and the planting depth. (3) Drive in the stake with a sledge hammer. (4) Position the tree and spread out its roots. (5) Check planting depth and adjust if necessary.

The tree must be held away from the stake with a buffer and the tie must be secure. Remember, the stake is meant to hold the tree in position, not the other way round.

Larger trees may be staked using three stakes positioned to form a triangle about 18 in. (50 cm) from the stem of the tree. The tree is then anchored to each stake, using soft ties. (See photograph, page 20.)

POSITIONING AND FILLING IN

Before backfilling the hole, check that the tree is planted to the same depth as it was before purchase, whether it was grown in a pot or in the open ground. Never plant a tree so deep that the graft or bud union (usually a bump low on the stem) is below the ground. This could cause suckering from the rootstock or damage to the graft.

Add some garden compost and general fertilizer to the soil heaped beside the hole. Mix and gradually fill in around the tree, firming the soil gently against the roots. Avoid firming on top of the rootball, as this can cause damage. Pile the soil around the tree to create a saucer, to direct water into the rootball of the tree.

See page 24 for pruning at the time of planting.

WATERING AND FEEDING

Thorough and regular watering is essential both after planting and during the following season. Initially, this settles the soil particles around the roots, enabling newly developed root hairs to take up water. Roots of bare-root trees will take time to develop and search out water, so adequate supply needs to be on hand as the new leaf canopy develops and the tree demands more water.

Young trees, and some mature specimens, on poor, fast-draining soils—especially sand—will benefit from occasional feeding after the planting stage. (This is not

Planting a bare-root tree: (1) Line up the tree with the stake. (2) Secure the tree to the stake using a tree tie with a buffer between the stake and the stem of the tree. (3) Add compost and fertilizer to the pile of soil. (4) Mix the soil and compost, and back-fill the planting hole. (5) Firm the soil carefully around the roots before filling completely. (6) Water thoroughly.

usually necessary on moister, richer soils.) A slow-release fertilizer should be applied annually over the soil surface, ideally around the drip-line of the tree (the extent of the branch canopy at ground level), as this is where the young roots are most active. A high-potash fertilizer should be used annually on shy-flowering trees on poor soils to promote flower production.

CHECK STAKES AND TIES

Tree ties and stakes must be checked regularly until they are eventually removed (after three years or so). Ties that are too tight restrict the movement of sap up the tree and can slow growth and cause damage. Equally, ties that are too loose mean that the tree will move in the wind, possibly rubbing against the stake, which can be harmful.

This weeping ash, *Fraxinus excelsior* 'Pendula', has been carefully pruned as a young tree to preserve its shape but restrict its spread.

PRUNING

Some formative pruning may be required in the early years of a tree's life. This is the best time to influence the future shape of the tree, and branch removal when young is unlikely to leave scars on the main stem. Always use sharp secateurs and a professional pruning saw, taking care not to rip the bark.

When it comes to larger, mature trees, pruning is usually best carried out by a qualified tree surgeon. The size of mature trees is deceptive, and what appears to be a small tree or a tiny branch will seem much larger and heavier when on the ground. Always choose a reputable, preferably recommended operator; if the job is substantial, get more than one quotation. Badly executed tree work is not pleasant to look at and you will have to live with the results for a long time.

Most deciduous trees are pruned in winter, when the leaves have fallen and the buds are dormant. This is the

DIFFERENT PRUNING METHODS

PRUNING WHEN PLANTING

Many trees, especially those that are sold bare-root, become established more quickly when the branches are cut back by one-third at the time of planting. *Acer platanoides, Acer saccharinum, Sorbus aucuparia,* and ornamental crab apples (*Malus*) all benefit from this. Cutting the branches back stimulates healthy growth and reduces wind-resistance, meaning that the stem is less likely to break. Also, the lack of foliage means that the tree channels all its energy into developing its roots.

Before planting, always prune out any damaged wood and remove any lower branches that interfere with the shape of the crown of the tree.

CROWN LIFTING

To raise the base of the tree's canopy further from the ground, perhaps to enable people to walk beneath it, you can remove the lower branches, preferably when the tree is young. Remember, the branches will often be lower under the weight of foliage than when they are bare. Crown lifting also allows more air circulation and light into the area beneath the tree.

CROWN THINNING

By removing certain branches throughout the tree's canopy, you can reduce the density of the crown. This allows air, light, and rainfall to pass through, improving the growing conditions beneath. It also reduces wind-resistance, making branches less likely to snap in gales. It does not affect the tree's overall size or shape.

CROWN REDUCTION

You can reduce the height and spread of the crown by removing the branch tips across the tree's head. This will create a balanced shape, control the size of the tree, and reduce its wind-resistance.

DEAD WOODING

This is the removal of dead and diseased wood throughout the crown of the tree, for safety as well as aesthetic purposes.

POLLARDING

A mature tree is cut back to the same point every couple of years or so. This promotes a dense head of straight branches, all emerging in close proximity from the end of the trunk. Pollarding is particularly good for willows (*Salix*), as it encourages long, pliable, brightly colored ornamental stems in winter.

easiest time to see where to prune without leaves getting in the way. Trees pruned at this time include sorbus, crab apple (*Malus*), beech (*Fagus*), and oak (*Quercus*). In some trees, the sap starts to rise after midwinter; pruning after this time will cause bleeding from any larger wounds, so affected trees are best pruned in late summer and fall, even if they are still in leaf, because the sap will be falling. Trees that should be pruned at this time include acer, birch (*Betula*), hornbeam (*Carpinus*), walnut (*Juglans*), laburnum, magnolia, and prunus.

Evergreen trees are usually pruned only to maintain shape, if necessary. This is done in early spring, just before the main annual flush of growth takes place.

TREES IN GRASS

If a tree is planted in grass, an area about 3 ft. (1 m) in diameter around the trunk should be kept clear of grass and weeds, to allow rainfall to penetrate easily and to reduce competition. Herbicides can be used around trees in accordance with manufacturers' instructions. However, these must be of a type that is inactivated upon contact with the soil, as opposed to residual herbicides that remain active in the soil after application. Alternatively, weeds and grass can be removed by hand. A string trimmer should never be used around the base of a tree without a guard as the line or blade may damage the bark. More trees are damaged this way in gardens and open spaces than through any other cause. Careless use of mowing equipment can also damage the bark, causing serious damage.

UNWANTED TREES

TREES AS WEEDS

Some trees seed prolifically, and it is surprising how quickly tree seedlings can get out of hand. Tree of heaven (*Ailanthus altissima*) and Siberian elm (*Ulmus pumila*) are the worst offenders. Seedlings should be removed at an early age, otherwise they quickly become undesirable trees in the wrong locations. Specimens that arise in this way often become the objects of tree preservation orders, much to their owners' dismay.

REMOVING MATURE TREES

Sometimes a mature tree becomes unsafe and needs removal. This is always a job for a qualified contractor. Large trees in confined spaces can be dismantled in stages to avoid damage to neighboring trees and buildings, rather than felling them in one operation. Trees are often subject to preservation orders and restrictions. Always consult your local authority before removing a tree or carrying out major pruning work. Qualified tree surgeons will normally undertake this consultation on your behalf.

PESTS AND DISEASES

ANIMAL PESTS

Some animals, especially deer and rabbits, can cause severe, sometimes fatal damage to newly planted and even mature trees. Tree guards are essential if animals are a problem. Spiral guards are useful because they open up as the tree grows in girth. However, with certain trees, in particular ash (*Fraxinus*), rabbits will gnaw the bark between the spirals of the guard, so higher wire-mesh guards may be necessary. Higher wire-mesh guards are also essential if deer are a threat, as they will eat or bite off young shoots and can destroy a young tree by rubbing against it with their emerging antlers.

Below ground, chafer grubs—the larvae of adult chafer beetles—feed on young roots. They are a particular problem in rough grass on sandy soils. Look out for them when you are planting new trees and remove by hand.

HONEY MUSHROOM (SHOESTRING ROOT ROT)

Honey mushroom (*Armillaria*) is widespread in woodlands and gardens, where it lives on decaying plant material. However, it can become parasitic on the living roots of many plants. It is particularly a problem in trees, where it causes loss of vigor and eventually death. Active beneath the ground, the fungus enters the tree at the base of the trunk and attacks the living vessels, destroying the transport system, and robbing the tree of water and nutrients. Yellowing of the foliage, early leaf fall, and a ring of honey-colored toadstools around the base of the tree are usually the first signs of the problem.

All affected plants must be completely removed, even the tree stumps. There is currently no chemical treatment available. Spread of the fungus may be contained by inserting a physical barrier of heavy polythene or butyl rubber into the soil to a depth of 12 in. (30 cm) or more surrounding the infected area. Feeding and encouraging the vigor of neighboring plants helps them to resist infection.

PLANTING WITH TREES

Trees create both a challenge and an opportunity when it comes to choosing planting companions. They influence the growing conditions by casting shade and they also take water from the soil, which causes problems if the wrong plants are chosen. Evergreen shrubs and plants from woodland habitats often relish the growing conditions beneath trees, transforming a potential wasteland into a verdant oasis. Flowering bulbs add color, and a tree's trunk and branches can provide support for climbing plants, which extend the season of interest and introduce further variety.

RIGHT: *Viburnum plicatum* f. *tomentosum* 'Mariesii'.

Successful planting

Establishing plants under trees requires considerable care to ensure success. A large mature tree is a powerful plant, its extensive root system greedily taking water and nutrients from the soil before smaller plants, with shallower roots, can claim their share. In addition, the heavy leaf canopy in summer excludes light from plants growing beneath them and impedes the penetration of rainfall, making the ground even drier.

Establishing plants under a young tree presents few problems, particularly if the tree and the plants beneath it are planted at the same time. Establishing plants under mature trees is more challenging, but it is still important to provide interest in the lower layer of the planting.

When planting trees, shrubs, and perennials in a mixed border, consider the impact that the trees will have as they grow and develop. How far will the tree's canopy spread, and how will this affect the surrounding plants? It could be that over the next few years the tree will gradually change the growing conditions in part of a border beneath it.

One approach is to adapt the planting as the tree matures. For example, if you want some color in the border in the first few seasons while the tree is still young, you could plant fast-growing flowering shrubs beneath the tree, such as cytisus, lavatera, ceanothus, and abutilon, to fill the space quickly. All are short-lived shrubs that need full sun. As the tree develops and takes up more space, these shrubs can be replaced by low-growing, shade-tolerant evergreens (see pages 30–35). Alternatively, you could plant shrubs that tolerate partial shade close to the tree at the outset (see pages 36–41); these will continue to thrive as the head of the tree develops.

GRASS UNDER TREES

Where trees are grown as specimens in a lawn, the surrounding grass is robbed of light and water when the tree is in leaf. This means that even once the leaves have fallen, the grass is often thin, weak, and unable to resist the invasion of moss.

To improve the situation, sow a shade- and drought-tolerant seed mixture. Existing grass can be oversown in autumn, after leaf fall, provided the weather is warm, or in early spring, before the tree is in leaf. The shade-tolerant seed mixture can be blended into the existing lawn in problem areas.

PLANTING UNDER MATURE TREES

Planting under large, mature trees can be particularly challenging. Late fall, early winter, or early spring is the best time to plant, after there has been some rainfall to soften the ground. At this time of year, roots have the winter to grow and establish before the tree comes into leaf and depletes the water supply.

• Choose plants that are well adapted to the environment under trees: Those with woodland ancestry are particularly good. (See pages 30–41.)

• The first challenge is to find planting positions where it is actually possible to dig a hole. Approach the job gently, when the soil is moist, and using a small border spade, find positions between major roots. Be prepared to adjust planting positions to places where there is sufficient depth of soil, rather than battling through densely rooted areas, where competition for water will be even greater.

• To get newly planted subjects off to the best possible start, make the planting holes as large as possible, and incorporate some well-rotted manure or good garden compost and slow-release general fertilizer.

• Plant firmly, to the same depth as the plants are growing in their containers. Water the plants into the ground thoroughly; this not only provides water around the roots but it settles the soil particles, enabling the root hairs to make close contact with them.

• Provide supplementary water during the first growing season after planting, and minimize water loss by mulching the surface with bark, gravel, or garden compost.

Hydrangea arborescens 'Annabelle' and *Cornus alba* 'Elegantissima' make an elegant combination in the dappled shade of a tree with a light, airy canopy.

DO NOT ATTEMPT THE IMPOSSIBLE

Be realistic in your expectations. Large mature deciduous and coniferous trees are not hospitable to new plantings around them. Establishing new planting under their canopy will not be easy and may be impossible. It is best to experiment with a few tough plants (see pages 30–41) before investing in a full-scale planting scheme and finding that it will not succeed. Autumn planting is always the best option: Plants have the winter to establish their root systems before competition from the trees increases in spring.

RAISED BEDS UNDER TREES

To avoid the problems associated with planting beneath trees, a frequently adopted approach is to build a raised bed around the trunk and plant into this, rather than directly into the ground. A bed that is constructed too tightly around the tree looks out of proportion, and soil heaped up against the tree can harm it. However, it can be successful if the level of the ground is raised no more than 16 in. (40 cm) and soil is not piled up against the trunk. Beds of this type look best when the diameter is at least 6 ft. (2 m) if built under a young tree, and more if it is under a mature specimen.

Plants growing in a raised bed will be given a good start, and the roots will gradually make their way down into the soil beneath. Regular watering is essential to establish the plants and will always be required when the tree is in leaf.

A shallow raised bed, constructed of rustic logs or landscape timbers and planted with low, evergreen ground-cover subjects (see pages 30–35) will provide a green 'pool' around the base of the tree. It can also become the setting for an ornament or feature that will create a focal point in the shade of the tree.

Ground cover under trees

Low ground-cover plants are often the best choice under large mature trees and are usually a better planting solution than grass. They can be used on their own, to provide a carpet of green and variegated foliage, or the leaves can be punctuated with clumps of spring-flowering bulbs for early color. Alternatively, ground-cover plants can be combined with evergreen shrubs to create a more undulating and varied landscape picture.

The white-edged leaves and red berries of *Cotoneaster atropurpureus* 'Variegatus' are crowded on low, spreading branches, ideal for covering the ground beneath trees.

ESTABLISHING GROUND-COVER SHRUBS UNDER TREES

Ground-cover shrubs are often supplied as small pot-grown specimens, to be planted in dense groups in order to establish a carpet of planting quickly and effectively. However, small plants tend to dry out more quickly and need more aftercare, so when planting under trees it is generally better to plant larger plants at a lower density. Solve any weed problems before planting; perennial weeds are virtually impossible to eradicate later.

Weed-control fabric, also known as landscape fabric, can be used to suppress weeds and retain moisture under trees, and works particularly well with the more vigorous ground-cover shrubs. Use a heavy-duty, professional-quality product. Anchor the fabric firmly to the ground, then plant through slits in the fabric. The surface of the fabric can be covered with bark or gravel, except on sloping ground. Keep the shrubs well watered at their planting stations.

EVERGREEN SHRUBS FOR GROUND COVER

Low, spreading evergreen shrubs that retain their leaves and stems in winter provide the most effective ground cover under trees.

Cotoneasters are easy to grow and succeed on virtually any soil, including chalk. *Cotoneaster dammeri* (Zones 4–7) is the best known for ground cover, with stiffly trailing stems and tiny, shining dark green leaves. White flowers stud the stems in spring, followed by large red

Cotoneaster dammeri

Cotoneaster salicifolius 'Gnom'

berries in fall. *Cotoneaster conspicuus* 'Decorus' (Zones 6–7) is a low-growing, arching shrub with small, dark green leaves, white flowers, and plenty of red fruits that persist into winter. The hybrid *Cotoneaster × suecicus* 'Coral Beauty' (Zones 5–7) has arching branches and glossy green oval leaves. Its orange-red fruits are prolific when produced. *Cotoneaster salicifolius* 'Gnom' (Zones 6–8) forms a low mound of arching purple shoots and narrow, dark green leaves. The foliage is bronze-tinted in winter and sprinkled with small, bright red fruits. *Cotoneaster horizontalis* (Zones 6–8), although deciduous, makes an excellent ground-cover plant with its spreading, herringbone branches and small, dark green leaves. The scarlet berries remain on the branches after the leaves have fallen. The similar *Cotoneaster atropurpureus* **'Variegatus'** (Zones 5–7) has white-edged leaves that flush pink in fall.

The variegated forms of *Euonymus fortunei* (Zones 5–8) are widely used in gardens as dwarf shrubs at the front of borders, in pots and containers, and at the base of walls as compact climbers. They are versatile and adaptable, and succeed in difficult growing conditions, for example, under the shade of trees, where they provide invaluable foliage color and year-round interest. All make

Euonymus fortunei 'Emerald 'n' Gold'

Euonymus fortunei 'Silver Queen'

Euonymus fortunei 'Kewensis'

Hedera colchica 'Sulfur Heart'

SMALL-LEAVED IVIES FOR GROUND COVER

Many small-leaved ivies make excellent ground cover. Some good ones are:

Hedera helix **'Glacier'** (**1**) (Z. 4–9) Gray-green leaves with white margins.

Hedera helix **'Little Diamond'** (**2**) (Z. 4–9) Diamond-shaped, gray-green leaves edged creamy white.

Hedera helix **'Green Ripple'** (**3**) (Z. 4–9) Pretty green foliage with pointed lobes and arching stems.

Hedera helix **'Manda's Crested'** (Z. 4–9) Wavy green leaves; turns bronze.

Hedera helix **'Persian Carpet'** (Z. 4–9) Vigorous, with light green leaves.

low, spreading shrubs, usually about 2 ft. (60 cm) in height with a spread of over 3 ft. (1 m). Planted near the base of the tree, they will climb up the lower part of the trunk to attractive effect. *Euonymus fortunei* **'Emerald 'n' Gold'** is the most popular, with dark green leaves with a bold, old-gold margin that becomes pinkish in winter. *Euonymus fortunei* **'Silver Queen'** has the finest foliage but is the slowest grower. It has oval leaves of soft green, broadly edged with creamy yellow in spring and becoming white as the year progresses. *Euonymus fortunei* **'Blondy'** has dark green leaves with bold golden blotches in their centers. *Euonymus fortunei* **'Emerald Gaiety'** has dark green leaves marbled and edged with paler green and white.

Euonymus fortunei **'Kewensis'** is an altogether more dainty plant, with fine, trailing stems and tiny, deep green leaves. It creeps over the ground, tree roots, and

stones, and will gradually form anthill-like hummocks, creating a miniature architectural landscape. It is a good choice to plant with ferns and epimediums.

Many varieties of ivy (*Hedera*) make excellent ground-cover subjects and most thrive in difficult conditions. For example, they are an excellent choice on slopes. Some have tiny leaves that look pretty at ground level (see box, left.) Large-leaved ivies can also be used for ground cover in bigger areas. *Hedera colchica* **'Sulfur Heart'** (Zones 6–9), with large, shiny green leaves liberally marked with yellow and lime, makes a lively ground-cover subject that will also happily climb up a tree trunk (see page 48 and Good Companions, page 33). *Hedera hibernica*, the Irish ivy (Zones 4–9), is a vigorous trailing plant with large green leaves. It is particularly useful in dense shade. *Hedera hibernica* **'Deltoidea'** has denser, more compact growth and leaves that bronze in winter.

Lonicera pileata

Prunus laurocerasus 'Zabeliana'

Mahonia aquifolium 'Apollo'

Rubus tricolor

Pachysandra terminalis 'Variegata'

Sarcococca confusa

upright stems carry whorls of leaves and form good ground cover. It spreads quickly on moist soil but will succeed in difficult positions, even under pine trees. *Pachysandra terminalis* 'Variegata' has leaves finely edged in creamy white. It looks particularly decorative when planted with other white- or cream-variegated shrubs, such as *Euonymus fortunei* 'Emerald Gaiety' or with white-flowered perennials like *Galium odoratum* (see Good Companions, opposite).

Prunus laurocerasus 'Zabeliana' (Zones 6–8) is a low, spreading form of the cherry laurel, with narrow, shiny dark green leaves. It makes an excellent ground-cover plant, particularly when grown with variegated ground cover such as *Vinca minor* 'Illumination' (see page 34).

Rubus tricolor (Zones 7–9) is one of the most useful ground-cover plants for growing under trees and will succeed in the most difficult situations, even under a beech (*Fagus*). It has long, trailing, bristly stems and shiny dark green leaves, white and felty beneath. The leaves often turn burgundy around the edges in fall at the same time as reddish blackberry fruits appear. *Rubus tricolor* is a vigorous ground-cover plant that overcomes weeds and is particularly successful on slopes.

Not all ground cover needs to be ground-hugging. Low evergreen shrubs, especially those that are dense and thicket-forming, provide some welcome height in ground-cover planting. Varieties of **sarcococca** (Christmas box; Zones 6–8) are ideal, with their tolerant nature and suckering habit. Sarcococca grows on any soil. It has upright stems and neat evergreen leaves, and tiny white or pinkish flowers that appear in late winter. Although these are not showy, they are wonderfully fragrant and will fill a garden with their sweet scent. *Sarcococca confusa* has shiny dark green, pointed, lightly wavy leaves and creamy white flowers followed by black berries; it usually grows to around 2 ft. (60 cm). *Sarcococca hookeriana* var. *digyna* is a little taller

Lonicera pileata (Zones 6–7) is a dwarf, spreading shrub with almost horizontal branches that carry small, densely packed, bright green leaves. It is semi-evergreen, and loses some of its foliage in winter, but this is quickly replaced by new, bright green leaves in spring. A good alternative to boxwood (*Buxus*), this honeysuckle is often overlooked for garden use. This is a pity, as it is an excellent choice for underplanting and tolerates dense shade.

Mahonia aquifolium 'Apollo' (Zones 6–8) is the best cultivar of the Oregon grape. It has a suckering habit, with

upright stems reaching about 2 ft. (60 cm) high. These carry dark green, hollylike foliage that turns rich plum purple in fall and winter. The coloration is less marked in dense shade. In spring, large clusters of bright yellow flowers appear at the ends of the stems. 'Apollo' is a bright and cheerful subject under trees, particularly when planted with gold-variegated evergreens. (See Good Companions, opposite.)

Pachysandra terminalis (Zones 5–8) is a suckering, spreading plant that looks like a perennial but is in fact a dwarf shrub related to boxwood (*Buxus*). Short, than *Sarcococca confusa*, with dark stems and narrower dark green leaves; the pinkish flowers are more conspicuous than those of *Sarcococca confusa*. *Sarcococca hookeriana* var. *humilis* (Zones 6–8) makes particularly successful ground cover, forming large, suckering clumps of densely branched upright stems. The leaves are rich, dark green and shiny in shade, whereas in sun they are a flatter yellow-green color.

PERENNIALS FOR GROUND COVER

In addition to ground-cover shrubs, there are also some excellent perennials for planting under trees (see also pages 42–45). *Euphorbia amygdaloides* var. *robbiae*, the wood spurge (Zones 7–9), is an evergreen perennial with upright stems, reaching 1 ft. (30 cm) long, that carry rounded, shiny leaves. Lime-green flowers appear in early spring at the top of the stems. This spurge spreads by means of creeping stems and forms extensive mats in areas of quite heavy shade under trees. It makes a good planting partner for the smaller-leaved ivies (see page 31).

Euphorbia amygdaloides var. *robbiae*

Galium odoratum

Galium odoratum, the woodruff (Zones 5–8), has creeping underground stems that form mats of short, upright shoots that carry whorls of narrow, bright green leaves and foamy white flowers in late spring. Although it dies down in winter, it is an attractive and effective ground-cover plant for fertile soils that are not too dry or acid. (See Good Companions, below.)

The **comfreys** are coarse-leaved perennials that retain some foliage during winter. They are useful for ground cover on moister soils in shade under evergreen trees and shrubs such as rhododendrons. Their main attraction is their bright flowers in early spring.

Symphytum caucasicum

Tiarella cordifolia

Symphytum caucasicum (Zones 3–7) is one of the finest, with bright blue flowers resembling anchusa and deeply veined leaves on 2 ft. (60 cm) stems. It is a good choice for a woodland garden.

Tiarella cordifolia (Zones 3–7), the foam flower, has clumps of bright green, semi-evergreen leaves and spikes of frothy white flowers that rise just above the foliage in mid- to late spring. It prefers reasonably moist conditions. *Tellima grandiflora* (Zones 6–8), on the other hand, will tolerate quite dry conditions. With its clumps of green leaves and 24-in.-

GOOD COMPANIONS

The dark, hollylike foliage of *Mahonia aquifolium* 'Apollo' (1) (Z. 6–8) contrasts with the bright green and yellow leaves of the ivy *Hedera colchica* 'Sulfur Heart' (2) (Z. 6–9). In spring, the mahonia's yellow flowers pick up the ivy's golden variegation.

The bright green leaves and white flowers of *Galium odoratum* (3) (Z. 5–8) complement the softer green and white foliage of *Pachysandra terminalis* 'Variegata' (4) (Z. 5–8), which provides evergreen interest in winter when the galium dies down.

GOOD FERNS TO GROW UNDER TREES

Adiantum venustum (Z. 9–11), the Himalayan maidenhair fern, is deciduous but retains its green foliage through most winters. The new fronds are pink-tinged but quickly turn green. It spreads by creeping rhizomes, therefore creating good ground cover up to 1 ft. (30 cm) in height.

Asplenium scolopendrium (**1**) (Z. 5–9), hart's tongue fern, is evergreen with shiny, tongue-shaped leaves up to 1 ft. (30 cm) high in a shuttlecock arrangement. It is useful to punctuate other ground-cover plants, such as small-leaved ivies (see box, page 31).

Dryopteris erythrosora (**2**) (Z. 5–8) is a lovely deciduous fern with coppery new foliage turning olive-green during summer. It grows to 2 ft. (60 cm).

Dryopteris filix-mas (**3**) (Z. 5–8), the male fern, is a deciduous British native. It is tolerant and easy to grow, forming vigorous clumps up to 3 ft. (90 cm) high.

Polypodium interjectum 'Cornubiense' (Z. 5–9) is a hybrid fern, forming large evergreen clumps of fine foliage up to 16 in. (40 cm) in height.

Polypodium vulgare (Z. 3–6), the common polypody fern, is low-growing and evergreen, with curled, leathery fronds. It spreads well and tolerates dry soils.

Polystichum aculeatum (Z. 4–8), the hard shield fern, forms broad shuttlecocks of evergreen foliage up to 3 ft. (90 cm) in height.

Polystichum setiferum (Z. 7–8), the soft shield fern, is an attractive fern with evergreen, spreading, finely cut fronds. It reaches 32 in. (80 cm) in height, more across. There are many forms: *Polystichum setiferum* Divisilobum Group 'Herrenhausen' is one of the finest, with its slightly shiny leaves with prominent midribs; *Polystichum setiferum* 'Pulcherrimum Bevis' (**4**) is a beautifully feathery fern with tall, arching fronds; *Polystichum setiferum* Plumosum Group has dense, feathery fronds that spread widely across the ground.

PERIWINKLES

The evergreen periwinkles, or vincas, are effective ground-cover plants in almost any situation, but they are particularly useful on shady slopes. They spread by means of creeping, low, arching stems that layer themselves to produce more plants, thereby covering large areas of ground. *Vinca major* (**1**) (Z. 8–9), with larger leaves and thicker shoots than *Vinca minor* (Z. 5–8), is a vigorous plant and can be invasive and overpowering, although in the right situation this may be exactly what is needed. *Vinca major* 'Variegata' (Z. 8–9) has emerald green leaves edged creamy white and clear blue flowers throughout spring. It is as vigorous as the green forms.

Vinca minor (Z. 5–8) has smaller leaves on fine stems and blue flowers throughout spring and early summer. There are many named forms with different-colored flowers and variegations. *Vinca minor* 'Alba' (**2**), with white flowers, is pretty in shade and looks particularly effective when planted with snowdrops (*Galanthus*). *Vinca minor* 'Argenteovariegata' (**3**) has blue flowers and creamy white variegated leaves. Again, it shows up well in shade. *Vinca minor* 'Illumination' (**4**) has the showiest foliage, with dark green leaves with bright golden centers. The blue flowers are of secondary importance.

Vinca difformis (**5**) (Z. 8–9) is less widely grown and can be herbaceous in cold areas. However, its more upright shoots and autumn flowers make effective ground cover under the shelter of trees. *Vinca difformis* 'Alba', with white flowers and blue-green foliage, is the most useful, especially when planted with white-variegated evergreens such as *Euonymus fortunei* 'Emerald Gaiety' (see page 31).

OTHER GOOD GROUND-COVER PLANTS *Ajuga reptans* • *Asarum europaeum* • *Epimedium* × *rubrum* •

(60 cm)-long spikes of greenish flowers in early summer, it is not showy but is a useful component in a planting carpet.

Many evergreen **ferns** succeed in the shade under trees (see box, opposite). They look at home in this situation, and create a naturalistic woodland picture when combined with epimediums,

Gaultheria procumbens

Leucothoe 'Lovita'

galiums, euphorbias, and dwarf woodland bulbs (see pages 42–43). Most prefer soil that is adequately moist, although some will withstand quite dry conditions as long as the soil is not dust dry.

GROUND COVER ON ACID SOILS

Heaths and **heathers** make excellent ground-cover subjects on acid soil. Although they flower more prolifically in full sun, they are tolerant of some shade and will grow under the dappled shade of trees. They associate well with light, deciduous trees such as birch (*Betula*) and sorbus, both natural choices for acid soil, and colonize beneath the high canopy of mature pines. **Callunas** (Zones 4–7) must have acid soil and flower in summer and early fall. Many varieties have attractive winter and early spring foliage, which can be as much a feature as the flowers. Most ericas, especially cultivars of *Erica carnea* (Zones 5–7) and *Erica × darleyensis* (Zones 4–7), are tolerant of some chalk, and flower in late winter and early spring. They are very effective beneath birches that are being grown for their attractive winter bark (see box, left).

All heaths and heathers benefit from a light trim after flowering, to remove faded flowers and stimulate bushy new growth.

For an acid soil rich in leaf mold, *Cornus canadensis* (Zones 2–7) is a charming

Cornus canadensis

ground-cover subject, with spreading underground stems that give rise to short, upright shoots which carry dark green leaves and flowers consisting of a darker center surrounded by four creamy white bracts. The shoots disappear in winter and are renewed in spring. Although this plant doesn't suppress weeds, it is still a choice subject for an acid woodland garden.

Gaultheria procumbens (Zones 3–8) forms spreading mats of fine stems that carry rounded, dark, shiny evergreen leaves. These are studded in fall and winter with large, round scarlet berries. *Leucothoe* 'Lovita' (Zones 4–7) and *Leucothoe* 'Scarletta' (Zones 4–7) are low-growing evergreens with small oval, pointed leaves; they turn rich shades of burgundy-red and scarlet respectively in winter. Both leucothoe and gaultheria are excellent plants for semi-shade, and make good ground cover on acid soils under rhododendrons and pieris.

GOOD HEATHS AND HEATHERS FOR GROUND COVER

Calluna vulgaris 'Mullion' (Z. 4–7) Bushy and spreading. Green foliage and masses of deep pink flowers.

Calluna vulgaris 'Sir John Charrington' (Z. 4–7) Vigorous and spreading. Yellow foliage that turns reddish in winter; lilac flowers.

Calluna vulgaris 'White Lawn' (above) (Z. 4–7) Spreading habit. Deep green foliage and white flowers.

Erica carnea 'Isabell' (Z. 5–7) Bushy and spreading. Bright green foliage and plentiful white flowers.

Erica carnea 'Myretoun Ruby' (Z. 5–7) Bushy and spreading. Deep green foliage and dark rose pink flowers.

Erica × darleyensis 'Darley Dale' (Z. 4–7) Taller than *Erica carnea*. Green foliage and pale pink flowers.

Erica × darleyensis 'Furzey' (Z. 4–7) Compact. Dark green foliage and deep pink flowers.

Erica × darleyensis 'White Perfection' (Z. 4–7) Tall and vigorous. Bright green foliage and white flowers.

Geranium macrorrhizum • *Hypericum calycinum* • *Lamium maculatum* • *Symphoricarpos × chenaultii* 'Hancock' •

Shrubs under trees

There are plenty of shrubs that will grow successfully under deciduous trees. Of course, some trees present more of a challenge than others, particularly those with a dense canopy or a vigorous, extensive root system. Trees with a lighter canopy that casts dappled shade are generally more hospitable and create an environment that some shrubs prefer to an open, sunny situation.

The lovely *Viburnum plicatum* f. *tomentosum* 'Mariesii' grows in the dappled shade of deciduous trees.

Aucuba japonica 'Marmorata'

EVERGREENS FOR DENSE SHADE

Many tough, versatile evergreens come into their own in heavily shaded situations and survive the competition of the canopy above and the roots beneath. *Aucuba japonica* (Zones 7–10), the spotted laurel, is useful in this situation. There are a number of cultivars, with varying degrees of variegation, from the plain, glossy green *Aucuba japonica* 'Rozannie' to the liberally gold-splashed *Aucuba japonica* 'Marmorata'. (See Good Companions, opposite.) Female forms produce attractive red berries; these, combined with the brightly variegated leaves, will add color to the gloomiest corner.

Aucubas grow into medium-sized, rounded shrubs and are easily pruned to control size and shape. They sometimes suffer from a blackening of the shoot tips in winter. This is a result of drought the previous summer and can occur under trees. However, the effect is short-lived and new growth soon comes through.

Most **berberis** grow in sun or shade, and the evergreen types are particularly tolerant plants. *Berberis darwinii* (Zones 7–9) has small, dark green, hollylike leaves and bright, jewel-like orange flowers in spring. It will grow to 6 ft. (2 m) or more but is usually smaller and of more open habit under trees.

All varieties of **boxwood** do well under trees. The growth is often lighter and airier than when they are grown in the open garden. *Buxus sempervirens*

TRIED AND TESTED

As with any challenging situation in the garden, it is better to choose a shrub that you know will succeed under a tree rather than a plant that you particularly desire. Many shrubs recommended for growing under trees are familiar landscape plants; the reason that they are widely used is that they are successful in most situations. Do not dismiss them as common and ordinary; use them because they work.

Berberis darwinii

Buxus sempervirens 'Elegantissima'

Danae racemosa

Buxus microphylla 'Faulkner'

Euonymus japonicus 'Bravo'

(Zones 6–9), the common boxwood, is invaluable as a small-leaved background shrub. The variegated forms are attractive but slower-growing. *Buxus sempervirens* **'Elegantissima'** is a small shrub with neat, dark green leaves edged with cream. *Buxus sempervirens* 'Latifolia Maculata' has much broader, dark green leaves that are irregularly splashed and edged with creamy yellow. It forms a rounded dome, up to 3 ft. (1 m) in height, and looks good rising out of a small-leaved ground-cover ivy such as *Hedera helix* 'Goldchild' (Zones 4–9). *Buxus microphylla* (Zones 5–9) has small, shining emerald green leaves and is ideal for clipping and shaping. *Buxus microphylla* **'Faulkner'** is a good cultivar because of its low, compact habit.

Danae racemosa (Zones 6–9), the Alexandrian laurel, is well adapted to dry shade. It has arching sprays of pointed, glossy dark green leaves that reach 3 ft. (1 m) high. Orange berries appear after warm summers. It is a lovely shrub for cutting and is altogether more attractive than the closely related butcher's broom, *Ruscus aculeatus* (Zone 8).

The evergreen **euonymus** grow anywhere on any soil. The variegated forms are versatile shrubs that bring foliage color to shady areas under trees. The cultivars of *Euonymus fortunei* (Zones 5–8) can be used as short climbers (see pages 47–48) and ground cover (see page 31). Cultivars of *Euonymus japonicus* (Zones 7–9) are useful to provide larger variegated

leaves and form rounded shrubs up to 5 ft. (1.5 m) high. *Euonymus japonicus* **'Latifolius Albomarginatus'** has dark green foliage that is broadly edged with white. *Euonymus japonicus* **'Bravo'** has leaves with broad, creamy white margins, and *Euonymus japonicus* **'Chollipo'** is the best gold-variegated form, the leaves edged with bright yellow. (See Good Companions, below.)

GOOD COMPANIONS

The bright, bold, gold-variegated leaves of *Euonymus japonicus* 'Chollipo' (1) (Z. 7–9) look striking combined with the more subtle, gold-sprinkled foliage of *Aucuba japonica* 'Marmorata' (2) (Z. 7–10).

The glossy dark green leaves of × *Fatshedera lizei* (3) (Z. 8–11) stand out against the soft gray-green and white variegated leaves of the ivy *Hedera helix* 'Glacier' (4) (Z. 4–9).

Fatsia japonica

× *Fatshedera lizei* 'Variegata'

× *Fatshedera lizei*

Hedera helix 'Arborescens'

Fatsia japonica (Zones 8–9), commonly known as the castor oil plant, grows well in heavy shade, and its huge, hand-shaped leaves are darker, greener, and glossier when unbleached by the sun. It also appreciates the protection from hard frosts that overhanging branches provide. Spectacular creamy white, ivylike flowers appear in early winter at the top of the stems, which can reach 6 ft. (2 m) or more. Fatsia is a large shrub that grows well under trees but does not cope with dry conditions, which may cause wilting. Larger specimens are more resilient; if you are buying a small plant, grow it in a container for a season or two before planting out.

A tougher plant, the hybrid of fatsia with ivy, × *Fatshedera lizei* (Zones 8–11), carries small, hand-shaped, dark green leaves on rather ungainly, sprawling stems. It eventually forms a low, spreading mound and is useful to add height and variety amid ivies planted as ground cover. (See Good Companions, page 37.) The cream and green variegated form, × *Fatshedera lizei* 'Variegata', is slower-growing and often better where it has some light. × *Fatshedera lizei* 'Annemieke' is a beautiful variety, with rich green leaves centrally splashed with bright lime.

Ivies have a reputation for growing anywhere, and they are well adapted to coping with competition from trees. Not all are vigorous climbers; there are

DARK EVERGREENS IN SHADE

Plain dark evergreen shrubs may seem a dull choice for planting in heavy shade, but they are usually the most successful. In reality, shiny deep green leaves look wonderful in low light, and they appear more defined without strong sunlight to rob them of their rich color. They also form a dramatic background for the lighter highlights of variegated evergreens and the seasonal color of flower bulbs.

more compact, shrubby forms, which are interesting evergreens that should be used more widely. *Hedera helix* 'Arborescens' (Zones 4–9) is a clone selected from adult growth of the common ivy. It develops into a broad mound up to 3 ft. (1 m) or more in height, with shiny, diamond-shaped evergreen leaves and green-black berries in winter after the green flowers. *Hedera helix* 'Conglomerata' (Zones 4–9) is dense and slow-growing, with upright stems up to 20 in. (50 cm) in height. The dark green leaves have a wavy margin and are regularly arranged close together up the stems. It is an attractive architectural plant that associates well with interesting pieces of natural wood and stone.

Most **hollies** are woodland plants, so they are well adapted to growing in shade under trees. Hollies of regular conical shape need enough headroom to develop. However, the shorter, bushier varieties succeed under low branches.

OTHER PLAIN EVERGREENS FOR SHADE *Choisya ternata* • *Cotoneaster franchetii* • *Cotoneaster lacteus* •

Ilex aquifolium 'Ferox Argentea'

Prunus laurocerasus 'Rotundifolia'

***Ilex aquifolium* 'Ferox'** (Zones 6–9), the hedgehog holly, has dark green leaves with spines over their surface as well as around the edges. It is a broad, bushy plant, growing to 5 ft. (1.5 m). The variegated form, ***Ilex aquifolium* 'Ferox Argentea'**, has leaves with creamy white edges and spines. It is very attractive when planted against other plain dark evergreens.

Often mistaken for hollies, varieties of ***Osmanthus heterophyllus*** (Zones 6–9) are more compact shrubs of bushier habit. They grow well in shade and, once established, will cope with dry conditions. ***Osmanthus heterophyllus* 'Variegatus'** produces attractive small, softly spiny, dark

Osmanthus heterophyllus 'Variegatus'

green leaves with creamy white margins. It forms a diminutive shrub, reaching 3 ft. (1 m) or more in height. The popular ***Osmanthus heterophyllus* 'Goshiki'** will

Prunus laurocerasus 'Otto Luyken'

grow in shade, but its foliage lacks the interesting yellow color variation that is exhibited in a sunnier situation.

Prunus laurocerasus (Zones 6–8), the cherry laurel, will grow in most sites and has become an invasive pest in woodlands in many areas. However, when controlled, it is useful where a large, heavy screening background shrub is needed under trees; or it may be clipped to form a solid structural shape. ***Prunus laurocerasus* 'Rotundifolia'** is particularly good for clipping. ***Prunus laurocerasus* 'Otto Luyken'** is a more suitable choice for the average garden. It grows to 5 ft. (1.5 m) and has narrow, glossy dark green leaves, and produces spikes of white flowers from virtually every leaf node in spring. It can also be trimmed to control its size and shape. (See Good Companions, left.) ***Prunus laurocerasus* 'Zabeliana'**, which is lower and more spreading, makes a good ground-cover plant (see page 32).

GOOD COMPANIONS

The shining foliage of *Prunus laurocerasus* 'Otto Luyken' (1) (Z. 6–8) contrasts with the matt dark green of *Viburnum tinus* 'French White' (2) (Z. 8–9). The white flowers of the prunus appear as those of the viburnum fade.

The bold, dark green leaves of *Viburnum davidii* (3) (Z. 7–9) are a dramatic contrast to the smaller, shiny green leaves of *Sarcococca confusa* (4) (Z. 6–8).

39

Daphne laureola • *Daphne pontica* • *Mahonia aquifolium* • *Mahonia japonica* • *Osmanthus decorus* • *Sarcococca confusa* •

SHRUBS FOR ACID SOILS UNDER TREES

Many acid-loving shrubs prefer to grow in the shade under trees, provided the ground is not too dry. These plants often originate from woodland habitats, where the soil is rich in organic matter from decaying leaves; also, because they have shallow roots, their fibrous rootballs rarely compete with the deeper roots of trees. **Rhododendrons** (**1**), deciduous and evergreen **azaleas,** and **pieris** all prefer light dappled shade.

Camellias (**2**) will grow in heavier shade and are more alkaline-tolerant than rhododendrons; however, they ideally need a neutral to acid soil. *Camellia japonica* (Z. 7–10) has broad, shiny evergreen leaves and glorious blooms in late winter and early spring. There are many varying cultivars; although they flower less freely in heavy shade, they are still valuable. Those with smaller, single flowers have charm and simplicity and fit more easily into an informal garden situation.

Gaultheria mucronata (Z. 6–7) is a wiry evergreen shrub with stiff stems and tiny, very dark green bristly leaves. On female plants, tiny white spring flowers produce colorful berries in late fall and winter. A male pollinator needs to be present if flowers and berries are required, so gaultheria is best planted in groups of male and female plants. There are a few hermaphrodite cultivars that are self-pollinating: one of the best is *Gaultheria mucronata* 'Bell's Seedling' (**3**), with profuse, cherry red berries.

Leucothoes are low-growing shrubs with evergreen foliage that often colors richly in winter, when temperatures fall and the light level under deciduous trees increases. *Leucothoe fontanesiana* 'Rainbow' (**4**) (Z. 4–7) has arching stems of elegant, pointed leaves in shades of dark green, cream, pink, and burgundy. The leaf color becomes richer in winter. Other leucothoes make excellent ground cover on acid soils (see page 35).

Ruscus aculeatus (Zone 8), the butcher's broom, is the ultimate shrub for dry shade. It forms dense clumps of tough, upright stems that are usually less than 3 ft. (1 m) high. The leaves are sharp and leathery and very dark green. These leaves are actually modified, flattened stems, and carry tiny white flowers that will develop into shiny red berries in winter. If all other shrubs have failed in a situation, the ruscus will probably succeed.

The dark green foliage of *Viburnum davidii* (Zones 7–9) might make it seem a rather dull subject for heavy shade. However, the leaves are so striking, with their rigid shape and deep ribs, that it stands out well in low light, particularly when partnered with a shrub that has smaller, brighter foliage. *Viburnum davidii* develops into a broad, well-structured dome. It usually grows up to 3 ft. (1 m) high but can reach larger proportions. (See Good Companions, page 39.)

Viburnum tinus (Zones 8–9) is a widely planted evergreen shrub; this is hardly surprising considering its versatility and long flowering period. It grows on any soil, including shallow alkaline ones, and is tolerant of heavy shade. There are various cultivars, some relatively compact, others more vigorous. All respond well to pruning after flowering, and all produce a wealth of white or pink flowers from midwinter through spring. *Viburnum*

Ruscus aculeatus

OTHER VARIEGATED EVERGREENS FOR SHADE *Elaeagnus pungens* 'Frederici' • *Fatsia japonica* 'Variegata' •

tinus is one of the best choices to grow under the most competitive deciduous trees such as oak (*Quercus*). *Viburnum tinus* 'French White' is a strong-growing form that reaches 10 ft. (3 m) or more, with dark green leaves and large heads of white flowers. (See Good Companions, page 39.) *Viburnum tinus* 'Gwenllian' is more compact, with smaller foliage and pink buds opening to white, pink-tinged flowers. *Viburnum tinus* 'Variegatum' has lighter green and cream variegated leaves. It is not as hardy and resilient as the plain green forms, but often succeeds under the shelter of trees.

Where there is sufficient space for a large, dramatic evergreen, try *Viburnum rhytidophyllum* (Zones 6–8). Stout, upright, light brown branches carry bold, corrugated, dark green leaves with light brown felty undersides. Small white, insignificant flowers in late spring can produce showy red fruits that turn black as they mature, but two or more plants are needed for reliable fruiting.

DECIDUOUS SHRUBS UNDER TREES

Most shrubs that thrive under the heavy shade of trees are evergreen. They need to retain their leaves during winter to make the most of the light when the tree above has lost its foliage. However, there are a few deciduous shrubs that do survive in shady conditions.

Where conditions are moist enough, hydrangeas will thrive in the shade of trees. *Hydrangea arborescens* 'Annabelle' (Zones 3–9) is surprisingly successful under trees. The upright stems reach 3 ft. (1 m), carrying soft pale green leaves and large, rounded, lime green flower heads that mature to white in summer. Stems often fall under the weight of the flowers, but if planted among low evergreen shrubs the effect is not spoiled. (See page 29.) *Hydrangea quercifolia* (Zones 5–9) has foliage that resembles large oak leaves

Viburnum rhytidophyllum

Viburnum opulus

Hydrangea quercifolia

Viburnum opulus 'Xanthocarpum'

and creamy white flowers in conical sprays at the end of upright branches, which can reach 5 ft. (1.5 m) high. In light shade the leaves turn scarlet and orange in autumn, while in deep shade they stay dark green.

The **snowberries** (*Symphoricarpos*) are reliable in shade under trees. They form dense thickets of fine, arching stems up to 5 ft. (1.5 m) high, depending on the variety. The leaves are oval to rounded, and the flowers, which are pink-white, are small and insignificant. The main feature of the plants are the spherical white, pink, or plum berries that remain on the stems in winter, after the leaves have fallen. *Symphoricarpos albus* var. *laevigatus* (Zones 3–7) is one of the tallest, with many large white berries. *Symphoricarpos × chenaultii* 'Hancock' (Zones 4–9) is dwarf and wide-spreading, with pinkish white berries. It makes excellent ground-cover. *Symphoricarpos × doorenbosii* (Zones 4–7) has a number of dwarf

varieties, including *Symphoricarpos × doorenbosii* 'Mother of Pearl', with large rose and white berries.

Viburnum opulus (Zones 3–8) is a British native shrub with maplelike leaves and lacecap heads of white flowers in spring, followed by glistening, red currantlike berries in fall and early winter. It is easy to grow on any soil. Occurring in woodlands and hedgerows in the wild, it has adapted to cope with competition from the roots of other woody plants. *Viburnum opulus* 'Xanthocarpum' has lovely golden yellow berries.

Like hydrangeas, *Viburnum plicatum* f. *tomentosum* 'Mariesii' (see page 36) does not cope with drought but succeeds on moister soils under trees. The horizontal branches carry veined green leaves and heads of white flowers in spring all along their length. The horizontally branched habit of the shrub makes it a natural choice to plant alongside a tree.

SHRUBS UNDER TREES

41

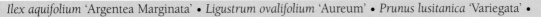

Ilex aquifolium 'Argentea Marginata' • *Ligustrum ovalifolium* 'Aureum' • *Prunus lusitanica* 'Variegata' •

Color under trees

In open, sunny borders you can add color with an endless variety of suitable plants. However, in shade under trees the choice is more restricted, particularly if the shade is heavy and the soil is dry. Variegated evergreen foliage is a reliable way to introduce color, enhanced by the addition of seasonal bulbs and flowers. In the dappled shade under light trees, such as birches, you can grow various grasses, sedges, and evergreen perennials to pleasing effect.

Camassia leichtlinii

Foxgloves, *Digitalis purpurea*, are woodland plants that thrive under the shade of trees.

Hyacinthoides non-scripta

SPANISH BLUEBELLS

The Spanish bluebell, *Hyacinthoides hispanica* (below), is more robust than the English *Hyacinthoides non-scripta* and will hybridize with it to its detriment.

The Spanish species should not be planted where it can invade English populations. In isolation it is a successful bulb and provides long-lasting color in dry areas under mature trees.

FLOWERING BULBS

Bulbs are an excellent way of brightening up the area under mature trees; most other subjects that succeed in this environment are foliage plants, so the addition of flowers is welcome. Many of the spring-flowering bulbs, particularly those from woodland habitats, thrive under mature trees. The bulbs store food and water through the dormant season, enabling them to grow, then they flower and set seed quickly at the first signs of spring, before the tree canopy robs them of light and water. They then die down and retreat beneath the surface until the following season. Some bulbs wait to flower until autumn, for example *Cyclamen hederifolium* (Zones 7–9) and *Colchicum autumnale* (see page 138). Both produce leaves after the flowers. By the time the bulbs' foliage appears, the tree canopy has thinned, allowing light through to the leaves and providing energy so the bulbs can survive through the following summer's dormant period.

Hyacinthoides non-scripta (Zones 5–8), the English bluebell, is a good choice for planting under trees, with its delicate arching spikes of sapphire flowers that stand out in light shade. It naturalizes well if allowed to seed. Large colonies can be established from very sparse bulb plantings after only a few years.

OTHER BULBS TO GROW UNDER TREES   *Anemone blanda* • *Anemone nemorosa* • *Chionodoxa luciliae* •

NARCISSI

Daffodils (*Narcissus*) are a good choice for damper sites, as they thrive on the heavy soil that is fatal to so many bulbs. For a naturalistic effect, choose those with graceful flowers. Always plant daffodils in drifts of several bulbs, leaving about 2 in. (5 cm) between the bulbs to give them space to multiply. Plant them approximately three times the depth of the bulb.

Narcissus 'February Gold' (**1**) (Z. 5–7) is an old variety, with golden yellow flowers held in a coy manner on slender 1-ft. (30-cm) stems. It is long-lasting, bright, and cheerful. *Narcissus* 'Jetfire' (**2**) (Z. 4–9) is an excellent variety with a bright orange trumpet and weather-resistant, long-lasting flowers. *Narcissus* 'Hawera' (**3**) (Z. 4–9) is later-flowering than most other daffodils, with fine, grasslike leaves and delicate, pale yellow flowers carried two or three on a stem. Unlike other daffodils, it does not leave obvious ugly foliage to die down after the flowers have faded. The British native *Narcissus pseudonarcissus* 'Lobularis' (**4**) (Z. 4–9) is one of the loveliest to naturalize. Growing to 8 in. (20 cm) or so, it has pale yellow, delicate blooms with slightly stronger yellow trumpets and starts to flower in early spring. All yellow daffodils complement golden-variegated evergreens, such as *Euonymus fortunei* 'Emerald 'n' Gold' (see page 31).

In a garden situation *Camassia leichtlinii* (Zones 3–8) offers an alternative to bluebells, with spikes of starry blue flowers emerging from grass or low ground cover in late spring. They are particularly effective set against the white bark of birches.

The sheltered area close to the trunk of deciduous trees provides a haven for small woodland bulbs, protecting them from wet conditions and often supplying soil rich in organic matter. The winter aconite, *Eranthis hyemalis* (Zones 3–8), is at home here, provided the soil is not too dry. In late winter it produces golden yellow, cup-shaped flowers ringed by emerald green ruffs. It seeds and spreads freely if happy. Snowdrops, including the widespread *Galanthus nivalis* (Zones 4–8), enjoy similar conditions, producing

Cyclamen hederifolium

Eranthis hyemalis

green and white blooms in late winter and early spring. The autumn-flowering *Cyclamen hederifolium* (Zones 7–9) is also happy here. Its ivy-shaped, marbled gray-green leaves are just as attractive in winter and spring as the pink and white flowers are in fall.

NATURALIZING BULBS UNDER TREES

Flowering bulbs such as bluebells (*Hyacinthoides*), daffodils (*Narcissus*), and snowdrops (*Galanthus*) (left) spread prolifically if allowed to seed. When they are grown in grass, avoid mowing until the seed is fully ripe and has fallen, usually by midsummer. In the early stages of establishing colonies of bulbs, it is worth collecting the seed and distributing it by hand to spread it more evenly. Do not use herbicides in the area, as these could damage the young seedling bulbs.

BULBS FOR WOODLAND CONDITIONS

Favored woodland conditions—rich in leaf mold and with some moisture throughout the year—provide the ideal growing environment for some exquisite bulbous perennials. The lovely creamy, backward-curving blooms of *Erythronium californicum* (**1**) (Z. 4–8) open in mid-spring above shining leaves. *Mertensia virginica* (**2**) (Z. 3–7), the Virginian cowslip, has smooth gray leaves and arching sprays of violet-blue flowers. Choicest of all are the trilliums, with their curious arrangement of petals and leaves in threes. *Trillium grandiflorum* (**3**) (Z. 5–7), the wake robin, is the best known, with large white petals against broad green leaves on 16-in. (40-cm) stems. Trilliums can be difficult to establish, but they prove their worth with their beautiful blooms in early spring.

Crocus chrysanthus 'Cream Beauty' • *Crocus tommasinianus* • *Leucojum aestivum* • *Narcissus bulbocodium* •

FLOWERING PERENNIALS

Some flowering perennials bloom along with the early bulbs under trees. The earliest to flower are the hellebores. *Helleborus foetidus* (Z. 6–8) is the most successful in shade, with attractive dark green palmate leaves and lime green flowers. The cultivar *Helleborus foetidus* **Wester Flisk Group** (**1**) is particularly fine, with plentiful red-tinged foliage and large heads of flowers above the leaves in late winter. It grows to 2 ft. (60 cm).

Iris foetidissima (**2**) (Z. 6–9) has green sword-shaped leaves, often rather scruffy in appearance, in irregular clumps of foliage 2 ft. (60 cm) high. The yellow-green flowers are flushed purple and are always rather hidden in the leaves when they appear in midsummer. The plant comes into its own in winter, when the seed pods split to reveal shining scarlet seeds that add a welcome splash of color in the shadiest areas.

Primula vulgaris (**3**) (Z. 6–7), the primrose, will seed itself and colonize the ground at the edge of the shade under trees. It produces its pale yellow, freshly fragrant flowers over a long period from late winter right through spring.

Pulmonarias (Z. 4–8), the lungworts, have delightful bright white, pink, or blue flowers in early spring, before their spotted and patterned leaves fully develop and provide interest for the remainder of the season. The white- and blue-flowered varieties are especially useful in shade, because the color of their flowers is so visible in low light. Good ones to choose include *Pulmonaria* **'Blue Ensign'** (**4**), with pale blue flowers, and *Pulmonaria* **'Sissinghurst White'** (**5**), in pure white.

Lamiums are good ground-cover plants, some having attractively patterned foliage. The tall-growing *Lamium orvala* (**6**) (Z. 4–8) is a valuable plant that establishes well under trees and covers the ground until midsummer. Upright stems carry nettlelike leaves and bruised-pink flowers that are surprisingly showy in shade. *Lamium galeobdolon* (Z. 4–8), the yellow archangel, has smaller, silver-etched leaves and soft golden yellow nettlelike flowers on 1-ft. (30-cm) stems.

Digitalis purpurea (**7**) (Z. 4–8), the biennial foxglove, will seed itself freely on virtually any soil. In the first year, it produces a rosette of evergreen leaves, and in the second a tall spike of tubular flowers. There are many selected varieties, but the British native species is unbeatable for naturalistic plantings. After flowering, allow the seed to ripen on the plant and scatter it freely where you want plants in following years. It often germinates better on disturbed soil, so it is worth stirring it into the surface with a hoe and watering lightly until the seedlings are established. These can be thinned or transplanted in late summer.

Geraniums that will grow in the shade under trees include *Geranium macrorrhizum* (**8**) (Z. 4–7), a good ground-cover plant, providing pink or white flowers in early summer and some foliage tints in late summer and fall. *Geranium phaeum* (**9**) (Z. 7–8), the mourning widow, is a much taller plant that will grow virtually anywhere. The small flowers, on delicate stems, vary from darkest maroon to white, and although not showy they are freely produced so make an impact.

Both the annual and perennial forms of **honesty** will grow in the dappled shade of trees. *Lunaria annua* (**10**) (Z. 7–9) is a biennial producing tall, branched stems up to 32 in. (80 cm) high in the second year, with simple flowers that are usually bright purple but sometimes white. Its silky seed heads last into winter and cast their round, flat brown seeds around the garden for coming seasons. The perennial honesty, *Lunaria rediviva* (**11**) (Z. 4–8), is more clump-forming but of similar height. Pale lilac or white flowers appear above a dome of bright green foliage. If happy, it will seed itself freely.

Epimedium × rubrum

Arum italicum ssp. *italicum* 'Marmoratum'

Carex comans bronze-leaved

Carex oshimensis 'Evergold'

SEASONAL BEDDING UNDER TREES

Most seasonal bedding plants need plenty of sun to flower well. Also, the conditions under trees are usually too dry for their delicate roots to fend for themselves. However, if grown in containers, or watered regularly, some will succeed and provide welcome color. All the various primulas are ideal in spring, and they associate well with bulbs. In summer, busy Lizzies (*Impatiens*) and begonias flower throughout the season in shade, continuing their display until the first frosts. Fuchsias are also excellent in shade, and will often establish successfully in the ground under lighter trees. Those with smaller flowers, such as the popular *Fuchsia* 'Mrs Popple' (Zones 7–9), will overwinter in the garden and perform again in following years.

Fuchsia 'Mrs Popple'

PERENNIALS AND SEDGES

A number of perennials flower in shade under trees (see opposite) but few display good foliage color. The shade-loving evergreen **epimediums** (Zones 5–8) are an exception in winter, when the shining green foliage of some varieties turns rich shades of copper and reddish brown. *Epimedium × rubrum* and *Epimedium × versicolor* 'Neosulphureum' produce particularly colorful winter foliage and reddish-bronze new leaves.

Arum italicum ssp. *italicum* 'Marmoratum' (Zones 5–8) is also useful for late winter and spring foliage interest. Its arrow-shaped leaves start to emerge in midwinter, producing clumps of emerald foliage up to 1 ft. (30 cm) high, delicately veined and patterned with silver; they are lovely with spring bulbs and primroses.

Where the ground is not too dry, some **sedges** succeed and add color with their graceful, grasslike foliage. *Carex comans* bronze-leaved (Zones 7–9) forms a light bronze cloud, with gently waving leaves up to 1 ft. (30 cm) high. It succeeds under trees with airy canopies, such as birches (*Betula*). *Carex oshimensis* 'Evergold' (Zones 5–9) has pale yellow, long, gently waved foliage and a prostrate habit. The leaves are edged green but appear light yellow.

Acorus gramineus 'Ogon' (Zones 10–11) has straight, pointed leaves 6 in. (15 cm) long. These are arranged in sharp fans forming dense clumps. Although the foliage is striped green and yellow, it appears lime green. It contrasts well with dark evergreen and ground-cover plants.

FOLIAGE COLOR IN SHADE

Many variegated evergreen and deciduous shrubs succeed in the shade of trees, retaining their color to good effect. Shrubs with plum or golden yellow foliage seem an obvious choice to add color in the absence of flowers, but these are not generally successful. In the shade, purple and red foliage loses its color and usually turns to a muddy brown-green, while yellow foliage tends to turn light green. In some cases, this can still be satisfactory. For example, the bright, strong yellow *Choisya ternata* 'Sundance' (right; Z. 8–10) can be overpowering in a garden, but in the shade of a tree becomes an attractive yellowish lime green color.

Planting climbers through trees

Climbers and trees make natural planting partners. In their native environment, vigorous climbers grow up into the tree canopy to take advantage of the light, and some weak-stemmed climbers use the trunk as a support. In gardens, climbers bring another dimension to the upper layer of planting—they add color and interest, in the branches and on the trunk of a tree.

Akebia quinata

Rambling roses such as *Rosa* 'Wedding Day' will cascade through the lower branches of birch trees.

Before planting a climber to grow through a tree, consider the long-term effects. A vigorous climber may compete too strongly with its host, smothering the tree and inhibiting its growth and development. For example, a rampant rambling rose grown through a tree makes an impressive statement when in bloom, but its weight and competitive growth can smother the branches, taking light and air from the leaves, while the roots draw water from the soil. Eventually, the tree will suffer. *Clematis montana* (Zones 6–9) is another climber likely to smother a smaller host tree. A picture when in flower in spring, it can quickly become a mass of untidy stems weighing down the branches. The same is true of *Fallopia baldschuanica* (Zones 4–9), the Russian vine.

The secret of success is to choose the right climber for the right tree. If you want a perfect specimen tree, avoid climbers, except possibly those that confine themselves to the lower part of the trunk.

Akebia quinata (Zones 4–8) is a twining climber with attractive light green leaves composed of several leaflets radiating from a central leaf stalk. The flowers are red-purple and fragrant, and hang from the twining stems in spring; they are sometimes followed by purple fruits in fall. Akebia can grow up to 40 ft. (12 m) in a tree; however, it is better growing through low trees or over dead tree stumps, because the flowers and foliage are light and delicate and are therefore lost when they are high up. It is a good choice for growing through a Japanese cherry (*Prunus*) such as *Prunus*

WHERE TO PLANT

Plant a climber as close to the tree's trunk as possible. The active feeding roots of the tree are out near the drip line (the extent of the branch overhang) of the tree, so there is far more competition for water and nutrients in this area than there is near the trunk. Use a border spade or fork to find a gap between the roots, and make a hole larger than the rootball of the climber. After planting, keep the climber well watered until established.

'Kanzan' (Zones 5–7); if the foliage of the tree starts to thin owing to bacterial canker, the akebia is light enough not to compete with the tree too severely.

Many of the larger-flowered **clematis** can be grown through small trees in mixed plantings. They add color around eye-level, below the tree canopy and above small shrubs and perennials. Clematis enjoy the shade that the tree provides over their roots, but they struggle if conditions are too dry, as is often the case beneath larger trees. Striking color effects are achieved by combining clematis with foliage trees in complementing or contrasting colors.

Spring-flowering *Clematis montana* (Zones 6–9) easily scales trees, draping its long garlands of flowers over the crown of the tree or hanging them from the branches. Once established, most varieties, including the popular *Clematis montana* **var.** *rubens*, are vigorous growers and can detract from the assets of the host tree when in leaf. But this is a good choice for larger trees and to scramble over dead trees and large stumps.

Clematis viticella (Zones 5–8) is the perfect choice to grow through any tree. It is easily maintained, as it is best cut down to within 2 ft. (60 cm) of the ground in late winter. The top growth can be carefully pulled from the bare branches of the tree when the plant is cut back. Vigorous new shoots then quickly emerge that will scale the trunk and branches and twine their way through the canopy. The growth is light and the leaves are dainty. All varieties are free-flowering, producing a profuse succession of dainty flowers from midsummer into fall. (See box, right.)

Euonymus fortunei varieties (Zones 5–8) are ideal ground cover beneath trees; they enjoy the shade and tolerate the dry conditions. Most will also climb if given support such as a tree trunk. *Euonymus fortunei* 'Emerald Gaiety', with green and gray-green leaves variegated with white, and *Euonymus fortunei* 'Emerald 'n' Gold', with dark

Clematis montana var. *rubens* is vigorous enough to grow into the branches of a large eucalyptus.

GOOD HOSTS FOR CLEMATIS VITICELLA CULTIVARS

Try these combinations to extend a tree's season of interest or to provide additional color.

Clematis '**Alba Luxurians**' (**1**) (Z. 5–7) White flowers. Adds interest to trees such as *Malus floribunda* (**2**) (Z. 4–8) after flowering.

Clematis '**Kermesina**' (**3**) (Z. 6–9) Crimson flowers. Good with purple foliage trees like *Prunus cerasifera* 'Nigra' (**4**) (Z. 3–8).

Clematis '**Purpurea Plena Elegans**' (**5**) (Z. 4–9) Double, soft red-purple flowers. Good with silver foliage trees such as *Pyrus salicifolia* 'Pendula' (**6**) (Z. 4–7).

Clematis '**Royal Velours**' (**7**) (Z. 3–8) Deep purple flowers. Complements golden foliage trees such as *Gleditsia triacanthos* 'Sunburst' (**8**) (Z. 3–9).

Fallopia baldschuanica

Hedera colchica 'Dentata Variegata'

Hedera colchica 'Sulfur Heart'

Humulus lupulus 'Aureus'

green and gold variegated leaves (see page 31), are the two most vigorous forms, climbing to 6 ft. (2 m) or more. *Euonymus fortunei* **'Silver Queen'** has strong creamy white variegation (see page 31). It is more striking than the others but slower. All give evergreen foliage interest on the tree trunk and an extension of ground-cover planting.

Fallopia baldschuanica (Zones 4–9), the Russian vine, is one of the most vigorous climbing plants. The stems reach 40 ft. (12 m) or more and growth is rapid. Sprays of tiny white, pink-tinged flowers appear in summer and fall. Although the effect is attractive, the plant smothers anything in its path. This climber should never be used over a valuable tree, but it can be a useful quick cover-up for a dead tree or an unwanted sycamore or ash.

Cultivars of *Hedera colchica* (Zones 6–9), the Persian ivy, have large, glossy, diamond-shaped leaves, often brightly variegated. They are strong-growing plants but rarely invasive, and are ideal for growing up the trunks of large mature trees. *Hedera colchica* **'Dentata Variegata'** has large green, marbled gray-green leaves broadly margined with rich cream. It is not as fast-growing as other varieties, so is good for less vigorous trees.

Its strong variegation shows up well in heavy shade. *Hedera colchica* **'Sulfur Heart'** has large leaves splashed with yellow and bright green, and dark green round the edges. It is strong-growing and reliable, and the foliage is perfect all year.

IVY: FRIEND OR FOE?

There are differing opinions regarding the effect of ivy on the health and growth of trees. Some gardeners fear its presence, considering that it eventually strangles and smothers the tree. Others claim that its presence is harmless to the tree and that it is beneficial in providing a habitat for birds and insects.

Some people argue that an old deciduous tree covered in mature ivy is more liable to be blown over in a gale, as the heavy, thick mass of the ivy's flowering shoots and leaves presents a barrier to wind, while the tree's bare branches would enable the wind to pass through unimpeded. On the other hand, the strong stems and roots of the ivy can help to anchor the tree as it weakens in old age. In reality, ivy is probably harmless to healthy trees that are still growing strongly with a good root system that anchors them firmly in the soil.

Gardeners need have no concern about planting the less vigorous variegated varieties of *Hedera colchica* and *Hedera helix* (see below). These attractive plants add color and interest to the trunk of a mature tree and thrive in the dry shade beneath its branches.

There are also many variegated varieties of *Hedera helix* (Zones 4–9), the common ivy. These are ideal growing on the lower trunk of a tree as an extension of ground-cover planting. Good varieties include: *Hedera helix* **'Glacier'**, with silver-green leaves edged white; *Hedera helix* **'Oro di Bogliasco'** ('Goldheart'), which has dark green leaves with central splashes of yellow; and *Hedera helix* **'Goldchild'**, which is pale green edged creamy yellow.

Humulus lupulus **'Aureus'** (Zones 5–8), the golden hop, is an herbaceous climber that dies down to the ground in winter. It grows quickly to 20 ft. (6 m) and has attractive soft yellow leaves and conelike clusters of hops in summer. The golden hop needs sun to develop the best leaf color, and is suitable for growing over smaller trees, hedges, and stumps. When established, it can produce a mass of heavy foliage to the detriment of the host tree. To prevent this, reduce the number of shoots in early summer. It goes particularly well with purple foliage trees.

The climbing hydrangea, *Hydrangea anomala* ssp. *petiolaris* (Zones 4–7), is usually associated with shady walls. Climbing like ivy, with the aid of aerial roots, it has tan-colored stems that are revealed when the heart-shaped, emerald green leaves fall in winter. The white flowers are like those of a lacecap hydrangea and appear in early summer. Given a tall tree to climb, it will reach 80 ft. (25 m), and it is a magnificent sight when in flower. It stays close to the trunk of the tree and rarely interferes with the leaf canopy of its host. Being deciduous, it does not present the problem of additional foliage weight and wind-resistance in winter. *Hydrangea seemannii* (Zones

Hydrangea anomala ssp. petiolaris

8–9) and *Hydrangea serratifolia* (Zones 9–10) are both evergreen species that will reach a height of 30 ft. (10 m). Natives of Central and South America, they are not suited to colder zones but are valuable evergreen climbers for woodland gardens. Both these species have leathery dark green leaves and creamy white flowers—

GOOD COMPANIONS

The deep velvety-red blooms of *Clematis* 'Rosemoor' (1) (Z. 4–8) are a striking contrast to the golden yellow summer foliage of *Ptelea trifoliata* 'Aurea' (2) (Z. 3–9).

The pink flowers of *Clematis* 'Comtesse de Bouchaud' (3) (Z. 4–9) are lovely with the soft silvery green leaves of *Sorbus aria* 'Lutescens' (4) (Z. 5–6).

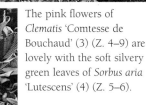

The sky-blue flowers of *Clematis* 'Blekitny Aniol' (Blue Angel) (5) (Z. 4–9) are bright and fresh with the white and green variegated foliage of *Acer negundo* 'Variegatum' (6) (Z. 2–9).

FAVORITE HONEYSUCKLES

There are a number of cultivars of *Lonicera periclymenum* and they vary in the timing and color of their flowers.

Lonicera periclymenum 'Belgica' (above; Z. 5–8), the early Dutch honeysuckle, has flowers that are reddish purple outside, yellow within, produced in early summer and again in late summer.

Lonicera periclymenum 'Graham Thomas' (Z. 5–8) has summer flowers that are creamy white and turn yellow.

Lonicera periclymenum 'Serotina' (Z. 5–8), the late Dutch honeysuckle, has flowers that are reddish purple outside, pale within, from midsummer into fall.

Lonicera periclymenum 'Sweet Sue' (Z. 5–8) blooms from early summer to early fall; creamy white flowers become yellow with age.

Hydrangea seemannii in domed flower heads edged with larger florets in summer, *Hydrangea serratifolia* in upright sprays that are produced in late summer.

Lonicera periclymenum (Zones 5–8), the woodbine, is a woodland native. It is a vigorous plant, scrambling and climbing across the woodland floor and scaling trees on its way. The sweetly fragrant, creamy yellow flowers are often flushed with pink or purple and appear throughout summer; there is no more delightful scent than that of honeysuckle on a summer's evening. A country garden plant, it looks good growing through apple trees, hawthorns, and hedges, although it may become too invasive in some areas.

VERY VIGOROUS ROSES TO GROW THROUGH TREES

All flower in early summer to midsummer.

Rosa **'Bobbie James'** (**1**) (Z. 5–10) A large, vigorous rambler reaching 40 ft. (12 m), with apple green leaves and very large heads of deliciously fragrant, creamy, semidouble flowers.

Rosa filipes **'Kiftsgate'** (**2**) (Z. 6–10) One of the biggest ramblers, growing to 50 ft. (15 m) or more. Very thorny, with gray-green leaves and large heads of small creamy white flowers followed by small orange-red hips.

Rosa **'Paul's Himalayan Musk'** (**3**) (Z. 4–9) Light, airy sprays of blush-pink, double flowers with a sweet fragrance, on trailing, thorny stems up to 40 ft. (12 m).

Rosa **'Wedding Day'** (**4**) (Z. 7–9) Small, dark green leaves on vigorous stems up to 30 ft. (10 m). Large clusters of apricot buds, opening to creamy yellow flowers, fading to white, followed by small orange hips. Good scrambling through old apple trees. (See page 46.)

Parthenocissus quinquefolia

Vitis coignetiae

Parthenocissus quinquefolia (Zones 3–10), Virginia creeper, goes unnoticed for much of the year, with its medium green leaves composed of five leaflets. It is a vigorous climber that will scale large trees, sending long vines over the canopy to cascade from the branches. In mid-fall its foliage suddenly erupts in brilliant shades of red. The effect is quite spectacular, like scarlet ribbons hanging from the branches. It is particularly effective when grown through mature yew trees, whose dark green foliage provide a dramatic background for the red display.

Roses are the obvious choice to grow through trees. Indeed, vigorous ramblers grow this way in the wild, being well equipped to climb unaided with their strong shoots, armed with grappling-hook thorns. Maintenance of roses growing through trees is virtually impossible, and pruning to remove some of the old stems is a major task, so choose carefully. In most cases, the rose eventually becomes the feature: the tree merely a means of support. This is a good way to incorporate roses into a garden where deer and rabbits prevent the successful cultivation of bush roses. There are many varieties to choose from: Those listed here are a few proven favorites (see boxes, above and opposite).

OTHER GOOD CLIMBERS TO GROW THROUGH TREES *Clematis tangutica • Cobaea scandens •*

LESS VIGOROUS ROSES TO GROW THROUGH TREES

All flower in early summer to midsummer.

Rosa 'Albéric Barbier' (**1**) (Z. 4–9) Almost evergreen, disease-free foliage and double clotted-cream flowers. Blooms in early summer and often again later. Grows to 25 ft. (8 m).

Rosa 'American Pillar' (**2**) (Z. 5–9) A vigorous rambler, reaching 20 ft. (6 m), with strong stems and sprays of single, deep pink flowers with white eyes. Striking with purple foliage.

Rosa 'Complicata' (**3**) (Z. 4–8) An old shrub rose with large, scented, deep pink dog-rose flowers in early summer. It is vigorous, reaching 16 ft. (4 m), and it will scramble into the boughs of a tree in even the most inhospitable conditions. Good in country gardens.

Rosa 'Rambling Rector' (**4**) (Z. 5–9) Dense, shrubby growth, reaching 20 ft. (6 m). Large clusters of creamy white, semidouble, very fragrant flowers are followed by small red hips in fall.

The vine *Vitis coignetiae* (Zones 5–8) is perhaps the best foliage climber of all. A vigorous grower, it can reach the top of tall trees, carrying its large, rounded, slightly lobed leaves on trailing vines secured by tendrils. The leaves are often as much as 1 ft. (30 cm) across, in soft green and lightly russet beneath. In fall they color ocher, orange, and red, lighting up the tree canopy. As autumn color is best when the vine is growing in poor dry soil, it is usually excellent planted below an oak or other large, greedy, thirsty tree.

Vitis vinifera 'Purpurea' (Zones 6–8) is at the other end of the scale. It is slow-growing, especially when first planted, with small leaves, green flushed purple, becoming more intense in color as the season progresses. It is suitable for growing through a small tree of modest growth and looks good with the weeping pear, *Pyrus salicifolia* 'Pendula' (see page 70).

Wisterias are often recommended for growing into old trees, and their vigorous growth will quickly take them into the

canopy of tall specimens. However, because the flowers hang down in long racemes, especially in the case of *Wisteria floribunda*, these are usually lost in the leaf canopy. *Wisteria brachybotrys* 'Murasaki-kapitan' (Zones 6–9) grows to 28 ft. (9 m) or more. The flowers are violet-blue and fragrant and carried in smaller racemes that hang to the side of the stems, making them more visible when growing in a tree. *Wisteria brachybotrys* 'Shiro-kapitan' (Zones 6–9) is similar, with large, fragrant white flowers.

Wisteria brachybotrys 'Murasaki-kapitan'

Wisteria sinensis

Wisteria sinensis (Zones 5–8), Chinese wisteria, has prolific fragrant mauve or dark lilac flowers in large, hanging clusters in late spring, before the leaves appear. It is therefore a good choice of wisteria for growing through a tree.

Lonicera similis var. *delavayi* • *Rosa* 'Félicité Perpétue' • *Schizophragma hydrangeoides* • *Schizophragma integrifolium* •

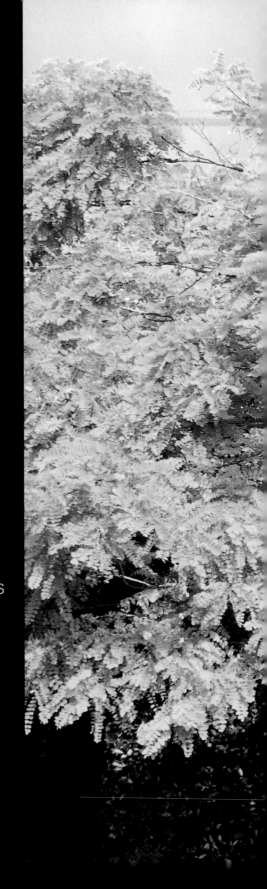

FOLIAGE EFFECTS

Blossom and fruit are frequently a tree's most spectacular assets, but their beauty is often very short-lived. In contrast, foliage provides interest for much of the year. There is an almost infinite spectrum of leaf color, in golden, purple, and silver hues as well as numerous greens. Variegated trees add eye-catching variety, and some evergreens from warmer regions have established themselves as permanent residents, adding further to the range of foliage effects in our gardens.

RIGHT: *Robinia pseudoacacia* 'Frisia' and *Prunus cerasifera* 'Nigra'

Golden foliage

Trees with golden foliage are not shy in coming forward in the garden. Some display their best color in spring, while others are at their peak in mid- to late summer. Whatever the time of year, yellow- and gold-leaved trees always bring lightness to a planting scheme and attract the eye.

Acer cappadocicum 'Aureum'

The ever-popular yellow-leaved *Robinia pseudoacacia* 'Frisia' is striking against a blue sky.

A golden foliage tree is essential to provide height in a yellow border. It is also a good choice for a focal point, perhaps placed at the end of the garden or a path, or beside a feature such as a statue, where it will draw the eye. Golden yellow foliage invariably demands attention. Consider its position carefully, because a single plant, particularly a tree, can dominate a garden and detract from the contribution made by other, more subtle subjects.

The **acers** boast a number of lovely golden-leaved trees that deserve wider planting, varying in stature from the diminutive Japanese maples to the yellow-leaved form of the large silver maple. All benefit from interesting leaf shape and they often have good autumn color.

Acer cappadocicum 'Aureum' (Zones 6–8) is an attractive broad-headed, medium-sized tree with shiny, sharply lobed leaves that are golden yellow in spring and early summer. The new growth is red, striking in contrast with the yellow mature leaves. The foliage becomes green in summer but turns rich butter yellow in fall.

Acer negundo 'Kelly's Gold' (Zones 2–9) is a form of the box elder. The divided, soft golden foliage looks lovely with the gray-green, upright stems. This bushy-headed acer can be grown as a multi-stemmed specimen or a standard tree and, like all *Acer negundo* cultivars, it responds well to pruning to keep growth in check, making it an ideal tree for a small space. (See Good Companions, opposite.) Although its coloring is not as vivid as that of *Acer negundo* 'Auratum' (Zones 2–9), the latter is liable to sunburn and is a less vigorous grower. *Acer negundo* is one species that seems to be resistant to honey mushroom (see page 25), a fact worth considering if you have had problems with this disease in the past.

The golden form of the Norway maple, *Acer platanoides* 'Princeton Gold' (Zones 3–7), is a good round-headed, medium-sized tree with large foliage. It is particularly striking in late spring, when the golden yellow leaves are at their best and are carried on red leaf stalks. The tree turns green as summer progresses but develops good yellow autumn color.

Acer pseudoplatanus 'Worley' (Zones 4–8), the golden sycamore, is an attractive medium-sized tree with soft yellow leaves

Acer platanoides 'Princeton Gold'

Acer saccharinum f. *lutescens*

Catalpa bignonioides 'Aurea'

that turn golden before reverting to green in summer. It can be slow to establish, so it is best to buy a container-grown specimen.

The yellow-leaved form of the silver maple, *Acer saccharinum* f. *lutescens*, (Zones 3–8) is a lovely choice where there is space for a large tree. It has a graceful, open habit, particularly when young, often with downward-sweeping branches and soft yellow, silver-backed leaves that shimmer as they flutter in the breeze. The color is best in spring and in fall, when the leaves turn to shades of gold, orange, and flame. Silver maples are not a good choice for a windy, exposed site, and their branches are easily damaged by strong winds as the trees mature.

The golden Indian bean tree, *Catalpa bignonioides* 'Aurea' (Zones 5–9), is one of the most exotic large trees for a temperate garden. The stiff, light brown branches are upright in young specimens but become more spreading with age. The foliage is late to appear: Often only small green buds are visible in late spring. Once the weather is warm enough, the large, velvety leaves quickly unfurl to form a soft, floating canopy of pure sunshine. On mature plants, glorious spikes of white, richly marked foxglovelike flowers appear in mid- to late summer, sometimes followed by long, beanlike fruits. Once the flowers appear, the leaves often develop a lime green hue, but plants in full sun still seem golden compared with neighboring plants. The leaves are shown at their best against a blue summer sky, or when the early evening sun shines

through them. Catalpa is easy to grow on any reasonably fertile soil. In very dry conditions, the leaves will be smaller; water and feed the tree with a slow-release fertilizer for best results.

OTHER WAYS OF GROWING CATALPA

Although a catalpa can ultimately grow into a large specimen tree, it can be grown as a shrub, as it responds well to hard pruning. If cut back hard at an early age, a multi-stemmed specimen results, with vigorous upright growth and large leaves, but usually at the expense of flowers. Catalpas are also successful when grown in a large tub.

GOOD COMPANIONS

The fine stems and tiny leaves of *Lonicera nitida* 'Baggesen's Gold' (1) (Z. 7–9) are light enough to partner *Acer negundo* 'Kelly's Gold' (2) (Z. 2–9), an airy tree with delicate, soft gold leaves.

Gold-variegated evergreens mix well with golden foliage trees. *Euonymus japonicus* 'Chollipo' (3) (Z. 7–9), an upright shrub, tolerates shade and thrives under the light canopy of trees like *Ulmus glabra* 'Lutescens' (4) (Z. 5–7).

Evergreen *Elaeagnus* × *ebbingei* 'Limelight' (5) (Z. 7–11) has leaves marked in yellow, which complement the golden foliage of *Robinia pseudoacacia* 'Frisia' (6) (Z. 3–8). It provides color after the robinia's leaves fall.

Metasequoia glyptostroboides 'Gold Rush'

Quercus rubra 'Aurea'

The golden foliage of *Gleditsia triacanthos* 'Sunburst' strikes the theme in this yellow border.

Fagus sylvatica 'Dawyck Gold'

There are a number of golden forms of beech. However, the most useful in gardens is *Fagus sylvatica* 'Dawyck Gold' (Zones 4–7). A dense, medium-sized, columnar tree, it is bright yellow in new leaf and becomes yellow-green in summer. It is useful in formal situations and as a strong but not overpowering statement in the garden.

Gleditsia triacanthos 'Sunburst' (Zones 3–9) is often mistaken for robinia. In fact it has more rigid, horizontal growth and smaller leaves. The light foliage canopy of this medium-sized tree suits mixed planting and allows cultivation of other plants right up to the trunk. If positioned in full sun, the color is retained all year. It is a considerably tougher character than robinia, and is a better choice for exposed sites. (See Good Companions, right.)

A tall and majestic tree, *Metasequoia glyptostroboides* 'Gold Rush' (Zones 4–8) is a yellow-leaved form of the dawn redwood. It needs a woodland setting on moist acid soil to perform well. The bright golden yellow new foliage is striking against the red-brown bark and is spectacular when sunlight shines through the branches.

For a sheltered, preferably semi-shady position, *Quercus rubra* 'Aurea' (Zones 4–8), the golden-leaved red oak, is a lovely small, spreading tree. In new leaf, it is unmissable: bright yellow against the lime green of other trees. As spring progresses, the color fades, becoming green by midsummer. The leaves color richly in fall on acid soil. A clone grown in Europe is less susceptible to scorch in full sun; this is known as *Quercus rubra* 'Limelight' at Hillier Nurseries in England.

GOOD COMPANIONS

The fine feathery foliage of *Gleditsia triacanthos* 'Sunburst' (1) (Z. 3–9) contrasts in texture with the bolder leaves of *Cornus alba* 'Aurea' (2) (Z. 2–8). The two make an excellent foundation for a border with a yellow theme.

The yellow foliage and flowers of the low, mat-forming creeping Jenny, *Lysimachia nummularia* 'Aurea' (3) (Z. 5–7), echo the yellow foliage canopy of *Ptelea trifoliata* 'Aurea' (4) (Z. 3–9).

MORE TREES WITH GOLDEN FOLIAGE *Alnus incana* 'Aurea' • *Fagus sylvatica* 'Zlatia' • *Laurus nobilis* 'Aurea' •

SMALL GOLDEN TREES

There are several golden trees that are under 12 ft. (4 m) and are therefore good for smaller gardens.

Both *Acer palmatum* 'Katsura' (1) (Z. 6–8) and *Acer palmatum* 'Orange Dream' (Z. 6–8) have bright orange-yellow foliage that turns rich yellow in fall. They are striking foliage plants, with soft, abundant leaves, which are richer in color at the end of the upright branches. Both of these acers are particularly effective in pots and in contemporary and Asian schemes.

Acer shirasawanum 'Aureum' (2) (Z. 5–9) is a beautiful small tree for dappled shade, ideally in a woodland garden on acid soil. Of bushy habit when young, it has rounded, many-lobed, soft golden yellow leaves. As the tree develops, the leaves and branches assume a horizontally layered habit. It is a good subject for a pot in a sheltered, semi-shaded position.

The golden hop tree, *Ptelea trifoliata* 'Aurea' (3) (Z. 3–9), is ideal for small gardens. In summer it bears loose sprays of small yellowish flowers that are richly scented, reminiscent of honeysuckle; winged green fruits often follow the flowers. The foliage is soft yellow and resembles large, pointed clover leaves. A low, spreading tree, growing to only 6–10 ft. (2–3 m) high, it is useful in a mixed border or as a small specimen. (See Good Companions, opposite.)

Robinia pseudoacacia 'Frisia' (Zones 3–8) is a popular medium-sized golden tree. Its softly divided leaves and sweeping growth are glorious all year, but they are at their richest towards late summer. In ideal conditions, *Robinia pseudoacacia* 'Frisia' makes an attractive specimen and is a dramatic contrast to purple foliage trees and shrubs, such as *Prunus cerasifera* 'Nigra' (Zones 3–8) and *Cotinus coggygria* 'Royal Purple' (Zones 4–8). The robinia is not

a tree for exposed situations: The branches may be brittle, especially under the weight of the foliage. In some seasons, robinias drop some of their foliage in summer, often in response to dry soil conditions and fluctuating temperature. This is not normally a problem, and trees usually recover the following spring, particularly if watered thoroughly and mulched with organic matter. (See page 54 and Good Companions, page 55.)

Ulmus glabra 'Lutescens'

Ulmus × *hollandica* 'Dampieri Aurea' (Zones 5–7) is a tall elm with a narrow, conical habit. The small, wavy leaves are crowded on the branches and are soft yellow, becoming greener where they join the twigs. It is an attractive tree, useful in a confined space and in a mixed border, with the branches casting little shade. It is resistant to Dutch elm disease. *Ulmus glabra* 'Lutescens' (Zones 5–7) is a lovely form of the Scotch elm, or wych elm. It grows quickly and develops a broad, spreading habit. The leaves are soft primrose yellow at first, becoming golden, then greenish yellow. (See Good Companions, page 55.)

GOLDEN EVERGREENS

Where a golden evergreen tree is needed, conifers are really the only choice. Most have branches and foliage to the ground, so the trunk is not visible, but they provide a strong presence and stature. Large golden conifers, such as **Chamaecyparis lawsoniana** 'Stardust' (1) (Z. 5–7), make a bold statement but do not suit rural settings. **Pinus sylvestris** Aurea Group (2) (Z. 2–8) is a slow-growing small tree, useful for its soft, golden yellow winter foliage that mixes well with gold-variegated hollies and gold-spotted aucubas. The foliage assumes a yellow-green shade in summer.

Liquidambar styraciflua 'Moonbeam' • *Quercus robur* 'Concordia' • *Sorbus aria* 'Chrysophylla' •

Plum foliage

Trees with dark, plum purple foliage are the most dramatic and awe-inspiring plants: the nearest thing to permanent autumn color in the garden. Far from being sombre or oppressive, they contribute richness to the planting and create a bold link with purple-leaved shrubs. Purple foliage trees make excellent screening plants; surprisingly perhaps, their deep tones recede into the distance rather than create a dense wall.

Acer palmatum var. *dissectum* 'Crimson Queen'

The new leaves of purple beech, *Fagus sylvatica* Atropurpurea Group, darken as summer progresses.

Acer palmatum 'Atropurpureum'

Acer palmatum 'Bloodgood'

The purple-leaved **Japanese maples** are grown as both shrubs and small specimen trees. *Acer palmatum* 'Atropurpureum' (Zones 6–8) is among the most popular. Fairly upright in habit and vigorous for a Japanese maple, it has rich crimson-bronze leaves that turn deep red in fall. Of the many named varieties of Japanese maple, *Acer palmatum* 'Bloodgood' (Zones 6–8) is one of the finest. The stems are dark purple-brown, and its elegant leaves are dark red-purple, retaining their color throughout the season. In summer, red fruits develop, hanging beneath the leaves. The foliage turns deep red in fall. (See page 92.)

The varieties with finely cut foliage, *Acer palmatum* var. *dissectum* (Zones 6–8), form mounded shrubs when allowed to grow naturally. However, if trained when young, or grafted on to an upright stem of *Acer palmatum*, they can make an attractive standard—a miniature weeping tree with cascading branches and feathery foliage. One of the best is *Acer palmatum* var. *dissectum* 'Crimson Queen', with deep reddish purple leaves clothing the branches.

Acer platanoides 'Crimson King' (Zones 3–7) is a widely planted, large-leaved purple foliage tree. Although large and heavy-headed, it is nonetheless elegant and stately when grown as a specimen. It is a lovely sight in spring, when the fluffy lime-colored flowers contrast with the translucent red new foliage. By summer, the leaves are purple-black and shiny on the upper surfaces, and reflect the light beautifully in full sun; in the low light of morning and evening, and in shade, the foliage assumes a muddy, purple-green hue, and the tree appears darker and bolder. In fall, the leaves develop shades of purple, red, and orange. (See Good Companions, page 60.) *Acer platanoides* 'Crimson Sentry' (Zones 3–7) is a more upright, narrow-headed tree, with similar reddish purple foliage that is lighter in color. *Acer platanoides* '**Deborah**' (Zones 3–7) is excellent as a large background or screening tree. It has light red-purple new growth that turns green, tinged with purple as it ages.

Catalpa × *erubescens* '**Purpurea**' (Zones 5–9) is of medium stature but big when it comes to impact, with its large velvety, heart-shaped leaves. The new shoots are dark chocolate-purple opening to purple-green, and the leaves become dark green flushed purple with age. As with all catalpas, the foliage is late to appear and is held almost horizontally on the branches. This cultivar produces foxglove-like flowers in summer that are similar to those of other catalpas; they are purple-brown, with white spots, and are smaller than those of *Catalpa bignonioides* (see page 82). *Catalpa* × *erubescens* '**Purpurea**' responds well to hard pruning to control size, resulting in vigorous growth with larger foliage. It is a good choice to provide dramatic height in mixed plantings, and this species also works well in exotic schemes with plants such as phormiums and cannas. (See Good Companions, page 60.)

Acer platanoides 'Crimson King'

Acer platanoides 'Deborah'

Catalpa × erubescens 'Purpurea'

PURPLE FOLIAGE EVERGREENS

There are not any true broad-leaved hardy evergreen trees with purple foliage. However, *Pittosporum tenuifolium* '**Purpureum**' (1) (Z. 9–10) would serve the purpose of a small tree in a confined space. It is a very upright, often rather sparse, evergreen shrub with shining dark purple leaves that are particularly richly colored in winter.

The foliage of some conifers changes color in the colder days of winter. *Cryptomeria japonica* Elegans Group (2) (Z. 6–8), the Japanese cedar, is a bushy small tree or large shrub, with clouds of soft foliage that is sea-green in summer and bronze in winter. It makes a superb specimen and goes well with broad-leaved shrubs in a mixed border.

The red foliage forms of *Cordyline australis* (Z. 7–11), the cabbage palm, will grow to single-stemmed or multi-stemmed specimens in time. In sheltered gardens, cultivars such as *Cordyline australis* '**Torbay Red**' (3) are good where an exotic, architectural tree is required and would not look out of place. (See pages 80–81.)

Cercidiphyllum japonicum 'Rotfuchs'

Cercis canadensis 'Forest Pansy'

Gleditsia triacanthos 'Rubylace'

Purple-leaved beeches are magnificent trees, with rich foliage color from the time when the young copper leaves unfurl in spring until the old leaves turn golden brown, clinging to the branches all winter. **Fagus sylvatica Atropurpurea Group** (Zones 4–7) and the named selections are large, stately trees that are good for big spaces (see pages 58 and 95).

Fagus sylvatica 'Purpurea Pendula' (Zones 4–7) is a small, weeping form. It is usually grafted to produce a compact, mushroom-headed weeping tree suitable for a small garden. The color is good, but this tree can be awkward to place; it looks best on the corner of a bed where a bold focal point is needed.

Fagus sylvatica 'Dawyck Purple' (Zones 4–7) is a fastigiate form, and one of the finest trees of upright habit. Narrow when young, it broadens with age and retains its branches to ground level. It can

Cercidiphyllum japonicum 'Rotfuchs' (Zones 4–8) is a fastigiate form of the Katsura tree, with small, heart-shaped purple leaves arranged neatly on upright stems. A medium-sized, slow-growing plant, it is ideal for providing vertical height in a mixed border, perhaps rising from low purple foliage plants like heucheras.

Cercis canadensis 'Forest Pansy' (Zones 5–9) is a showy, slow-growing large shrub or small tree, with a broad, round head, ideally suited to mixed planting. The magnificent leaves are heart-shaped and delicate, velvety ruby-purple, and thin enough to allow light to shine through them. The new leaves are redder and remain shiny until they reach their ultimate size, forming an attractive contrast to the silky mature leaves. This is an ideal tree for a small, sheltered garden, positioned out of the hot, midday sun. If planted as a young specimen, its leader should be staked to help it to achieve the desired height. (See page 137 and Good Companions, right.)

GOOD COMPANIONS

The silvery foliage of *Elaeagnus* 'Quicksilver' (1) (Z. 3–9) is a dramatic contrast against the dark purple leaves of *Prunus cerasifera* 'Nigra' (2) (Z. 3–8).

The sea-blue flowers and wine-flushed foliage of *Hydrangea serrata* 'Bluebird' (3) (Z. 5–7) make a soft and subtle combination with the rich purple leaves of *Cercis canadensis* 'Forest Pansy' (4) (Z. 5–9).

Purple-leaved trees, like *Acer platanoides* 'Crimson King' (5) (Z. 3–7) and *Catalpa* × *erubescens* 'Purpurea' (Z. 5–9), complement purple shrubs such as *Physocarpus opulifolius* 'Diabolo' (6) (Z. 2–7).

OTHER PLUM FOLIAGE TREES *Acer platanoides* 'Schwedleri' • *Betula pendula* 'Purpurea' •

also be trimmed to clear the lower stem and make an upright purple tree suitable for a restricted space. (See page 110.)

The delicate, fernlike foliage of *Gleditsia triacanthos* 'Rubylace' (Zones 3–9) is ideal in the mixed border with roses and herbaceous perennials, and is a more subtle contrast to shrubs with golden foliage than trees with strong plum-purple foliage. The leaves, which emerge late on the wiry horizontal branches, are green at first, becoming coppery red by midsummer. As summer progresses, the foliage in the heart of the tree reverts to green, but the leaves at the ends of the branches remain red. The weight of the foliage in midsummer gracefully bends the branches. 'Rubylace' is less vigorous than the yellow-leaved *Gleditsia triacanthos* 'Sunburst' (see page 56), so is better in a small space, although its tardiness to come into leaf may be a disadvantage.

There are numerous small, purple-leaved ornamental **crab apples**. Sadly, many are ruined by their susceptibility to canker and mildew. *Malus* × *moerlandsii* 'Profusion' (Zones 4–7) is still planted and cherished for its wine red fragrant flowers, small red fruits and pretty, coppery crimson young leaves. However, it is susceptible to both diseases. *Malus* 'Profusion Improved' (Zones 4–8) and *Malus* 'Directeur Moerlands' (Zones 4–8) are improved forms, similar to 'Profusion' but more resistant to disease. The latter has softly serrated leaves of coppery plum, redder at the tips of the branches. It has an open habit, exposing dark purple-black stems.

Malus 'Royalty' (Zones 3–7) is a small, upright tree with pointed, glossy dark purple leaves that turn red in fall. The large, crimson-purple flowers are followed by dark red fruits. *Malus* 'Royal Beauty' (Zones 3–7) is a weeping alternative. The hanging stems are dark purple and carry red-purple leaves that age to dark green but retain their purple color on the undersides. The dark red-purple flowers are followed by small, dark red fruits.

In this garden, the purple-tinted leaves of *Malus* 'Directeur Moerlands' provide foliage interest and light height alongside a pergola of rambling roses.

The **ornamental cherries** are known for their short flowering season, but there are a number of varieties that have decorative, red-purple foliage. Since leaves provide interest for longer than blossom they generally make better garden plants than other cherry trees, especially where space is at a premium. All the red-purple cherries are small and round-headed. *Prunus* × *blireana* (Zones 5–7) has attractive, coppery purple shining leaves and a graceful habit. The leaf color is retained through summer. The flowers, which open with the leaves in mid-spring, are relatively large and double, rose-pink and fragrant.

Prunus cerasifera 'Nigra' (Zones 3–8) is perhaps the most versatile purple foliage tree and being small will fit into most gardens. It has blackish stems and neat, black-purple leaves; in full leaf, it is rounded and billowing, and provides drama without weight. The small pink flowers appear on the bare branches in early spring. (See page 120 and Good Companions, opposite.) *Prunus cerasifera* 'Pissardii' (Zones 3–8) is similar but has white flowers (see page 121). The two are often confused. Both make excellent shrubs and can be used for hedging. The lovely *Prunus* 'Royal Burgundy' (Zones 5–7) has deep purple summer foliage that turns bronze in fall. It is less vigorous than *Prunus* 'Kanzan' (Zones 5–8), from which it originated as a sport, but still has the same large, double pink flowers. It is a good choice for those who enjoy frothy cherry blossom in spring, with the bonus of foliage that provides further interest through summer and fall.

61

Fagus sylvatica 'Purple Fountain' • *Fagus sylvatica* 'Rohanii' • *Malus* 'Rudolph' • *Prunus padus* 'Colorata' •

Variegated foliage

Variegated trees occur rarely in the wild and are a phenomenon of gardens, where they provide a beautiful, often year-round display. The cream, white, yellow, or pink in their foliage adds delicate color, and they are ideal for lightening the tree canopy. Since variegated leaves have relatively low levels of chlorophyll, which helps to manufacture food for growth, they are often less vigorous than their entirely green counterparts.

The graceful *Acer* 'Silver Cardinal' has beautiful foliage and hanging clusters of winged fruits.

Acer campestre 'Pulverulentum'

Acers, always at the forefront when it comes to colorful foliage selections, include some of the best variegated trees. *Acer campestre* (Zones 4–8), the field maple, has some very attractive variegated forms. The neat, round, lobed leaves and loose, rounded head combine to form a small to medium-sized tree that is relatively slow-growing and suitable for smaller gardens. *Acer campestre* 'Carnival' has leaves with broad cream margins. *Acer campestre* 'Pulverulentum' is more unusual, with leaves that are thickly speckled and blotched with white, giving an overall silvery green appearance.

VARIEGATED BOX ELDERS

The variegated forms of *Acer negundo* (box elder; Z. 2–9) have smaller leaves and create a lighter effect than *Acer platanoides* (see page 108). They grow relatively quickly, but respond well to pruning. All need regular attention to remove reverted plain green growth.

Acer negundo 'Variegatum' has white margins to the leaves. It is a light and pretty tree, and can be grown in a container. (See Good Companions, page 66.) *Acer negundo* 'Elegans' (1) has creamy yellow edged leaves. It is usually more vigorous and provides a bolder effect than 'Variegatum'. *Acer negundo* 'Flamingo' (2) is the most widely grown box elder, with soft salmon pink margins to the young gray-green leaves, the margins becoming white as the leaves age. It is often grown as a shrub; hard prune to maintain vigorous growth and good leaf color. As a tree, it is better pollarded: Cut all the branches back to the main stem in winter.

Some of the Japanese maples, varieties of *Acer palmatum* (Zones 6–8), display variegated foliage, but these rarely achieve more than medium-sized shrub proportions. *Acer palmatum* 'Asahi-zuru' is one of the fastest-growing, with a spreading habit and leaves blotched with white and pink. *Acer palmatum* 'Butterfly' is more upright and compact in habit, with small gray-green leaves edged with cream and tinged pink at the tips of the branches. It needs a sheltered position in dappled shade to protect the leaves from being scorched.

The Norway maple, *Acer platanoides* 'Drummondii' (Zones 3–7), is perhaps the most striking and popular of all variegated trees. The emerald green leaves have broad cream margins, creating a light and showy effect. This acer can lack vigor when young, taking several seasons to get going. However, it eventually becomes a showy, round-headed, medium-sized tree if it is well maintained (see box on Reversion, below). Its bold appearance will always attract attention in the garden, and it makes an excellent focal point. (See Good Companions, page 66.)

Acer palmatum 'Asahi-zuru'

Acer palmatum 'Butterfly'

Acer platanoides 'Drummondii'

Acer pseudoplatanus f. *variegatum* 'Leopoldii'

Acer pseudoplatanus f. *variegatum* 'Nizetii'

Acer pseudoplatanus f. *variegatum* 'Esk Sunset'

REVERSION

Most variegated plants have a tendency to revert, or produce plain green shoots. These all-green shoots must be cut out as they appear, because they are more vigorous than the variegated growth and, if left on the plant, will eventually take over. *Acer platanoides* 'Drummondii' specimens (Z. 3–7) and the variegated forms of *Acer negundo* (Z. 2–9) are often ruined by leaving the plain green shoots to develop.

RESISTANCE TO HONEY MUSHROOM (SHOESTRING ROOT ROT)

Acer negundo and its cultivars (Z. 2–9) appear to be resistant to honey mushroom. Use them where honey mushroom is present and to replace a tree that has been killed by the fungus.

There are a number of good variegated **sycamores**, particularly for more exposed situations. Their showy foliage is eye-catching in the garden, even on young plants. Winged fruits, which are usually salmon pink on cultivars with pink variegation, sometimes hang from the spreading branches. *Acer pseudoplatanus* f. *variegatum* 'Leopoldii' (Zones 4–8) has leaves that are splashed and streaked with salmon pink and yellow. *Acer pseudoplatanus*

f. *variegatum* 'Nizetii' (Zones 4–8) has similar variegation of pale green and white, often purple on the underside of the leaves. (See Good Companions, page 66.) *Acer pseudoplatanus* f. *variegatum* 'Simon-Louis Frères' (Zones 4–8) is a lovely cultivar, with pink young leaves becoming blotched and streaked with green and white as they age. All mature to medium-sized trees of compact habit. *Acer pseudoplatanus* f. *variegatum* 'Esk Sunset' (Zones 4–8) is a

Aralia elata 'Aureovariegata' can successfully be grown in a pot.

Bright variegated trees look even more striking when underplanted with dark-leaved evergreens. These also provide foliage interest in winter, when the leaves of deciduous trees fall. *Prunus laurocerasus* 'Otto Luyken' (1) (Z. 6–8) is a low-growing shrub, with upright stems bearing narrow, dark green leaves and spikes of white flowers in spring. It grows well in shade and tolerates the dry conditions under the canopy of a tree. Any of the sarcococcas are ideal under deciduous trees. *Sarcococca confusa* (2) (Z. 6–8) has wavy, dark green leaves on upright green stems up to 3 ft. (90 cm). It has a suckering habit, and will slowly colonize the ground under trees, where it enjoys the shade in summer. Fragrant tiny white flowers in winter are a bonus.

Aralia elata 'Variegata'

Castanea sativa 'Albomarginata'

much slower-growing cultivar that is often grown as a shrub. The leaves are salmon pink when young, becoming dark green mottled and streaked with salmon, sage, and white, with purple undersides.

Acer 'Silver Cardinal' (Zones 5–8; see page 62) is a lovely medium-sized tree that is becoming popular. The new shoots and leaf stalks are red, and the bark develops chalky stripes as it matures, like a snake-bark maple (*Acer capillipes*). The leaves are shining and dark green with subtle lobes; the upper surface is splashed and streaked with white. As the tree matures, it develops gracefully drooping branches, showing off the lovely foliage to advantage.

The Japanese angelica tree, *Aralia elata* 'Variegata' (Zones 3–9), is usually seen as a shrub, but will grow into a small, exotic, open tree. The leaves are carried in a palmlike arrangement at the top of slender thorny stems, and the leaflets are edged and blotched creamy white. *Aralia elata* 'Aureovariegata' (Zones 3–9) is similar, but with yellow variegation, fading to white later in the season. Mature specimens produce large sprays of white flowers in fall. This is a good tree for a small garden. It suits contemporary schemes, and is effective planted as a group of three specimens of varying heights rising out of gravel.

The exotic foliage of the rare variegated sweet chestnut, *Castanea sativa* 'Albomarginata' (Zones 4–9), is particularly fine, with dark green leaves edged in creamy white. It is a fast-growing, medium-sized, broadly columnar tree that does not reach the large proportions of other chestnuts. Unfortunately, *Castanea sativa* is susceptible to chestnut blight, so avoid it if this is a problem in your area.

Cornus controversa 'Variegata' (Zones 5–8) is usually regarded as a shrub, but it matures into a beautiful small variegated tree. The leaves are strikingly variegated with creamy white, and they hang elegantly from sweeping horizontal branches. The tree has a lightness and grace, and makes a delightful specimen, particularly against darker background planting. As a young shrub, growth can be slow, and the habit is very horizontal until a strong leading shoot appears. However, it is highly ornamental at all stages of its life. Where space is limited, try growing *Cornus alternifolia* 'Argentea' (Zones 3–7) as a single-stemmed specimen. The foliage is smaller and softer, but the layered habit produces a similar effect.

Ligustrum lucidum 'Excelsum Superbum' (Zones 7–10) should be one of the most popular choices for a garden tree. A form of Chinese privet, it is evergreen, with attractive creamy-edged leaves that appear soft yellow when seen from a distance. It grows into an elegant, broad-headed small tree of regular shape, and produces attractive white flowers in late summer and early fall. This ligustrum is an excellent choice for alkaline soils but is not good for cold areas, where frost damage can result in leaf drop.

Cornus controversa 'Variegata' is often known as the wedding-cake tree because of its layered branches.

Liquidambars are normally selected for the impact and beauty of their autumn color. Although the variegated forms are not noted for this, they nonetheless offer some interesting foliage effects during much of the year. *Liquidambar*

styraciflua 'Silver King' (Zones 5–9) is a small, broadly conical tree with white-edged, gray-green leaves. The overall effect is almost one of silver foliage that flushes rose pink in late summer and fall. *Liquidambar*

styraciflua 'Variegata' (Zones 5–9) is more vigorous, with leaves striped and mottled with yellow. The soft, attractive color gives the overall effect of a golden foliage plant but with the bonus of reasonably attractive autumn color.

Liriodendron tulipifera 'Aureomarginatum'

Populus × *jackii* 'Aurora'

the green form, *Liriodendron tulipifera* 'Aureomarginatum' displays good golden autumn color.

Populus × *jackii* **'Aurora'** (*Populus* × *candicans* 'Aurora') (Zones 2–5) is the variegated form of the Ontario poplar, or balm of Gilead poplar, so called because of the balsamlike fragrance of the new leaves. The young leaves are predominantly creamy white tinged with pink, becoming green streaked with white, and finally green. Pruning in late winter stimulates new growth and promotes better color. The variegation does not always appear in the first season after planting. This poplar is a small, broad-headed tree and can be disease-prone in some areas.

One of the most admired and also most reviled of all small trees, *Salix integra* **'Hakuro-nishiki'** (Zones 4–8) is undeniably eye-catching. Usually seen clipped into a lollipop shape, top-grafted on a slender stem, it explodes as a mass of small leaves,

Salix integra 'Hakuro-nishiki' can be a striking small tree in a sheltered spot.

GOOD COMPANIONS

The pretty green and white variegated leaves of *Acer negundo* 'Variegatum' (1) (Z. 2–9) are perfect with the apple green foliage and clear white flowers of *Rosa* 'Iceberg' (2) (Z. 4–9).

The salmon pink in the leaves of *Acer pseudoplatanus* f. *variegatum* 'Nizetii' (3) (Z. 4–8) picks up the pretty strawberry pink blooms of *Rosa* 'Cornelia' (4) (Z. 4–10).

The lime and cream flowers of *Hydrangea arborescens* 'Annabelle' (5) (Z. 3–9) create a harmonious combination with the cream-variegated midsummer canopy of *Acer platanoides* 'Drummondii' (6) (Z. 3–7).

The variegated tulip tree, *Liriodendron tulipifera* **'Aureomarginatum'** (Zones 4–9), makes a magnificent medium-sized, broadly columnar tree. The tulip-shaped leaves are edged with bright yellow in spring and early summer, the color fading to yellow-green by late summer. Like

OTHER VARIEGATED FOLIAGE TREES *Crataegus laevigata* 'Gireoudii' • *Crataegus monogyna* 'Variegata' •

profusely blotched with white, carried on straight twigs. The shoots are pink at the tips, and the overall effect is one of cotton candy on a stick. It is at its best in late spring and summer, but when the leaves fall in winter the twigs turn an attractive red-brown. This is a weak plant, susceptible to damage by sun, wind, and frost, and in all but the most sheltered situations it will be disappointing. However, in a courtyard garden, where it is happiest, it makes a striking small tree, ideal for a container.

VARIEGATED HOLLIES

Where a variegated evergreen tree is needed, a holly is a natural choice for the patient gardener. Hollies are initially slow-growing, but most grow into elegant conical trees, about 15 ft. (5 m) tall, and retain their branches almost to ground level. *Ilex × altaclerensis* 'Golden King' (Zones 6–9) is one of the finest, with

Ilex × altaclerensis 'Golden King'

Ilex × altaclerensis 'Lawsoniana'

Ilex aquifolium 'Argentea Marginata'

bright, golden-edged leaves that lack spines. It produces prolific red berries that contrast brilliantly with the foliage. *Ilex × altaclerensis* 'Lawsoniana' (Zones 6–9) is similar, but with gold-centered, green-edged leaves. *Ilex aquifolium* **'Handsworth New Silver'** (Zones 6–9) is one of the best white-variegated varieties, with dark stems and long, dark green leaves mottled with gray and edged creamy white; it also produces plenty of bright red berries. *Ilex aquifolium* **'Argentea Marginata'** (Zones 6–9) has broad, dark green leaves edged with pale cream, and dark red berries.

SMALL VARIEGATED TREES

These variegated trees are all under 12 ft. (4 m), and are therefore good choices for a smaller garden or courtyard, and for growing in large containers in a sheltered situation. When growing trees in pots, always use a loam-based potting mix—this retains water and nutrients well, and has sufficient weight to anchor a top-heavy tree in a container.

Acer negundo 'Flamingo' (**1**) (if pruned) (see page 62)

Acer palmatum 'Asahi-zuru' (**2**) (see page 63)

Acer pseudoplatanus f. *variegatum* 'Esk Sunset' (**3**) (if pruned) (see page 63)

Aralia elata 'Variegata' ✿ (**4**) (see page 64)

Liquidambar styraciflua 'Silver King' (**5**) (see page 65)

Salix integra 'Hakuro-nishiki' (**6**) (see page 66)

Fagus sylvatica 'Albomarginata' • *Ligustrum lucidum* 'Tricolor' • *Prunus cerasifera* 'Hessei' • *Quercus robur* f. *variegata* •

Silver foliage

Trees with silver foliage suit sunny situations and often tolerate dry soils and coastal locations. They provide soft contrast to darker trees and shrubs, lightening the darker greens and enhancing the richness of purple foliage; many are evergreen. Although silver trees often originate in warmer climates, they mix well with the deciduous broad-leaved trees of temperate gardens and rarely look out of place.

Eucalyptus gunnii

Eucalyptus parvifolia

Eucalyptus dalrympleana is a fast-growing, robust tree with wonderful bark.

Mostly natives of Australia, **eucalyptus** are fast-growing evergreen trees that are widely planted in temperate climates. Many species are very tough, and they combine attractive bark with beautiful leaves, which are often different in shape and color in their juvenile and adult forms. The leaves, although heavy and plentiful, are carried on fine stems and move with the breeze. Their leathery surface is reflective and shimmering in bright sunlight, giving the blue-green color of most species a silver sheen.

Eucalyptus gunnii (Zones 8–10), the cider gum, is the most widely planted eucalyptus. It is easy to grow and looks attractive as a young specimen in a pot—hence its appeal in garden centers. The young leaves are rounded and silver-blue initially, becoming sickle-shaped and blue-green as the tree matures. Left unpruned, this fast-growing, spreading tree becomes far too big for the average garden, but if grown as a multi-stemmed specimen (see box, right) its size can be controlled by cutting back selected stems to ground level every year or two.

Eucalyptus parvifolia (Zones 7–9) is less widely grown than *Eucalyptus gunnii*, but it is one of the most tolerant of all eucalyptus, surviving low temperatures and alkaline soils. It grows to a medium-sized, spreading tree, with blue-green narrow leaves. The peeling bark is particularly attractive and is especially noticeable in winter.

Eucalyptus dalrympleana (Zones 8–10), the mountain gum, is a fast-growing, medium-sized, broadly columnar tree, with gray-green leaves that are bronze when young. The attractive patchwork bark becomes white as it matures. This is one of the hardiest eucalyptus species, and it copes with exposed sites, especially if grown as a multi-stemmed specimen.

Eucalyptus pauciflora (Zones 8–10), the snow gum, is another hardy species from high altitudes. It is smaller in stature than many eucalyptus, so is therefore easier to accommodate, and it has a spreading habit. *Eucalyptus pauciflora* **ssp. *debeuzevillei*** bears long, lance-shaped leaves and white bark. *Eucalyptus*

Eucalyptus pauciflora ssp. debeuzevillei

pauciflora ssp. *niphophila* is the slowest-growing, with gray-green, sickle-shaped leaves on blue-green shoots. This is perhaps the best of all eucalyptus for bark effect: a patchwork of sage green, cream, and gray.

Eucalyptus perriniana (Zones 9–10), the spinning gum, is another small tree with white bark marked with darker blotches. The juvenile foliage is particularly striking: The leaves are rounded and form discs that are joined together by a fine, straight stem that passes through the middle of each leaf. Some of the older juvenile leaves dry and remain loosely attached to the plant, causing them to spin in the wind, hence the common name. This is regarded as one of the best eucalyptus for silver-blue foliage.

Hippophae rhamnoides (Zones 3–7), the sea buckthorn, can be grown as a shrub or a small tree. It has an upright habit with stiffly ascending, often angular branches and silver, willowlike leaves. An adaptable plant, it grows on any soil and is particularly useful in exposed coastal situations. Some trees produce yellow berries in the winter that persist on the stems after the leaves have fallen.

Now that winters have become milder, the olive tree, *Olea europaea* (Zones 8–9), is more and more widely grown in warmer parts of North America and the British Isles. Its silver-green evergreen foliage and silver-gray stems are attractive

Hippophae rhamnoides

The silver foliage of the olive tree, *Olea europaea*, rises above a cloud of white *Centranthus ruber* 'Albus' flowers.

all year, and it suits a variety of situations. Olives can be grown untrained as large, round-headed shrubs or informal trees, their size controlled by pruning. They are also good in containers—an ideal choice for a sunny courtyard garden—and can be trimmed and trained as topiary subjects. (See Good Companions, page 71.)

CULTIVATING EUCALYPTUS

A eucalyptus is best planted as a young container-grown plant. When grown as a single-stemmed specimen, it will achieve height quickly, often without establishing a stable root system to provide sufficient anchorage; this can result in the plant toppling over in exposed situations. To avoid this, cut the plant back hard after planting, and select the strongest shoot to grow on.

Alternatively, you can grow a eucalyptus as a multi-stemmed tree. This restricts its size, provides greater stability, and makes more impact in those forms with attractive bark. To create a multi-stemmed tree, cut it back in early spring after planting: Preserve three or four stems and allow these to develop into multiple trunks emerging from the same root.

Most eucalyptus can be grown as shrubs, resulting in contained plants with vigorous, juvenile foliage year after year. Cut back all the stems to the base every couple of years (a process known as 'stooling'); eucalyptus have the ability to regenerate from the base of the plant. *Eucalyptus gunnii* (Z. 8–10) is particularly successful grown like this: its rounded, silver-blue leaves on graceful stems are superb for cutting for floral decoration.

Populus alba

Salix exigua

The weeping branches of the weeping pear, *Pyrus salicifolia* 'Pendula' are clothed in soft, silver willowlike leaves from spring to fall.

Sorbus aria 'Lutescens'

Although the white poplar, **Populus alba** (Zones 3–8), has a rather sparse, unattractive habit, it is a good, large tree for exposed sites and coastal situations. Its most attractive feature is its foliage, which looks dramatic when the white, woolly undersides of the leaves are seen against a blue summer sky. The tree's foliage is useful for making an impact on the edge of a large rural garden.

The weeping silver pear, **Pyrus salicifolia 'Pendula'** (Zones 4–7), is a popular silver-leaved tree. Its diminutive stature and attractive habit make it a natural choice for smaller gardens, where it makes a good specimen tree and provides height in mixed beds and borders. The grayish branches can be awkward when young, but they weep gently when mature and are generously clothed in narrow silver, willowlike leaves. Creamy flowers appear in clusters in spring. To control the size of this tree, prune the branches in winter; alternatively, if you want a neater, more formal shape, trim the shoots regularly. Underplanting with *Santolina chamaecyparissus* (Zones 6–9) is effective and amplifies the silver effect.

The willow **Salix alba** var. **sericea** (Zones 2–9) is a delightful tree for wet sites, and it looks particularly striking from a distance. Smaller and less vigorous than *Salix alba*, this form is more compact and round-headed, with whippy stems and intensely silver narrow leaves. Like most willows, it can be pollarded to contain its size and promote a round-headed shape. **Salix exigua** (Zones 2–9) is often grown as a shrub but it will make an elegant slender tree that provides height without weight. The fine brown stems are clothed in narrow silver leaves that sway in the

OTHER SILVER FOLIAGE TREES *Chamaecyparis lawsoniana* 'Columnaris' • *Elaeagnus* 'Quicksilver' •

SILVER-BLUE CONIFERS

Where space permits, *Cedrus atlantica* Glauca Group (**1** and **2**) (Z. 6–9) is a magnificent large tree with horizontal, slightly down-swept branches of silvery blue needles. It is attractive and appealing at an early age, but often quickly outgrows its site. Many specimens are spoiled by pruning, and this should be avoided.

The various forms of *Picea pungens* Glauca Group (**3**) (Z. 2–7) grow into regular, conical, small to medium-sized trees with stiff but elegant branches and bristling needles in shades of silver-blue. The color is best on neutral to acid soils and in areas with clean air and cold winter weather. *Picea pungens* 'Hoopsii' is an excellent form with vivid silver-blue needles, particularly intense towards the ends of the branches. *Picea pungens* 'Koster', the most popular cultivar, is almost identical. (See page 151.)

The silver-blue forms of *Chamaecyparis lawsoniana* (Z. 5–7) are useful where a large columnar or conical subject is needed. Their softly colored foliage makes them easier to integrate into a planting scheme than the golden varieties, and they sit more happily in informal plantings. *Chamaecyparis lawsoniana* 'Pembury Blue' (**4**) is considered one of the best. It grows to form a tall, feathery cone of silver-blue foliage in light sprays.

Sorbus thibetica 'John Mitchell'

GOOD COMPANIONS

The dark green leaves of *Osmanthus* × *burkwoodii* (**1**) (Z. 6–8) complement the silver-green foliage of the whitebeam *Sorbus aria* 'Lutescens' (**2**) (Z. 5–6). The osmanthus has fragrant flowers in spring, when the tree is at its loveliest.

The silver-green foliage and white stems of the olive *Olea europaea* (**3**) (Z. 8–9) create a Mediterranean picture with the silver foliage and blue flowers of the lavender *Lavandula angustifolia* (**4**) (Z. 5–8).

breeze. It is a wonderful subject for mixed plantings, and it combines well with shrub roses and herbaceous perennials.

The **whitebeams** are stunning in spring, when the silver-gray buds swell on the dark stems. The leaves unfurl silver-green, becoming green above and silver beneath by late summer. *Sorbus aria* 'Lutescens' (Zones 5–6) is a beautiful tree, with rounded, slightly pleated leaves, but it can be susceptible to leaf drop owing to scab. White flowers in spring are followed by red fruits, which show up well against the rich yellow shades of the autumn foliage. (See page 111 and Good Companions, left.) *Sorbus aria* 'Majestica' ('Decaisneana') (Zones 5–6) has larger, more oval leaves and is more resistant to scab and early leaf drop. It grows well in exposed sites and coastal locations. Both make small to medium-sized, round-headed trees.

A substantial, rounded tree, *Sorbus thibetica* 'John Mitchell' (Zones 5–7) unfurls magnificent large, rounded foliage, which gives it an exotic appearance. The leaves are silver when they emerge, but the upper sides turn green with age. It is an excellent choice for specimen planting.

Eucalyptus coccifera • *Picea pungens* 'Moerheimii' • *Pittosporum* 'Garnettii' • *Populus* × *canescens* • *Pyrus nivalis* •

Evergreen foliage

The appeal of evergreen trees is obvious: no bare branches in winter, no major leaf fall, and a permanent presence in the garden. Where screening is required, an evergreen is generally the best choice, as it provides a solid barrier and enduring privacy. Some evergreens lend themselves to trimming and shaping, so the size and appearance of the plant can be tailored to the situation.

A mature holly, *Ilex aquifolium*, makes a bold, broadly conical tree of great beauty. Hollies can live to a great age, developing more character as they mature.

The silver wattle or florist's mimosa, ***Acacia dealbata*** (Zones 10–11), is best known for its glorious sprays of fluffy golden yellow flowers produced in late winter and early spring (see page 152). It is a slender, fast-growing tree that broadens with age, with long branches and ferny blue-green foliage. It is evergreen unless severe winter weather causes defoliation. This is one of the loveliest of the small trees, but it needs a sheltered site and sufficient space to reach its potential.

Arbutus unedo (Zones 8–10), the Killarney strawberry tree, is a small spreading, ornamental tree with dark green, glossy foliage. In maturity it often becomes gnarled, with a beautiful stem of deep red-brown, shredding bark. Small white, hanging pitcher-shaped flowers are borne at the same time as strawberry-like fruits in late fall. Although reminiscent of an ericaceous plant in its flowers and foliage, it is alkaline-tolerant and does well on poor soil; it is also an excellent coastal plant. *Arbutus unedo* usually spends its early years as an attractive bushy shrub before reaching treelike proportions. (See Good Companions, page 75.) ***Arbutus unedo* f. *rubra*** has pink flowers and abundant fruit.

Arbutus × andrachnoides (Zones 8–11) is a beautiful, spreading hybrid with cinnamon-colored bark.

Acacia dealbata

Arbutus unedo

Arbutus × andrachnoides

Arbutus unedo f. rubra

Arbutus menziesii

Cotoneaster frigidus 'Cornubia'

Cotoneaster 'John Waterer'

Cotoneaster 'Hybridus Pendulus'

Arbutus menziesii (Zones 7–9) also has a spreading habit and smooth reddish bark that peels in late summer and fall to reveal emerald shades beneath. The flowers appear in clusters in late spring, followed by orange-yellow fruits. The leaves tend to be larger and more succulent than those of *Arbutus unedo*, but *Arbutus menziesii* is fussier, needing a sheltered site and acid or neutral soil.

Although usually viewed as large shrubs, some **cotoneasters** take on treelike habit and proportions. In spring all have clusters of white flowers, which attract pollinating insects, and in fall they bear showy berries that are appreciated by the birds. *Cotoneaster frigidus* 'Cornubia' (Zones 7–9) is semi-evergreen and grows to 20 ft. (6 m) high; in fall its upright branches are weighed down by large red fruits. (See Good Companions, page 75.) *Cotoneaster* 'Hybridus Pendulus' (Zones 6–9) is often grown as an attractive small weeping tree with trailing branches; large, dark red berries nestle in the glossy green leaves in fall. (See page 87.) *Cotoneaster × watereri* 'John Waterer' (Zones 5–7) is another semi-evergreen tree with long, spreading branches that carry plentiful big red berries. It needs space, and is an excellent choice for a specimen in an area of rough grass.

EVERGREEN TREES FOR SCREENING

When planting an evergreen tree for screening, you need to remember that evergreen trees are usually slower-growing than deciduous trees. For example, a mature arbutus will make an excellent screening plant but it takes years to reach a height that will screen, for example, a building. Large imported specimens of trees such as *Quercus ilex* (see page 97), *Laurus nobilis* (1) (Z. 8–9) and *Photinia* × *fraseri* 'Red Robin' (2) (see also page 77) are readily available; however, these often suffer a severe transplanting check if soil preparation and aftercare are not carried out properly.

Generally, for quicker results, it is better to partner an evergreen screening shrub or tree with a larger, faster-growing deciduous tree. For example, grow the deciduous *Sorbus* × *commixta* 'Embley' (3) (Z. 6–8) alongside *Arbutus unedo* (4) (Z. 8–10). The former can be planted as a standard tree, and will quickly give a light canopy of fernlike foliage and masses of red berries in fall. The arbutus will provide evergreen interest and will slowly mature to a beautiful tree when the life of the sorbus is coming to an end.

The many species of **eucalyptus** are obvious choices where evergreen trees are required (see pages 68–69). They sit well in most landscapes because of their light habit and softly moving foliage, and they grow quickly, making an impact from an early age; bear in mind that some reach massive proportions. Eucalyptus are best planted as young container-grown specimens. If planted when mature, they are often unsteady on their roots and become top-heavy.

In reasonably sheltered locations on neutral or acid soils, **eucryphias** (Zones 8–10) grow into evergreen trees of great beauty. Most are narrow and upright in habit, particularly when young, so they are ideal in more confined spaces or to bring height to plantings of ericaceous plants such as rhododendrons and azaleas. Their flowering time of late summer is a welcome extension to the flowering season of most ericaceous plants, and they are ideal subjects for woodland gardens. (See page 105.)

One of very few British native evergreens, the holly *Ilex aquifolium* (see page 72) has long been cultivated. It is hardly surprising that ancient man was in awe of this plant: The fact that it produced glowing red fruits and retained its leaves throughout winter, when other trees were bare and dormant, seemed to defy the elements. *Ilex aquifolium* (Zones 6–9) has charm at all stages of its life, but it eventually grows into a medium-sized tree of broadly conical habit. It thrives in any soil, and is tolerant of dry shade

Ilex aquifolium 'J.C. van Tol'

Ilex × *altaclerensis* 'Camelliifolia'

and industrial pollution. The female forms produce berries, but they always need a male form to pollinate them. The fruits are usually red but are sometimes various shades of yellow and orange. There are fewer female trees than males among seed-raised hollies, and if berries are required it is important to acquire a female clone or a self-pollinating variety. The numerous variegated forms are among the most decorative and long-lived shrubs or trees grown in gardens. Of the clones with plain green foliage, *Ilex aquifolium* 'J.C. van Tol' is the most popular, because it is self-pollinating and reliably sets a good crop of red berries without the need for a partner. It has dark, shiny, spineless leaves. *Ilex* × *altaclerensis* 'Camelliifolia' (Zones 6–9) has broader, larger leaves and big red berries. It is tolerant, pyramidal in habit and suited to coastal and industrial areas.

OTHER GOOD EVERGREEN TREES *Araucaria araucana* • *Cedrus atlantica* Glauca Group • *Cordyline australis* •

The variegated hollies (Zones 6–9) are generally more popular in gardens than those with plain green foliage. Good types include *Ilex aquifolium* 'Handsworth New Silver', *Ilex aquifolium* 'Argentea Marginata', *Ilex × altaclerensis* 'Golden King', and *Ilex × altaclerensis* 'Lawsoniana'. (See page 67.)

The sweet bay, *Laurus nobilis* (Zones 8–9), is a magnificent aromatic plant, with dark green oval, pointed leaves. Depending on how it is trained, it will either develop into a broad, loose cone of upright stems branching from the ground, like a shrub, or it will grow into a small evergreen tree on a single stout stem. It can be trimmed

Laurus nobilis

Ligustrum lucidum

Luma apiculata

THE MAGICAL POWERS OF HOLLY

Magical powers have been attributed to holly since ancient times. Branches of holly were cut and used around livestock pens to ward off wild animals and evil spirits, and holly trees were planted outside cottage doors to keep witches at bay. Both berries and leaves have also been used medicinally. It is said that to cut down a holly tree may result in the "death of the feller or one of his family," so hollies have traditionally been left to grow to a great age.

and trained into virtually any shape, but is most often seen as a formal trimmed standard, useful for the smallest of spaces. It grows on any soil and tolerates coastal conditions, and it even thrives when confined to a container.

Ligustrum lucidum (Zones 7–10), the Chinese privet, has a broad, conical habit and grows into a small or medium-sized tree that will be happy on any soil. It has large, glossy, pointed, elegant leaves and big conical sprays of fragrant white

GOOD COMPANIONS

The shiny dark evergreen foliage of *Arbutus unedo* (1) (Z. 8–10) contrasts well with the sword-shaped, gray-green leaves of *Phormium tenax* (2) (Z. 8–11). The latter's striking red-brown flower spikes reflect the color of the arbutus bark.

The gold foliage of *Sambucus racemosa* 'Plumosa Aurea' (3) (Z. 3–7) looks good with the dark green leaves of *Cotoneaster frigidus* 'Cornubia' (4) (Z. 7–9). The red cotoneaster berries are at their best after the sambucus leaves have fallen.

flowers in fall. Mature specimens develop an attractive fluted trunk. (See Good Companions, page 77.) There is a very handsome variegated form, *Ligustrum lucidum* 'Excelsum Superbum' (see page 65).

Luma apiculata (Zones 9–10), a type of myrtle, is a beautiful small tree for milder zones. It has small green leaves and pretty creamy white flowers in late summer and fall, followed by edible berries on some plants. Its loveliest feature is its light cinnamon-gold bark, which peels to reveal cream-colored patches beneath. A native of Chile, it thrives in gardens that get plentiful rainfall.

Cryptomeria japonica • *Eucryphia × nymansensis* 'Nymansay' • *Picea pungens* 'Hoopsii' • *Trachycarpus fortunei* •

GROWING MAGNOLIA GRANDIFLORA

Magnolia grandiflora (Z. 7–9) comes from the southern states and dislikes cold, wet conditions. In colder zones and on heavy soils, it often fails to establish if planted too deeply. *Magnolia grandiflora* can take 15 years or more to flower. If you want blooms, choose a named clone that produces flowers early in life, such as 'Exmouth' or 'Goliath'. It responds well to training and to shaping if carried out from an early age. Prune to shape in early spring, using pruners rather than shears, shortening the new growth back to two or three leaves.

Maytenus boaria is a lovely evergreen tree from South America. The foliage is said to be irresistible to cattle.

Magnolia grandiflora

The beautiful **Magnolia grandiflora** (Zones 7–9) has the most magnificent foliage of all the evergreen trees. The large, leathery leaves are glossy olive- to dark green above and reddish brown on the underside. The flowers, which are large, fragrant, waxy, and creamy white, are borne in summer and fall, but only on mature specimens. Often grown as a wall plant, this magnolia enjoys a sheltered position. It is alkaline-tolerant but needs fertile soil to succeed. **Magnolia grandiflora** 'Exmouth' has long, oval leaves that are lighter in color, and it flowers from an early age. (See Good Companions, opposite.) **Magnolia grandiflora** 'Victoria' is one of the hardiest magnolias, with flowers in summer and leaves that are very dark green on the upper sides and rich brown underneath. All are usually grown as short-stemmed trees with large heads.

Maytenus boaria (Zones 8–10) deserves much wider planting. A native of Chile, it is not hardy in cold zones but is a wonderful small evergreen tree for mild areas and grows on any soil. The branches are slender and graceful, lightly clothed with narrow, emerald green shining leaves. The habit is variable: usually the branches hang from the crown like those of a weeping willow, but it can be upright. Masses of tiny green flowers appear among the leaves in spring.

Southern beeches (*Nothofagus*) are also beautiful evergreen trees that should be seen more often in gardens. They are not very hardy, particularly as young specimens, but are worth experimenting with in milder locations. **Nothofagus betuloides** (Zones 7–9) is a medium-sized tree, dense and columnar in habit, with rounded, dark green shiny leaves. **Nothofagus dombeyi** (Zones 8–9) is large

Quercus ilex

and vigorous; it is similar to *Nothofagus betuloides* but is wider-spreading and more open in habit. Nothofagus may lose some or all of their foliage in cold winters.

Photinia × fraseri 'Red Robin' (Zones 7–9) is a lighter, more colorful alternative to sweet bay (*Laurus nobilis*, see page 75). Trained as a standard, this photinia makes a dense-headed evergreen tree that can be shaped and trimmed. The white flowers in spring and bright red new shoots make it a colorful subject for year-round interest. It succeeds on almost any soil.

Also good on most soils, **Prunus lusitanica** (Zones 7–9) has glossy, dark green leaves on red stalks and grows into an attractive conical, small tree that can be shaped for informal effect and is good in a big pot.

Quercus ilex (Zones 7–9), the holm oak, is a versatile evergreen. If left to grow and mature, it will form a large, majestic tree that will sit happily alongside substantial landscape subjects such as other oaks and beech. Dark in foliage and outline, it provides a useful contrast to large deciduous trees. It can also be

Nothofagus betuloides

clipped and shaped from an early age—in the form of a lollipop, for example (see page 91). The leaves are highly variable: They are dark green and leathery, often gray on the undersides, and may be oval with smooth lines, or toothed and more oaklike; this variability often results in confusion in identification. The holm oak tolerates shade, grows well on alkaline soils, and succeeds in coastal situations, but it does not tolerate severe cold.

GOOD COMPANIONS

The arching habit and small dark green foliage of *Abelia* × *grandiflora* (1) (Z. 6–9) contrasts with the big leathery leaves and upright growth of *Magnolia grandiflora* 'Exmouth' (2) (Z. 7–9). The abelia's flowers add color when the magnolia blooms are over.

The creamy white foliage of *Cornus mas* 'Variegata' (3) (Z. 4–8) shows up well against the dark-green-leaved *Ligustrum lucidum* (4) (Z. 7–10). The latter also makes a good background for the tiny yellow cornus flowers in early spring.

CONIFEROUS EVERGREEN TREES

Many broad-leaved evergreens hail from warmer climates and do not cope with the severe winter weather of colder zones. However, conifers have adapted their foliage to harsher conditions; the smaller surface area of their narrow leaves makes them less susceptible to desiccation and damage in cold, drying winds. Some conifers, such as pines, have spiky needles, while spruces have bristling branches, and chamaecyparis have soft sprays or curious strands of overlapping, scalelike leaves. Conifers can mix well with other garden plants, but most of them do not sit comfortably in naturalistic settings.

Cedars are the most magnificent evergreen trees, but they are far too large for most gardens and are trees to plant for the future rather than for immediate effect. *Cedrus deodara* (**1**) (Z. 7–9), the deodar, has perhaps the softest appearance of all the conifers and is beautiful from an early age. It has elegantly drooping branches and the foliage is blue-tinged when young, turning dark green with maturity. This cedar will eventually mature to a large, stately tree. As with all cedars, pruning can spoil the shape of this tree, so it is essential to allow plenty of space when you plant it.

Cupressus sempervirens (**2**) (Z. 7–9), the Italian cypress, is essential in any Mediterranean planting scheme. Its tall, narrow columnar habit and unique silhouette are evocative of the region, particularly when it is planted to rise out of low underplanting, rocks and gravel. It is hardier on well-drained soil, but can be damaged in cold, exposed areas. The large, round fruits are prone to weigh down the slender upright branches; prune the shoots out regularly to maintain the shape. The Italian cypress is best planted as a young pot-grown specimen, preferably no higher than 6 ft. (2 m); larger plants can be top-heavy and fail to make good mature specimens. (See page 90.)

The long needles of **pines** and their dark, cloudlike profiles differ from the more rigid appearance of most other conifers. As mature trees, they are more similar in shape to most deciduous trees, but as adolescents they usually have a broad, conical habit. Few are grown as garden trees, although they excel in coastal areas, where their needles help them to cope with salt-laden air better than broad-leaved trees. *Pinus nigra* (**3**) (Z. 5–8), the Austrian pine, is one of the most widely grown for landscape purposes. It has a large, dense head of dark green foliage and makes an excellent windbreak. Growing on virtually any soil, it is a good choice for inhospitable sites.

Pinus pinaster (Z. 7–9), the maritime pine, is a medium-sized tree of open habit, with red-brown, textured bark. The long needles are soft gray-green, and the large cones persist on the branches for several seasons. It is a good choice for sandy soil and coastal areas. For the same situations, *Pinus pinea* (**4**) (Z. 9–10), the umbrella pine, is a slightly smaller-growing alternative, with shorter, darker needles and shiny brown cones. It develops a compact, umbrella-shaped head and is a tree of great character. *Pinus wallichiana* (**5**) (Z. 7–8), the

Bhutan pine, has much longer blue-green needles and a softer appearance. It makes a large, elegant tree but will not grow on dry, shallow soils. *Pinus engelmannii* (**6** and **7**) (Z. 4–8), the Apache pine, is one of the most striking foliage trees, with needles over 1 ft. (30 cm) long carried in a chimney sweep brush arrangement at the end of the branches. It is usually a large, spreading, open tree with low branches.

The **spruce** most commonly planted in gardens is *Picea abies* (Z. 2–8), the Norway spruce; many find their way there after use as Christmas trees and all too soon grow into large, ungainly specimens of little ornamental value. They take up a considerable amount of space and little will grow beneath them. *Picea omorika* (Z. 4–7), the Serbian spruce, is a far better choice if this is the shape of tree that is wanted in the garden. It is tall and fast-growing, and has elegant branches that turn up at the tips; the needles have attractive silver-blue highlights. As a mature specimen it retains a narrow shape, and it grows well on most soils. *Picea breweriana* (**8**) (Z. 6–8), Brewer's weeping spruce, is another narrow, conical tree with elegant down-swept branches and long, hanging branchlets carrying dark blue-green needles. It is a beautiful small to medium-sized specimen tree and is impressive even when young.

The common yew, *Taxus baccata* (Z. 6–7), appears in gardens in many forms, often shaped into hedges or topiary. Its appeal is its dark raven green color, that makes a superb background for other plants. It is less often grown as a garden tree in the true sense of the word, but for the patient gardener it makes a superb formal trimmed tree of any size. *Taxus baccata* 'Fastigiata' (**9**), the Irish yew, has the same dark green foliage but grows as a dense column. It is an excellent specimen tree that lends itself to use as a statement plant or focal point, and sits more happily in traditional English schemes than the Italian cypress (*Cupressus sempervirens*) (Z. 7–9). (See page 90.)

The western hemlock, *Tsuga heterophylla* (**10**) (Z. 6–8), is a large, fast-growing tree that provides a good alternative to a cedar, making an impressive specimen in about ten years. This tsuga forms a slender, elegant, conical tree with down-swept branches carrying small, flat, soft green leaves that are silvery beneath. It does not succeed on alkaline soils, and is too large for the average garden unless planted as a short-term subject.

Exotic foliage

Palms, tree ferns, and trees with large or palmlike foliage create wonderfully exotic, subtropical effects in the temperate garden. In the 19th century the pioneering Irish plantsman William Robinson used exotics to add a different dimension to his naturalistic traditional planting schemes. Today, exotics are still used extensively, to enliven contemporary schemes and to add a sense of lushness to seasonal plantings.

Araucaria araucana

The tree fern, *Dicksonia antarctica*, retains its long, palmlike fronds throughout the year in mild areas. New leaves unfurl from the crown in spring.

PALMS AND TREE FERNS

The cabbage palm, *Cordyline australis* (Zones 7–11), has become one of the most widely planted exotics in today's gardens. As a young plant, it is used as an accent subject in seasonal bedding schemes and containers. More mature plants are used as specimens, particularly in coastal and Mediterranean schemes. If left to mature, it grows quickly into a splendid single-stemmed, small tree with an impressive head of long, swordlike leaves. If the crown of the plant is damaged in any

Cordyline australis

THE MONKEY PUZZLE

Araucaria araucana (Zones 8–10), the Chile pine or monkey puzzle, has long attracted admiration because of its unique appearance. The long, dark green, severely bristly branches and symmetrical shape are strongly architectural, and grab the attention of those who are normally oblivious to the presence of trees in the landscape. The monkey puzzle was widely planted by the Victorians, often in unsuitably small gardens; anyone considering including one of these should first look carefully at a mature specimen to ensure they have the space to accommodate it. In urban areas it usually loses its lower branches, while on moist, fertile soil in a large country garden it may retain them. Monkey puzzles are more likely to do well if planted as small, container-grown specimens.

way, it will branch, producing a multi-headed specimen; older plants do this of their own accord. This cordyline is strong-rooted and wind-resistant, and when mature produces large inflorescences in summer; the tiny flowers are pinkish white and heavily scented, the smell reminiscent of suntan lotion. An excellent plant in the right place, its growth potential is often underestimated (a mature specimen can be difficult to remove). The forms with colored foliage are particularly decorative. *Cordyline australis* 'Torbay Dazzler', with cream and green striped leaves, is striking but smaller in stature, rarely reaching tree proportions. Other good colored forms include *Cordyline australis* 'Torbay Red' (see page 59), *Cordyline australis* Purpurea Group, and *Cordyline australis* 'Red Star': All have red-brown foliage and in mild areas will grow into small, branched trees.

The tree fern, *Dicksonia antarctica* (Zones 9–11), has become a contemporary garden essential. A slow-growing plant, it is ideal in small gardens and courtyard settings. The heavy, fibrous brown trunk and head of splendid fern leaves can convey an instant tree effect with a lush subtropical feel. Tree ferns are not new to cultivation—in the 19th century, they were planted extensively in the valley gardens of Cornwall in England, where they enjoy the mild climate, copious rainfall, and sheltered environment. Tree ferns are imported as mature specimens from Australia, where they are collected from the wild under license. They arrive as semi-dormant logs: The length of the trunk usually sets the price of the tree. (See Good Companions, page 83.)

Trachycarpus fortunei (Zones 9–10), the windmill palm, is the toughest of the large true palms. A mature specimen is a magnificent sight, with a straight trunk up to 15 ft. (5 m) or more clad in dark brown fibres, which are the remains of old leaf bases. The head consists of large, dark green, fan-shaped leaves with pointed

GROWING TREE FERNS

Much of the root system of *Dicksonia antarctica* (Z. 9–11) is in the trunk of the fern, so some of the trunk needs to be buried in the ground to anchor the plant. Tree ferns need moisture, especially around the crown; regular spraying with water will encourage the leaves to emerge. In mild, sheltered locations tree ferns are evergreen, but they shed some of the oldest leaves during the course of the season. In colder conditions, the leaves die away and the plant becomes dormant until the following spring. Straw or fleece around the crown and trunk will help to protect it in severe weather.

Trachycarpus fortunei

fingers. Although this is a surprisingly weather-resistant palm, the leaves are battered and spoilt by strong winds, so the finest specimens are usually those planted in a sheltered location. Mature plants produce impressive inflorescences of tiny yellow flowers in early summer. These hang from the crown of the plant, forming an attractive contrast with the trunk and leaves.

PALMS FOR MILDER GARDENS

There are numerous other palms that can be grown as trees, but many require mild winters to survive. *Butia capitata* (1) (Z. 10–11) is one of the most beautiful palms, a small tree with graceful arching leaves and long, hanging leaflets of soft sage green; it will withstand a touch of frost. *Phoenix canariensis* (2) (Z. 11) is a familiar sight in coastal locations in southern Europe, and it grows happily in the mildest regions. Its elegant shuttlecock form is dramatic, and the tree is quick to grow to a size that will make an impact.

Ailanthus altissima

Catalpa bignonioides

BROAD-LEAVED TREES WITH BIG LEAVES

Some broad-leaved trees, usually those with large luxuriant leaves, create an exotic effect in the garden. The tree of heaven, *Ailanthus altissima* (Zones 4–8), grows to be very large and imposing, resembling ash, but with bigger leaves. It has become widely naturalized, and is an invasive pest in some parts of the world with hot summers, which result in the female plants producing large quantities of red fruits. It is good in urban gardens because of its resilience to pollution, and it is often seen growing to great height in

Aralia elata

EXOTIC PLANTING SCHEMES

You can create stunning exotic schemes in any garden, provided the plants are protected from frost—for example, in a frost-free greenhouse or a conservatory during the dormant season. After the danger of frost has passed, you can take the plants outside. An exotic scheme may consist of a few pots grouped together, or a large planted border. Cannas, alocasias, dahlias, coleus, and lilies all provide colorful, exotic-looking flowers and impressive foliage.

the tiniest spaces. Grown as a short-term subject, it quickly gives the effect of an exotic, architectural tree. It is best when young, when it produces massive leaves that can be up to 3 ft. (1 m) long.

The Japanese angelica tree, *Aralia elata* (Zones 3–9), has stout, vertical, spiny stems with a palmlike arrangement of large, heavy, fernlike green leaves at the top of each one. It often produces suckers, resulting in a group of stems of varying heights, like a small tropical forest. This can be very effective rising out of low ground-cover planting or gravel. Large sprays of tiny white flowers appear from among the leaves in autumn, before the leaves color and fall. The variegated forms are more sought after (see page 64), but the plain-leaved species should not be overlooked. (See Good Companions, opposite.)

Catalpa bignonioides (Zones 5–9), the Indian bean tree, normally appears in gardens as the gold-leaved form, *Catalpa bignonioides* 'Aurea' (see page 55). The plain green form is equally beautiful, with its large, soft, heart-shaped green leaves that move gently in the breeze. A mature specimen is broad and wide-spreading; young plants are more upright, and can be pruned hard to control size and promote

OTHER TREES WITH EXOTIC FOLIAGE *Eriobotrya japonica* • *Koelreuteria paniculata* • *Magnolia grandiflora* •

BANANAS

Bananas always grab attention with their huge lush leaves and subtropical appearance. They are herbaceous perennials rather than woody plants, so are not trees at all in the true sense of the word. However, in garden terms they sit alongside palms, cordylines, and other trees of exotic appearance. In the mildest zones, the hardiest forms can be overwintered outside, especially if given some protection. *Musa basjoo* (1) (Z. 7–10) is one of the hardiest bananas: a slender plant growing to 12 ft. (4 m). The leaves may die back in winter (2), leaving a stem resembling a withered leek; warm weather the following summer will promote a fresh crop of leaves. *Musa lasiocarpa* (Z. 7–10) is regarded as the hardiest banana but reaches only 5 ft. (1.5 m), so it tends to be more suitable for a pot.

GOOD COMPANIONS

The brown and brown-green fronds of the royal fern *Osmunda regalis* (1) (Z. 2–8) complement the leaves and trunk of the tree fern, *Dicksonia antarctica* (2) (Z. 9–11); both enjoy damp conditions in light shade.

The bamboo *Sasa veitchii* (3) (Z. 6–10) is ideal underplanting for *Aralia elata* (4) (Z. 3–9): It provides evergreen winter interest, and its foliage creates a striking contrast with the aralia leaves.

larger leaves. Grown in this way, they are sometimes used as exotic container and bedding subjects. Mature specimens produce spikes of beautiful white, delicately marked, foxglovelike flowers in late summer. Both the gold- and the green-leaved form become medium-sized trees.

Paulownia tomentosa (Zones 5–9) is the ideal tree for an exotic border or for a surprising focal point in traditional planting. Although it has become an invasive problem in places, it is treasured and nurtured in colder regions. Mature specimens produce spectacular spikes of lavender blue flowers in spring. The buds form the previous fall, so they can be vulnerable in severe weather. Paulownia's greatest assets are its vast leaves: To encourage even more magnificent foliage, cut the plant back to the ground in spring. A number of suckering shoots arise, so remove these, but leave a single stem to grow and develop. This stem can reach 10 ft. (3 m) in a single season and will carry leaves up to 2 ft. (60 cm) across.

Paulownia tomentosa

Magnolia macrophylla • Pseudopanax ferox • Pterocarya fraxinifolia • Rhus typhina • Toona sinensis •

SITUATIONS

As with any other plant, the success of a tree depends on whether it is the right one for the right situation. Small gardens need compact or narrow trees, or those with a tall, light canopy that rises above the space without cutting out all the light. Big spaces offer scope to plant majestic specimens, or groups of trees. Country gardens need trees that sit comfortably in a rural setting, while urban gardens can accommodate trimmed and trained subjects. Some growing environments require trees that are tolerant of a particular soil type or of wet, dry, or windy conditions.

RIGHT: *Pterocarya fraxinifolia.*

SITUATIONS

Small gardens

Even if you have a small garden, you should always try to make space for at least one or two trees. Their height, form, and structure are just as important in a small, confined space as in a larger one and, if the garden is overlooked, trees also play a key part in creating a feeling of privacy.

A weeping silver pear, *Pyrus salicifolia* 'Pendula', brings height to a bed of perennials and low-growing silver foliage shrubs. Light pruning in winter keeps the tree in shape and controls its spread.

In small gardens, trees are often planted for privacy: A well-positioned tree can prevent the garden from being overlooked by neighboring houses. Evergreen trees are an obvious choice for this purpose. However, a deciduous tree with an attractive branch structure is often just as effective. Consider the position of the tree carefully. Planting the tree as far from the house as possible, perhaps on the boundary, may seem the best option. However, by bringing the tree closer to the house, the overlooking windows of neighboring houses are often screened more effectively.

In a small garden, every plant has to earn its place if the garden is to have year-round interest. As there may be only one or two trees, they have to work hard. A tree that has glorious blossom for a week in spring and is ordinary for the rest of the year is not a good choice in this situation; instead, choose one that has other features—perhaps interesting bark or good autumn color. (See also Tree Companions box, opposite.)

CHOICE TREES FOR CONFINED SPACES

Amelanchier lamarckii (Zones 4–8), the snowy mespilus, is a popular small garden tree. It is often grown as a multi-stemmed specimen but can also be trained as a standard. The graceful branches carry copper-colored new leaves in spring at the same time as many heads of starry white flowers. In fall, the small oval leaves

Amelanchier lamarckii

USING TREES IN A SMALL SPACE

There are several ways that a tree can be used in a small space. The most obvious option is to choose a narrow, columnar tree with minimal spread. This will provide height and structure but casts little shade. Alternatively, a spreading tree with a light canopy casts dappled shade, changing the environment and enabling a different range of plants to grow. Small, compact, weeping trees, such as a weeping pear (*Pyrus salicifolia* 'Pendula', above; Z. 4–7) may be used as specimens or focal points. They do not suit naturalistic schemes, but they are ideal where limited height and spread are essential. In very restricted spaces, the effect of a tree can sometimes be achieved by choosing a trimmed and trained plant, planted in the open ground or in a container.

often color well, especially when the tree is grown on a moist, well-drained, acid soil. Although normally recommended for acid conditions, it often thrives on alkaline soils. *Amelanchier* × *grandiflora* 'Ballerina' (Zones 4–7) has larger flowers and improved foliage color (see page 125).

In dry and inhospitable conditions, *Caragana arborescens* (Zones 2–7), the pea tree, is a good choice. It is a

Caragana arborescens 'Walker'

Cercis siliquastrum

small, shrubby species with light foliage and yellow pealike flowers in summer. *Caragana arborescens* 'Walker' is a prostrate form with finer foliage. It is often top-grafted on to a stem of the species to produce a very small weeping tree; if grown in this way, it is ideal used to add height in a small, dry area of the garden combined with gravel and low, sun-loving plants.

Cercis siliquastrum (Zones 6–9), the Judas tree, is a lovely small species with charcoal-colored bark and rounded, heart-shaped leaves. A native of the eastern Mediterranean, it was introduced into cultivation in the 16th century; fine old

TREE COMPANIONS

If you have space for two trees, choose plants that differ in terms of their shape and main season of interest. Below are some suggestions for good combinations.

Photinia × *fraseri* 'Red Robin' (**1**) (Z. 7–9) with *Sorbus* 'Sunshine' (**2**) (Z. 5–7). The photinia is evergreen and has bright red shoots in late spring. The sorbus has good color in fall and golden fruits.

Cotoneaster 'Hybridus Pendulus' (**3**) (Z. 6–9) with *Prunus cerasifera* 'Nigra' (**4**) (Z. 3–8). The cotoneaster is evergreen and bears bright red fruits in fall, and the cherry (*Prunus*) has pink spring blossoms and rich purple foliage in summer and fall.

Pyrus calleryana 'Chanticleer' (**5**) (Z. 4–8) with *Ligustrum lucidum* 'Excelsum Superbum' (**6**) (Z. 7–10). The pyrus has white spring blossom and good autumn color. The ligustrum is evergreen and flowers in late summer and early fall.

GOOD AND BAD WEEPING TREES

Salix caprea 'Kilmarnock' (Z. 4–9), the Kilmarnock willow, is attractive in early spring, when the golden yellow, pussy-willow catkins appear on the dark weeping branches. The tree is usually top-grafted on a 5-ft. (1.5-m) stem and is appealing as a young plant, which is when it is offered for sale. As a long-term garden plant, however, it has little to recommend it. The foliage is dull and the season of interest is short. If left unkempt, it becomes an untidy, top-heavy specimen that takes up space and contributes little. After the catkins have fallen, selective hard pruning of half the branches right back to where they emerge from the main stem is essential.

Cotoneaster 'Hybridus Pendulus' (right; Z. 6–9) is a better choice. It is evergreen, has white flowers in spring and sealing-wax-colored fruits in fall. It requires little care apart from occasional selective pruning of some of the branches; a few should be cut back quite hard each year. If they are just trimmed, ugly divided growth will result near the base of the canopy.

Cornus florida f. rubra

Malus floribunda

Malus 'Royal Beauty'

SITUATIONS

There are a number of named clones selected for the quality of their flowers and foliage: **Cornus florida 'Cherokee Chief'** has deep rose-red bracts; **Cornus florida 'Sunset'** has pink young leaves that mature with a broad yellow margin. The autumn color of the foliage of all f. *rubra* clones is pink, red, and purple.

The hawthorn **Crataegus persimilis 'Prunifolia'** (Zones 4–7) is a superb small, spreading tree of compact habit with more than one season of interest. The glossy green foliage develops fantastic autumn color, and the white spring flowers are followed by large red berries that persist after the leaves have fallen. It is a good choice for a small garden, but beware of its long thorns. (See page 138.) **Crataegus × lavalleei 'Carrierei'** (Zones 4–7) is another good hawthorn, with glossy green leaves that often remain on the tree into winter and persistent orange-red fruits.

Some of the less vigorous **crab apples** are suitable for smaller gardens. **Malus floribunda** (Zones 4–8), the Japanese crab, is one of the loveliest and is deservedly popular. The long, graceful branches have a horizontal habit and are garlanded in spring with crimson buds that open to blush-pink and white fragrant flowers. It is very slow-growing.

Weeping varieties include **Malus × scheideckeri 'Red Jade'** (Zones 4–8), with white and pink flowers, followed by red cherrylike fruits, and **Malus 'Royal Beauty'** (Zones 3–7), with deep red-purple flowers and small, dark red fruits. The latter also has the advantage of dark purple stems and red-purple young leaves.

Prunus 'Amanogawa' (Zones 6–9) is probably the most widely recommended flowering tree for a confined space. It is a small, upright tree, usually with ascending branches from just above ground level and green-bronze new foliage becoming green when mature. The semidouble, fragrant, shell pink flowers cover the branches in mid-spring, and a good specimen in flower is a lovely sight. Occasionally, the

specimens are to be found in many great English gardens. Even young specimens often adopt a gnarled character and have an air of maturity. It will grow in poor, well-drained soil, thrives on alkaline soils, and is often grown against a wall. The pealike flowers appear in clusters on the bare wood in late spring, just before the leaves emerge; they wreathe the branches, even on young plants. Flattened, reddish, pealike seed pods develop under the cover of the leaves during the summer; in fall,

they remain on the branches after the leaves have fallen. **Cercis siliquastrum 'Bodnant'** is a particularly fine form, with profuse larger flowers of lilac-purple.

The **flowering dogwoods** make excellent small trees for most gardens. **Cornus florida f. rubra** (Zones 5–9) is one of the finest, making a narrow, conical tree with superb pink blooms in early summer and rich autumn foliage. The branch framework is elegant and architectural. (See Good Companions, opposite.)

OTHER GOOD TREES FOR SMALL GARDENS *Acer griseum* • *Arbutus unedo* • *Betula pendula* 'Tristis' •

Prunus 'Amanogawa'

Prunus sargentii 'Rancho'

Prunus 'Spire'

Pyrus calleryana 'Chanticleer'

leaves develop reasonable autumn color. Narrow and upright when young, it tends to open up with age.

Prunus sargentii 'Rancho' (Zones 5–9) is an excellent small to medium-sized tree. An upright clone of *Prunus sargentii*, it has the same red-brown polished bark, masses of single pink flowers in mid-spring, and vivid early autumn leaf color.

Prunus 'Spire' (formerly *Prunus × hillieri* 'Spire'; Zones 6–7) is a wonderful tree for a small space; it is often grown as a landscape plant and deserves wider use in gardens. It develops a narrow, elegant vase shape and has a robust character. The soft pink flowers appear in mid-spring and the leaves develop rich red-purple autumn color. In winter, the shape of the tree has a strong architectural presence.

Prunus × subhirtella 'Autumnalis Rosea' (Zones 5–8) used to be widely grown and cherished for its delicate, pale pink blossom in winter. A small, light-framed, spreading tree, it is ideally suited to a small garden but unfortunately

it suffers from bacterial canker, which causes wilting of the blossom and periodic defoliation. In a small space, where every plant is important, it is not worth the risk. (See pages 152–53.)

Pyrus salicifolia 'Pendula' (Zones 4–7), the weeping silver pear, is frequently planted in small gardens and is a good choice for its light, silvery, willowlike foliage. It has a graceful habit and is small in height, but in time its weeping branches can have a broad spread and be greedy for space. However, selective pruning can control this; it can also be trimmed if a more formal effect is desired. (See pages 86, 70 and Good Companions, left.)

Pyrus calleryana 'Chanticleer' (Zones 4–8) has become one of the most widely used subjects for general landscape planting, but this should not exclude it from garden use. Of medium height, it is an elegant, slender tree that develops a narrow, flame-shaped head when young, broadening with age. White flowers in early spring are quickly followed by

GOOD COMPANIONS

The purple leaves and bushy habit of *Cotinus coggygria* 'Royal Purple' (1) (Z. 4–8) set off the elegant form and pink-tinged leaves of *Cornus florida* f. *rubra* (2) (Z. 5–9). The cotinus foliage looks best in summer, after the cornus has flowered. Both color well in fall.

The soft purple leaves of *Vitis vinifera* 'Purpurea' (3) (Z. 6–8) combine well with the narrow silver leaves of the weeping pear, *Pyrus salicifolia* 'Pendula' (4) (Z. 4–7). As the vine is not too vigorous, it will not swamp the tree.

Laburnum × watereri 'Vossii' • *Malus* 'Golden Hornet' • *Prunus* 'Accolade' • *Sorbus* 'Joseph Rock' •

NARROW COLUMNAR EVERGREENS

Upright, narrow conifers are ideal to provide height and vertical structure in restricted situations.

The Italian cypress, *Cupressus sempervirens* (1) (Z. 7–9), grows to form a tall, pencil-shaped column with upright branches of dark green foliage that ascend close to the trunk. The round green fruits, particularly evident in late summer but present year-round, tend to weigh down the branches, creating a more open, feathery appearance; this can be prevented by selectively cutting out the spreading branches. There are a number of named clones, but *Cupressus sempervirens* 'Green Pencil' is one of the toughest. It is an ideal choice for Mediterranean schemes and dry gardens. (See page 78.)

For a more traditional setting, choose *Taxus baccata* 'Fastigiata' (2) (Z. 6–7), the Irish yew. As a young tree, this forms a narrow column of dark green foliage carried on upright branches; it broadens with age. Red fruits stud the plant in the latter part of the year. The Irish yew is a versatile, small to medium-sized tree. It makes a wonderful specimen, works as a focal point in a mixed border, and looks good with low, evergreen ground cover.

fresh green leaves that turn deep green and glossy; it is disease-free. The foliage develops good autumn color, which is usually butter yellow but sometimes flame and orange, and the leaves are held on the tree well into winter. It is a drought-tolerant tree, and establishes quickly from container-grown or bare-root stock.

Robinia × *slavinii* 'Hillieri' (Zones 5–8) is a lovely compact, summer-flowering tree with pink wisterialike blooms and

Robinia × slavinii 'Hillieri'

soft green foliage. It is a good choice for a small, sheltered garden and produces results quickly. (See page 132.)

Deciduous trees with small leaves are more suitable for a small garden or a confined space, as they are less of a problem at leaf fall than larger-leaved species. There are many species and cultivars of *Sorbus* that possess this quality and also have attractive flowers and autumn fruits.

Sorbus aucuparia 'Fastigiata'

Several cultivars of *Sorbus aucuparia* (Zones 3–7) are upright and compact. *Sorbus aucuparia* 'Fastigiata' has a tight columnar habit. White spring flowers are followed by large bunches of scarlet fruits. *Sorbus aucuparia* 'Streetwise' is a Hillier selection with similar compact qualities and bright orange berries. *Sorbus* 'Chinese Lace' (Zones 5–7) is a small, upright tree with deeply cut and divided leaflets that turn red-purple in fall—a handsome background for the dark red fruits.

Sorbus cashmiriana (Zones 4–7) is a very desirable small tree of open habit, often only reaching 10–12 ft. (3–4 m)

OTHER TREES FOR TRIMMING *Camellia japonica* (standard) • *Olea europaea* • *Photinia* × *fraseri* 'Red Robin' •

TRIMMED AND TRAINED TREES

Many deciduous and evergreen trees can be trimmed and shaped, making them suitable for confined spaces. All the plants described below are good for growing in containers, so they can be used where planting in the ground is impossible.

The hornbeam, *Carpinus betulus* (**1**) (Z. 4–8), is widely used for this purpose. Its fine twigs and small, fresh green leaves make it suited to clipping into a variety of shapes, both rounded and angular. *Carpinus betulus* **'Fastigiata'**, with upright branches, suits shaping into a narrow, pointed column. (See page 109.)

Laurus nobilis, bay (Z. 8–9), is a widely used evergreen for training as a small tree: Classic lollipop standards grace the entrances of many urban and country houses. Green and variegated forms of *Ilex aquifolium* (**2**) (Z. 6–9) and *Ilex* × *altaclerensis* (Z. 6–9) also make great standards, some with the added bonus of berries in fall and winter. *Ilex aquifolium* **'Green Pillar'** is an upright, narrow holly with dark green, spiny leaves and red berries; it is a good choice where a columnar shape is needed rather than a standard. (See pages 74–75.)

Buxus sempervirens (**3**), boxwood (Z. 6–9), makes a dense-headed standard, ideal trained as a lollipop (see pages 36–37).

In sheltered locations, *Ligustrum delavayanum* (Z. 7–9) is a good alternative to boxwood for trimmed pyramids and also makes a good standard. The leaves are tiny and dark green. White summer flowers are followed by black berries, which nestle in the foliage on trimmed plants.

The silver leaves of *Sorbus aria* **'Lutescens'** (**4**) (Z. 5–6) make a striking column if the side branches are pruned regularly from an early age. It can be grown with branches right down to ground level or on a stem as a columnar tree. (See page 71.)

For a larger trimmed evergreen tree, choose *Quercus ilex* (**5**) (Z. 7–9), the holm oak. This makes a splendid formal standard with a square, rounded, or columnar head. Buy a good-quality specimen of the size and weight needed for the situation—these plants take years to grow and train. Although they are expensive, the investment will be worthwhile. (See page 77.)

high. Pink flowers in spring are followed by large white berries, which remain long after the leaves have fallen. It is superb when planted against a background of dark evergreens, such as a yew hedge.

Sorbus hupehensis var. *obtusa* **'Pink Pagoda'** (Zones 6–8), a broadly columnar, medium-sized tree, has blue-green leaves and long-lasting pink berries, which become paler as winter progresses.

MAINTENANCE OF TRIMMED TREES

Trimmed and trained trees need regular maintenance to preserve the effect; consider this before you plant. A small standard can be trimmed with a pair of one-handed sheep shears; a full standard-shaped tree may need a long-armed power trimmer. The frequency of cutting depends on the plant. Deciduous subjects are usually trimmed in winter, when the leaves have fallen, and then again after the first flush of growth in spring; one or two more cuts may be required during the growing season to keep them in shape. Evergreens are trimmed after the first flush of growth in spring and then again in summer. Trimming late in the year should be avoided in zones where severe winter weather is a possibility.

Prunus lusitanica • *Pyrus salicifolia* 'Pendula' • *Taxus baccata* • *Tilia cordata* • *Viburnum tinus* (standard) •

Acer palmatum 'Bloodgood' makes an excellent small tree for a pot. Its rich red-purple foliage is a striking contrast to other plants from spring through to fall.

POTS AND CONTAINERS

Growing a tree in a pot is an excellent way of restricting its size; the Japanese have been doing just that for centuries through the art of bonsai. Placing a small tree in a container above ground level can create an illusion of greater height and stature and give the plant real presence.

The right tree partnered with an appropriate container can introduce a particular theme to the garden. For instance a Japanese maple in a Chinese pot creates an Asian feel; an olive in a terra-cotta pot suggests the Mediterranean; a multi-stemmed birch in a polished zinc container would fit a contemporary design. There is a vast range of containers available, enabling the gardener to enhance the chosen tree in a variety of ways.

The **Japanese maples**, cultivars of *Acer palmatum* (Zones 6–8), are obvious choices for pots. *Acer palmatum* 'Bloodgood' is a reliable purple-leaved cultivar and will form an elegant specimen in

Prunus incisa 'Kojo-no-mai'

a large container. The more recent introduction *Acer palmatum* 'Shiraz' is an excellent variety with wine-colored foliage and good autumn color. As a rule, *Acer palmatum* var. *dissectum* and its forms—those with finely cut foliage—are broader-spreading. Pruning is best avoided, but if branches must be removed, do it when the plants are in full leaf; cuts made in winter can allow disease to enter. (See page 58.)

A bay, *Laurus nobilis* (Zones 8–9), trained as a standard is a classic small tree for a pot. It is a tolerant plant, resistant to drought and air pollution. (See page 75.)

Olea europaea, the olive (Zones 8–9), thrives in poor, dry soil, so suits planting in a pot, particularly where there is a chance of neglect. Its attractive gray wood and silver-green foliage look good in a sunny situation. It responds well to trimming and training, and specimens are available in a range of shapes. (See page 69.)

Photinia × *fraseri* (Zones 7–9) is attractive when grown as a standard. Clipping in late spring and fall stimulates bright red young shoots. Mature specimens produce less leaf growth but often flower prolifically in late spring. *Photinia* × *fraseri* 'Red Robin' is one of the best cultivars. (See page 77.)

Prunus incisa (Zones 5–7), the Fuji cherry, is a charming subject for a pot. It has elegantly angular twigs and small,

Olea europaea

OTHER GOOD TREES FOR POTS *Acer capillipes* • *Acer negundo* 'Elegans' • *Acer shirasawanum* 'Aureum' •

serrated leaves that are beautifully tinted in fall. The flowers are small and white, tinged pink, freely borne in early spring on bare branches. The beautiful dwarf *Prunus incisa* 'Kojo-no-mai' can be used as a bonsai-style subject for a pot and will reward with beautiful blossom in spring and glowing autumn leaf shades.

Palms and **cordylines** will create an exotic effect from an early age. The tree fern, *Dicksonia antarctica* (Zones 9–11), will create the same effect instantly if planted as a mature specimen. As it does not have roots in the normal sense of the word, a large specimen can be fitted into

Laurus nobilis

Photinia × fraseri

Dicksonia antarctica

CONTAINERS AND COMPOSTS

Choose as large a container as possible—one that is in proportion with the tree you have chosen, allowing for the tree to grow. A deciduous tree in leaf is top-heavy in a pot, therefore a container that is sufficiently large and heavy is vital. Loam-based potting mixes are heavier and better at holding water and nutrients, and are therefore always the best choice. A top-dressing with some fresh potting mix and controlled-release fertilizer will be required at the beginning of each growing season.

FRUIT TREES IN POTS

Fruit trees can be grown in pots, as long as they are on dwarf rootstocks. Apples, pears, plums, cherries, peaches, and nectarines are all available on rootstocks that will restrict their size; they will, however, provide a satisfactory crop of fruit if given the right conditions. All are best in a reasonably sheltered situation; many dwarf rootstocks have brittle roots that are easily broken if the wind rocks the plant. Adequate feeding with a high-potash fertilizer is essential to promote flowers and fruit, and attention needs to be paid to watering: if the plants are allowed to dry out during fruit formation, the embryo fruits may be shed. Source the plants from a reputable garden center or from a specialist nursery.

---

a relatively small container, providing that the pot is heavy enough to anchor the plant. (See page 81.) *Catalpa bignonioides* 'Aurea' (Zones 5–9), although late into leaf, is striking in a large tub. Its large, softly felted leaves will bring the jungle to a courtyard garden. (See page 55.)

Where a larger tree in a container is required, multi-stemmed trees are a good choice. These are produced by hard pruning at an early age or by planting three or more young specimens in the same container. The effect is that of a small grove, and they appear more naturalistic than a single specimen in a pot. Various **birches** are grown in this way; *Betula utilis* var. *jacquemontii* (Zones 4–7) is particularly effective with its white stems. *Eucalyptus* also make wonderful multi-stemmed trees, and can be cut back to pot level if they get too large. Since they grow quickly, they are a good choice for those who do not wish to invest in a ready-grown specimen. Another good multi-stemmed specimen is *Prunus serrula* (Zones 5–8), with polished mahogany bark and a relatively light head that will not cast too much shade in a small space. (See pages 68–69, 148 and 150.)

Catalpa bignonioides 'Aurea'

Cordyline australis • *Cornus* 'Porlock' • *Cotoneaster* 'Hybridus Pendulus' • *Magnolia grandiflora* •

Large gardens

Big, open spaces offer the opportunity to plant really large trees. Majestic specimens, such as horse chestnut, copper beech, oak, and linden, can grow to their full stately proportions, and you can plant trees that take a long time to reach maturity, perhaps a giant redwood or a group of incense cedars, which may take up to three generations to develop fully. Trees normally chosen for smaller gardens still have their place here, perhaps in groups, or in more confined areas within the divisions of a large space.

Aesculus × carnea

Aesculus hippocastanum 'Baumannii'

Aesculus indica 'Sydney Pearce'

The cedar of Lebanon (*Cedrus libani*) is a magnificent large tree, often found in the grounds of English stately homes—here at Montacute House in Somerset. It takes years to develop shape and maturity.

The **horse chestnuts** are magnificent trees for large gardens and parkland. They are at their most beautiful in late spring, when their rounded crowns are decorated with showy candles of flowers against a canopy of large, softly held, hand-shaped leaves. However, they are also stunning in early spring, when the fresh apple green leaves first open from sticky brown buds; and also in fall, when the leaves turn to gold and brown. On some trees, polished chestnuts, the large shiny seeds, emerge as the spiky green fruits split open.

TREES AND VIEWS

When planting large-growing trees that take time to mature, pay particular attention to their impact on vistas and views in the longer term. Often, large trees rob a garden of the views over surrounding countryside as they grow to maturity, and the garden owner has to decide between retaining the tree and retrieving the view. Losing a fully grown tree has an adverse impact on the maturity of the garden, and a replacement tree in a different location takes time to make an impact (see Consider Timescale, page 15).

Red horse chestnut, *Aesculus × carnea* (Zones 3–7), is a hybrid between the stately common horse chestnut, *Aesculus hippocastanum* (Zones 3–7), and the red buckeye, *Aesculus pavia* (Zones 5–8). The latter is responsible for the deep pink color of the splendid semi-upright flower spikes that appear against the dark green leaves in late spring. *Aesculus × carnea* 'Briotii' is the most widely grown form, as it is more compact in habit and slower-growing than *Aesculus × carnea*. It makes a stunning tree for an avenue as well as an impressive individual specimen. Red horse chestnuts are best planted in grass, because the roots near the surface can lift paving or tarmac.

Aesculus hippocastanum (Zones 3–7), the horse chestnut, is much bigger and is one of the most splendid large specimen trees when mature. It is exotic and flamboyant when in flower, with its large candles of creamy white flowers, speckled and blotched with golden yellow and red. *Aesculus hippocastanum* 'Baumannii' has even showier double flowers and does not set seed.

Aesculus indica (Zones 7–9), the Indian horse chestnut, is a good choice for alkaline soils. It has pink-flushed flowers in large spikes in midsummer, and the foliage, which is glossier and stays in better condition than that of other horse chestnuts, displays lovely orange

Fagus sylvatica Atropurpurea Group

and yellow autumn color. *Aesculus indica* 'Sydney Pearce' has larger flowers, a more upright habit and dark green leaves.

Castanea sativa (Zones 3–7), the sweet chestnut, was probably introduced to Britain by the Romans from southern Europe, and to the West afterward. It is a big, broadly columnnar, fast-growing tree with long, oval, shining leaves with serrated edges. Creamy green catkins decorate the branches in midsummer. In hot summers these are followed by edible chestnuts in green prickly seed cases. It is a tolerant tree but is susceptible to chestnut blight in many areas and does not thrive in shallow alkaline soils.

There is no lovelier sight than the beech *Fagus sylvatica* (Zones 4–7) in full leaf; it is a natural choice for a large garden. Purple-leaved cultivars are attractive as

Fagus sylvatica 'Riversii'

young trees but take many years to develop their mature shape and stature. *Fagus sylvatica* Atropurpurea Group is the name given to purple-leaved forms selected from seed-raised plants. To be certain of the depth of color, acquire these as container-grown plants in leaf, as the color can vary considerably—in some cases, it may be a light brown-purple and rather disappointing. When planted bare-root, the color is often poor in the first season. There are many named clones that have been selected for the quality of their foliage. *Fagus sylvatica* 'Riversii' is the finest selection, growing into a magnificent large tree with dark, shining purple leaves. Beeches are accommodating trees, growing on most well-drained soils; they are not a good choice for damp sites or heavy clay soils.

CHOOSING TREES FOR A BIG SPACE

It is as important to select the right tree for a large garden as it is for a small area. Whether the tree is planted on its own or in a group, its size has to be in proportion to the surrounding space. Large trees tend to take more time to reach maturity, so timescales are often longer when the garden is big; however, to ensure instant impact a combination of fast-growing trees and slower, longer-lived subjects is ideal. Large trees that mature quickly include *Acer platanoides* (Norway maple; Z. 3–7) (**1**), *Acer saccharinum* (silver maple; Z. 3–8), *Eucalyptus gunnii* (cider gum; Z. 8–10), *Platanus × hispanica* (London plane; Z. 4–8), and the willow *Salix alba* var. *vitellina* 'Britzensis' (Z. 2–9). Large trees to plant for the future include *Cedrus libani* (cedar of Lebanon; Z. 6–9) (**2**), the beech *Fagus sylvatica* 'Riversii' (Z. 4–7), *Juglans regia* (common walnut; Z. 4–9), *Liriodendron tulipifera* (tulip tree; Z. 4–9), and *Quercus robur* (common oak; Z. 5–8).

Ginkgo biloba

Liriodendron tulipifera

Liriodendron tulipifera

Platanus × hispanica

Liriodendron tulipifera, the tulip tree (Zones 4–9), is a wonderful, fast-growing large tree native to North America. It is upright in habit when young, becoming broader but maintaining a high, bushy crown. The leaves are medium green and unique in shape, being indented at the tips, not unlike flattened tulip flowers. The foliage turns rich butter yellow in fall. The flowers appear in summer on mature trees; they are tulip-shaped and yellowish green, marked with orange at the base of the petals. The tulip tree grows on any fertile soil and is a superb choice for an individual specimen in a large space.

Platanus × hispanica (Zones 4–8), the London plane, is common in cities, with its flaking mottled bark and bold, acerlike leaves. Round, prickly fruits hang from the branches in thin clusters, appearing in early summer and persisting on the tree after the leaves have fallen in winter. It is a large, fast-growing tree, tolerant of atmospheric pollution and exposed windy conditions, and growing on virtually any soil (its size is restricted on shallow chalk). If pollarded (see left), its flaking trunk and trimmed branches create a dramatic architectural effect in winter.

TREE HOUSES

A tree house is a consideration where a large, mature tree in good condition already exists. Tree houses offer children a wonderfully adventurous play environment and adults the ultimate refuge, with a different perspective on the surrounding garden and countryside. They should always be installed professionally, safety being of paramount importance. Pay particular attention to the condition of the supporting tree and to the ground beneath it; bark chips are a good idea to provide a softer surface. Damage to the tree must be avoided at all costs, and thought should be given to the possible future removal of the structure; a tree is likely to outlive the use of any tree house.

Ginkgo biloba (Zones 3–9), the maidenhair tree, is of great historical interest; it is a living fossil, unchanged since prehistoric times. As a garden plant, it is awkward when young but has a certain charm, with its gangly habit and unusual fan-shaped leaves. It grows quickly into a narrowly conical specimen, with widely spaced branches at right angles to the main stem. The leaves turn rich yellow in fall, when mature female trees also produce unpleasant-smelling fruits. It is a good choice where a tall, narrow tree is required that will not block a vista, and where a contrasting shape is needed, perhaps against broad-headed trees. Maidenhair trees are also hardy, easy to grow, and tolerant of atmospheric pollution.

Pterocarya fraxinifolia

Quercus frainetto 'Hungarian Crown'

Quercus robur

Platanus orientalis (Zones 7–9), the oriental plane, has more deeply lobed leaves. It is a large, broad, long-lived tree with attractive flaking bark and a magnificent stately crown. It is a striking tree to plant for future generations.

Pterocarya fraxinifolia (Zones 5–8), the wingnut, is a beautiful large, widely spreading tree that resembles the closely related common walnut, *Juglans regia* (see page 102). It has deeply furrowed bark and dark green leaves made up of numerous leaflets arranged along each side of long central stalks. In summer, long green female catkins hang from the branches, creating a delightful effect under the canopy. The fruits that follow are winged, hence the common name. The wingnut is not widely planted—the common walnut is a more popular choice, perhaps because of the possibility of it producing nuts. However, the wingnut is a more decorative tree when in flower and also has handsome foliage. It will

sit happily in a naturalistic setting, and is an excellent choice to plant by a river or lake as it enjoys moist conditions. It will generally tolerate dry soils.

There are many species of oak, mostly deciduous and some evergreen. *Quercus frainetto* (Zones 5–7), the Hungarian oak, is a big, fast-growing tree with a broad, oval crown of ascending branches carrying large, lobed leaves that color orange-yellow in fall. It is a robust tree that will succeed on any soil, including chalk. The most widely planted cultivar is *Quercus frainetto* 'Hungarian Crown'—an excellent, faster-growing alternative to the common oak, *Quercus robur* (Zones 5–8).

Quercus ilex (Zones 7–9), the holm oak, is a wonderful large, evergreen tree that forms a big, broad-headed specimen with loose, often drooping branches. It tolerates exposed and coastal situations and grows well on any soil, including alkaline ones, but it is a tree for the long term because of its slow rate of growth.

The holm oak can be grown as a multi-stemmed tree, a form that suits more naturalistic plantings. (See page 77.)

Quercus robur (Zones 5–8), the common oak, is a large, slow-growing, long-lived tree with a lovely rugged profile. Its lobed leaves and acorn fruits are well known, and it deserves a place in any large garden where trees can be planted for future generations. It is best planted as a root-balled or container-grown specimen and only transplants successfully bare-root as a very young plant.

Lindens are large, tolerant trees that are good on most soils including heavy clay and alkaline conditions. Most are fast-growing and produce attractive pale greenish yellow flowers in summer. Some are delightfully fragrant, but varieties such as *Tilia tomentosa* (Zones 4–7) are narcotic to bees. *Tilia* × *europaea* (Zones 4–7) and *Tilia platyphyllos* (Zones 5–8) are often attacked by aphids, resulting in sticky honeydew falling from the branches.

TREES FOR AVENUES

Large gardens and estates may offer the opportunity to plant an avenue, perhaps to line a drive. This type of formal planting demands trees of uniform growth to maintain the effect. It is a long-term project, so long-lived reliable trees are needed. Suitable trees include *Aesculus × carnea* 'Briotii' (red horse chestnut; Z. 3–7), *Carpinus betulus* 'Fastigiata' (fastigiate hornbeam, left; Z. 4–8), *Platanus × hispanica* (London plane; Z. 4–8), *Quercus frainetto* 'Hungarian Crown' (Hungarian oak; Z. 5–7), *Sorbus thibetica* 'John Mitchell' (Z. 5–7), and the lindens *Tilia cordata* 'Greenspire' (Z. 3–7) and *Tilia platyphyllos* 'Streetwise' (Z. 5–8).

Tilia × europaea 'Wratislaviensis'

Tilia × europaea

Tilia × europaea (Zones 4–7), common linden, was often planted as a street tree and for avenues all over Europe. It is large and vigorous, but responds well to pruning and pollarding. *Tilia × europaea* 'Pallida', the Kaiser linden, grows to form a broad, conical crown. The leaves are yellow-green beneath and the twigs are red in winter. *Tilia × europaea* 'Wratislaviensis' is a lovely large, slower-growing tree with a rounded head of emerald green leaves, golden yellow when young.

    Tilia platyphyllos (Zones 5–8), the broad-leaved linden, is a large, vigorous tree with rounded leaves with toothed edges. *Tilia platyphyllos* 'Rubra' is

an excellent form, particularly suited to planting as an avenue tree. The young shoots are bright red-brown and catch the winter light. *Tilia platyphyllos* 'Streetwise' is a large, upright form with dark, glossy foliage that turns purple-

brown in autumn. It has brightly colored red-brown shoots in winter and a more compact regular habit, making it ideal for avenue planting. (See pages 132–33.) All these lindens produce pale yellow flowers in midsummer.

TREE SEATS

A tree seat is an option if you have a big, mature tree set in spacious surroundings. Simple design and durability are the secrets of success. Slatted seats are always better than solid ones, which tend to collect fallen leaves and the debris from the tree and visiting birds. The inner circumference needs to be large enough to allow for expansion of the trunk, and the seat must be carefully fitted to compensate for variation in ground level around the tree.

OTHER GOOD TREES FOR BIG SPACES *Eucalyptus dalrympleana* • *Juglans nigra* • *Pinus nigra* •

LARGE CONIFEROUS TREES

Cedars are an excellent choice for a large space, as they are big, majestic trees that take about three generations to develop fully, from the sleek shape of youth through the broad, powerful proportions of middle age to the craggy silhouette of maturity. As mature specimens, both the Atlas cedar (*Cedrus atlantica*) and the cedar of Lebanon (*Cedrus libani*) form large, spreading, flat-topped trees with spectacular tiered branches. They are highly desirable for large gardens and parkland, and their strong, distinctive profile is sufficiently striking to set against the backdrop of a large, imposing house. As a young tree, **Cedrus atlantica** (Z. 6–9) grows quickly into a regular conical form. It has gray-green foliage that crowds the pliable branches, which tend to be upright when young and start to spread with maturity. **Cedrus atlantica** Glauca Group (**1**) has silver-blue foliage and is the most popular form (see page 71). **Cedrus libani** (**2**) (Z. 6–9) is slower-growing than the Atlas cedar. It is similar in shape when young, and wonderfully wide-spreading as a mature specimen (see page 94.). **Cedrus deodara** (see page 78) has a softer, more drooping habit and is perhaps more attractive as a young plant.

Calocedrus decurrens (**3**) (Z. 5–8), the incense cedar, makes an impressive specimen tree and a stunning feature when planted in a group in a larger space. It grows to a tall, dark column, the foliage in deep green, fanlike sprays. It is attractive as a young specimen and magnificent as a mature tree, when the lower branches are lost, leaving a very tall, narrow head on a short, stout trunk.

Sequoia sempervirens (Z. 7), the coast redwood, is a very tall, conical, evergreen tree with red-brown, fibrous bark and dark green foliage on downward-sweeping branches. It is extremely long-lived and regarded as the world's tallest living tree.

Sequoiadendron giganteum (**4**) (Z. 6–7), known as wellingtonia or mammoth tree, is a familiar sight in parks and estates, where it can attain a very large size; as a young tree, it is dense and conical in habit. It will grow on any soil apart from shallow alkaline conditions. The wellingtonia is shorter than the coast redwood, but it attains a greater girth and has more downward-sweeping, widely spaced branches; otherwise, the two trees are very similar in appearance. Both redwoods and wellingtonias need plenty of space to mature and are wonderful trees to plant for the distant future rather than for immediate effect—both are amazingly long-lived, surviving for 2,000 years or more.

Pinus sylvestris • *Populus* × *canadensis* 'Aurea' • *Quercus palustris* • *Quercus rubra* • *Tilia tomentosa* •

Country gardens

In a rural setting it is important to select trees that work as a transition between the garden and the surrounding landscape. Some garden trees, particularly those with highly colored foliage and exotic flowers or a formal shape, can look out of place in the countryside. Light, informal trees sit most happily and blend best with native species and hedgerow subjects. Whether selecting trees for a small country garden or a large paddock, the same principles apply.

SITUATIONS

Spring blossom in the orchard at West Green House, Hampshire, in England.

Acer campestre

Alnus glutinosa 'Imperialis'

Acer campestre (Z. 6–9), the field maple, is a lovely small to medium-sized tree ideal for a rural setting, particularly to provide height in a hedgerow. It is bushy-headed, sometimes rounded and often spreading in habit. The leaves are dark green, turning golden yellow, sometimes flame and orange in fall. The winged fruits are prolifically produced in some specimens and provide a splash of color in fall. (See page 62.)

Alders are often associated with wet conditions. However, many are tolerant plants that cope with dry soils as well as waterlogged sites (see page 109). *Alnus glutinosa* 'Imperialis' (Z. 3–7) is a lovely form of the common alder, with finely cut leaves and a graceful open habit. It grows into an elegant small tree that casts only light shade. This alder is excellent for planting close to a pond or stream in a smaller country garden.

Birches are such versatile trees, at home in virtually any setting, from a contemporary urban garden to an informal country plot. Perhaps the best

Betula pendula

Crataegus laevigata 'Paul's Scarlet'

choice of all for a country garden is the silver birch, *Betula pendula* (Z. 3–7), with its tracery of dark twigs and silver-gray bark with charcoal furrows and crevices as the tree matures. Young trees may have tan or almost golden brown stems before the characteristic silver bark develops at maturity. The silver birch grows to a medium-sized, narrowly conical tree and works well as a solitary specimen or planted in a group of three or more. Multi-stemmed specimens that branch into three or more main stems from ground level create the effect of a small copse when planted in a group of three or five. *Betula nigra* (Z. 4–9), the river birch, which is more spreading with shaggy copper-colored bark, also has a rustic character and is particularly useful near water. (See pages 146 and 147.)

Crataegus monogyna (Z. 4–7), the common hawthorn, is widely used as a rural hedging plant throughout the British Isles. It is spectacular in late spring, when the branches are garlanded with white or pink 'May blossom', followed by dark red berry fruits (known as 'haws') in fall. These often last into winter after the leaves have fallen. *Crataegus laevigata* (Z. 4–7) is similar, and any of its cultivars work well as garden trees in an area where hawthorn is used as a hedging plant. *Crataegus laevigata* 'Paul's Scarlet', with double red flowers (see Good Companions, page 103), and *Crataegus laevigata* 'Rosea Flore Pleno', with double pink flowers, are the most popular. Both grow into round-headed, small trees with gracefully arching branches and emerald green leaves. (See page 126.)

Some varieties of **ash** look at home in a rustic setting. *Fraxinus angustifolia* 'Raywood' (Z. 6–9) is a good choice of medium-sized tree for a country garden. Although it is quite tall, spreading, and vigorous, it is also light and airy. The fine, shiny green, fernlike foliage stays in good condition all summer and turns rich shades of purple and red in fall (see page 139). This ash needs a sheltered position, because it has a tendency to be quite brittle and branches can be broken by the wind in an exposed situation. It is a good choice to plant against a backdrop of native woodland, where its lighter habit will add foreground interest against heavier trees such as oak (*Quercus*) and beech (*Fagus*).

Fraxinus excelsior 'Jaspidea' (Z. 5–8), the form of ash with golden yellow

PLANTING IN GROUPS

For a natural effect in large country gardens and paddocks, plant groups of trees of the same type. They achieve greater impact in less time than individual specimens of different species planted across a large area of grass. Suitable trees to plant in this way include *Acer campestre* (Z. 4–8), *Amelanchier lamarckii* (Z. 4–8), *Betula pendula* (Z. 3–7), *Prunus avium* (Z. 4–8), and *Sorbus aucuparia* (Z. 3–7).

PLANTING IN HEDGES

A hedgerow often marks the boundary of a country garden. This is a good situation to include a tree as a link with the surrounding landscape. The right tree will provide a focal point in the picture, break the solid line of the hedge, and take the eye to the view of the landscape beyond. Good trees to plant in hedgerows include *Acer campestre* (Z. 4–8), *Corylus avellana* (Z. 4–7), *Crataegus laevigata* 'Rosea Flore Pleno' (Z. 4–7), *Prunus avium* (right; Z. 4–8), and *Sorbus aucuparia* (Z. 3–7).

Fraxinus ornus

Malus hupehensis

Juglans regia

shoots, also fits well in a rural setting in time. As a young tree, the striking color of the shoots and the regular habit can look out of place, but as the tree matures the habit becomes looser and more informal. Where space allows, this large tree is worth planting just for the golden yellow autumn color (see page 139). It is a good choice in front of coniferous trees such as plantation spruce (*Picea abies*). **Fraxinus ornus** (Zones 5–6), manna ash, is a lovely medium-sized tree with light green, fernlike foliage and fluffy heads of creamy white flowers in late spring, produced in abundance all over the head of the tree.

In a big country garden, **walnuts** are beautiful trees to plant for the future. They mature to elegant, round-headed, medium-sized to large, majestic trees. The big leaves are wonderfully aromatic when crushed; they consist of a strong central rib that carries a number of oval leaflets, which are green when mature and often copper-tinted when young. **Juglans regia** (Zones 4–9), the common walnut, has been cultivated in England since Roman times for its tasty nuts; these are produced on mature trees only and are much loved by squirrels. The age when nuts are produced varies in seed-raised trees, but grafted

named clones that fruit early are available. **Juglans regia** 'Buccaneer' is a popular variety. *Juglans regia* is slow-growing and should be planted as a young pot-grown or B&B specimen; bare-root trees often fail. **Juglans nigra** (Zones 4–8), the black walnut, is faster-growing, with larger leaves and deeply furrowed bark. It is reputedly resistant to honey fungus.

Most **ornamental crabs**, with their apple-blossom flowers and attractive autumn fruits, work well in country gardens. **Malus hupehensis** (Zones 4–8) is a medium-sized tree with upright branches when young, forming a loose, round head with age. It is a superb flowering crab, with profuse fragrant white flowers in late spring and small red fruits in fall. Resistant to scab and mildew,

NATURALIZING AROUND TREES

Trees planted in naturalistic settings look at home when underplanted with drifts of bulbs or perennials that are associated with the local countryside. Native wildflowers are an obvious choice; however, there are also some cultivated species that lend themselves to this use because of their habit and suitability for the growing conditions.

Where trees are planted in thin grass, the following naturalize successfully: *Anthriscus sylvestris* (Z. 7–10), *Digitalis purpurea* (**1**) (Z. 4–8), *Hyacinthoides non-scripta* (**2**) (Z. 5–8), *Lunaria annua* (**3**) (Z. 7–9), *Nectaroscordum siculum* (**4**) (Z. 6–10), *Primula veris* (**5**) (Z. 5–7).

If the grass is thick and lush around the trees, mow it regularly and remove all cuttings for a couple of years—this will reduce the fertility of the soil near the surface, resulting in less vigorous grass and therefore less competition for the underplanting as it gets established.

OTHER TREES FOR COUNTRY GARDENS *Acer platanoides* • *Alnus cordata* • *Amelanchier lamarckii* •

Prunus avium

Prunus avium 'Plena'

Prunus padus 'Watereri'

and easy to grow, it is an ideal tree for a paddock or wildflower meadow. *Malus transitoria* (Z. 4–7) is a lovely small tree, with broadly spreading branches that seem to float above the ground. In spring, the branches are smothered in honey-scented apple blossoms, followed by tiny golden yellow, cherrylike fruits in fall. If space allows, plant *Malus transitoria* in a group of three in the corner of a meadow or paddock. (See page 128.)

Prunus avium (Z. 4–8), gean or wild cherry, is a British native woodland tree. The upright trunk carries a rounded head of straight branches that are wreathed in spring with small white, single flowers and copper-tinted unfurling leaves. The autumn color is soft and rich, a mix of apricot-orange-red and amber. Birds quickly devour the small red, cherrylike fruits. It grows on any soil but is susceptible to canker and die-back. The double form,

Prunus avium 'Plena', is more resistant. It produces masses of double white flowers of great beauty but lacks the fragile charm of the single species. It is a good choice for an avenue in a rural situation, looking spectacular in both spring and fall.

Prunus padus 'Watereri' (Z. 6–9) has a totally different flower form from most other flowering cherries; the blooms are more akin to those of the cherry laurel (*Prunus laurocerasus*)—long, drooping racemes of small, almond-scented white flowers are produced among the fresh green leaves. It is a medium-sized tree of light, rounded but spreading habit. *Prunus padus* 'Colorata' (Z. 6–9) has pale pink flowers—a most attractive combination with the dark purple shoots and copper-purple new leaves.

GOOD COMPANIONS

Crataegus laevigata 'Paul's Scarlet' (1) (Z. 4–7) flowers well in late spring, but it does not fruit and the leaves do not color in fall. *Viburnum opulus* (2) (Z. 3–8) is the perfect partner, with white flowers in early summer followed by red fruits that last into winter. The leaves turn red and orange in fall.

Prunus padus (3) (Z. 6–9) has white flowers in spring but the foliage does not color well in fall. *Euonymus europaeus* 'Red Cascade' (4) (Z. 3–7) has insignificant flowers, but the fruits, pinkish red with orange seeds, persist after the leaves turn scarlet and fall.

Carpinus betulus • *Crataegus persimilis* 'Prunifolia' • *Liquidambar styraciflua* • *Malus floribunda* • *Prunus* 'Snow Goose' •

Acid soils

Those gardening on acid soil are blessed with the ability to grow rhododendrons, camellias, pieris, and many more of our most exotic flowering shrubs. In addition, some of our most beautiful trees require, or perform better, on acid soil. These include those with exquisite summer flowers and also the best trees for autumn color. Bear in mind that acid soils vary—they can be light and sandy, moist and peaty, or even clay—and certain choice trees require specific conditions to thrive.

Embothrium coccineum Lanceolatum Group

Rhododendrons thrive on acid woodland soil in the dappled shade of deciduous trees and shrubs.

A woodland garden on acid soil provides the shelter, light shade, and humus-rich soil enjoyed by the most discriminating acid-loving trees. Few are large in stature, preferring to keep below the higher tree canopy, often of pines and oaks. Their planting partners are usually rhododendrons and evergreen and deciduous azaleas. Many trees that require acid soil bloom after these have finished flowering, making them valuable for extending the season.

Cercidiphyllum japonicum (Zones 4–8), the Katsura tree, grows on any reasonably fertile soil but is an ideal choice for sheltered woodland gardens on acid soil. The delicate, heart-shaped foliage emerges translucent and pink, becomes soft green, and eventually turns to shades of pink, salmon, flame, or yellow in fall. A small to medium-sized, spreading tree, it is often at its best as a feathered specimen with branches to ground level. In this form, it is ideal to plant among other mature trees, which will afford protection against cold winds and frosts that can damage the emerging foliage. Dry conditions cause premature leaf fall. (See page 137.)

A plant for the enthusiast, *Embothrium coccineum* Lanceolatum Group (Zones 8–10) is a member of the protea family and native to Chile. It is hardy and grows into a small, slender, upright tree. The light, airy branches carry willowlike leaves

PATIENCE IS NEEDED

Most of the gems that require moist but well-drained acid soil are tricky to establish and resent disturbance once they are more mature; therefore they are best planted as young container-grown specimens. This means that patience is required, as they will take time to reach tree proportions and may need several years before they can produce a good display of flowers.

and bright orange-scarlet, grevillea-like flowers in early summer. It favors a sheltered, acid woodland location.

The **eucryphias** are less fussy than most of the other trees in this section. They prefer a loamy soil and will grow in open situations, provided they have some shelter. Although they are usually grown as shrubs, some mature into handsome evergreen trees. Their narrow, columnar habit makes them ideal in restricted areas and for mixed plantings, as they cast little shade over neighboring plants. *Eucryphia* × *intermedia* 'Rostrevor' (Zones 8–10) has dark green leaves with blue-green undersides and grows into a small but broad, dark column. Fragrant white flowers smother the slender branches in late summer—a welcome surprise late in the year. *Eucryphia* × *nymansensis* 'Nymansay' (Zones 8–10) is a popular hybrid, originally raised at Nymans Garden in Sussex, England. It grows quickly, assuming a columnar habit, and eventually reaches 30 ft. (10 m) or more. The leaves are relatively large and dark glossy green. The large white flowers resemble small single

Eucryphia × intermedia 'Rostrevor'

Halesia monticola var. vestita

Eucryphia × nymansensis 'Nymansay'

camellias and are produced profusely in late summer. A good specimen in full flower is a magnificent sight. (See Good Companions, page 107.)

Halesia monticola var. *vestita* (Zones 5–8), the snowdrop tree, is an elegant, small, spreading tree with hanging white, snowdroplike flowers along the branches in late spring. It needs a moist but well-drained, non-alkaline soil. It is a beautiful tree, similar to styrax, but only worth planting in the right soil conditions.

TREES FOR SANDY ACID SOIL

Sandy acid soils are often dry for much of the year and are low in nutrients. Some trees struggle to survive in these conditions, while others are well adapted if the soil of their native habitat is similar. *Acer negundo* (box elder; Z. 2–9) does well on dry acid soils, as do *Castanea sativa* (sweet chestnut; Z. 4–9), hollies (*Ilex*), birches (*Betula*), gleditsia, and robinia. *Cercis siliquastrum* (Judas tree, right; Z. 6–9), a Mediterranean native, is also a very drought-tolerant plant. Light, sandy acid soils can be improved by adding organic matter, but it is worth checking the pH of manure or compost before applying it around chalk-hating plants.

MAGNOLIAS

In large woodland gardens, the magnificent, spreading *Magnolia campbellii* (1) (Z. 8–10) is a must. A native of the Himalayas, it prefers warmer regions—in the United States, the finest specimens are found in gardens in the Deep South and California. This magnolia takes over 20 years to flower, so patience is needed, but the handsome large, cup-shaped blooms are worth waiting for. The species usually produces pink flowers, but there are several named clones in white or deeper pink. Since the flowers are borne in early spring, hard frosts can damage the blooms. All forms of *Magnolia campbellii* grow into large trees. For most gardens, *Magnolia* 'Star Wars' (2) (Z. 6–9), the excellent hybrid between *Magnolia campbellii* and *Magnolia liliiflora*, is a better choice. A small tree, it flowers from an early age, producing huge blooms that are deep pink on the outside, palest pink within.

Magnolia 'Elizabeth' (3) (Z. 4–9) is a glorious small tree for acid soil. A hardy variety, it was raised in the Brooklyn Botanic Garden, New York. It has a compact, conical habit, and the flowers are elegant and slender in bud, opening to cup-shaped blooms of clear primrose yellow. They open in late spring, before the leaves. (See Good Companions, opposite.)

Magnolia 'Heaven Scent' (4) (Z. 3–8) is a small to medium-sized, spreading tree producing profuse slender, cup-shaped flowers that are deep pink on the outside and pale pink within. They are richly scented and more weather-resistant than many magnolia flowers.

Magnolia salicifolia 'Wada's Memory' (Z. 4–8) is perhaps the best white magnolia. It grows into a small, spreading tree that produces a profusion of large white, delightfully fragrant flowers. Because of its size, it is a good choice for a smaller garden on acid soil. 'Wada's Memory' makes a stunning subject planted against a background of dark evergreens or the white stems of Himalayan birches.

The familiar *Magnolia* × *soulangeana* (Z. 4–9) is usually grown as a large shrub, with several main stems forming a large, broad, spreading plant that needs a lot of space (see pages 126–27). It is excellent on clay soils, tolerating even heavy clay, but prefers neutral to acid conditions and does not like chalk or alkaline soil. Its appeal is its large, waxy, goblet-shaped flowers in spring, usually white flushed with purple-pink. There are a number of superb varieties (see below).

CHOICE MAGNOLIA × SOULANGEANA VARIETIES

There are numerous cultivars of *Magnolia* × *soulangeana* (Z. 4–9), but those listed below are among the best. Varieties with dark flowers do not show frost damage as dramatically as those with white or pale pink flowers and may be the best choice for colder, more exposed gardens.

Magnolia × *soulangeana* 'Alba' (1) is one of the earliest varieties, with pure white, waxy flowers.

Magnolia × *soulangeana* 'Brozzonii' has large, elongated white flowers shaded purple at the base; it is the largest and latest-flowering variety.

Magnolia × *soulangeana* 'Lennei' (2) is vigorous and spreading. The large, goblet-shaped flowers are rosy purple outside, white within. It sometimes flowers again in fall.

Magnolia × *soulangeana* 'Rustica Rubra' (3), often regarded as the best variety, is vigorous, with cup-shaped, rich rosy red flowers.

MORE TREES FOR ACID SOILS   *Ailanthus altissima* • *Amelanchier lamarckii* • *Betula utilis* var. *jacquemontii* •

AUTUMN COLOR ON ACID SOILS

Acid soils produce the best autumn color and many of the finest trees and shrubs for autumn color grow only on acid soil. *Nyssa sylvatica* (**1**) (Z. 3–9), the tupelo, is one of the best, the leaves turning rich shades of flame and scarlet. The many varieties of *Acer palmatum* (**2**) (Z. 6–8) are also noted for their autumn color, and they are at their best in dappled shade on acid soils.

Stewartia pseudocamellia

Styrax japonicus is a beautiful early-summer flowering tree for a sheltered position on acid soil.

Stewartia pseudocamellia (Zones 4–8), related to the camellia, is a small to medium-sized tree of attractive open habit. The flowers resemble single white camellias with a mass of yellow stamens in the center of each flower. They are freely produced in mid- to late summer, and although they fall quickly—covering the ground under the tree—they are replaced by further abundant flowers. The tree also boasts attractive flaking bark and good red and gold autumn leaf color. *Stewartia pseudocamellia* Koreana Group is similar but with larger flowers and particularly attractive bark. *Stewartia sinensis* (Zones 5–7) is smaller but otherwise similar. These stewartias require a semi-shaded position, particularly over their roots. They resent disturbance, so once established they must be left alone.

Styrax japonicus (Zones 5–8), the Japanese snowbell, is an exquisite small, spreading tree of graceful habit with neat apple green leaves that are oval with pointed tips. In early summer, white bell-shaped flowers with yellow stamens hang from the branches in profusion. Styrax needs a moist, loamy acid soil, ideally in the dappled shade and shelter of a woodland garden. It is most beautiful when planted where the flowers can be admired from beneath: perhaps at the top of a bank or hanging over a pathway.

GOOD COMPANIONS

The delicate, primrose-scented flowers of *Corylopsis pauciflora* (1) (Z. 6–8) give early color beneath *Magnolia* 'Elizabeth' (2) (Z 4–9). Both are even lovelier in the presence of blue ground-cover such as *Pulmonaria* 'Mawson's Blue' (Z 4–8).

The dark green foliage of *Eucryphia* × *nymansensis* 'Nymansay' (3) (Z 8–10) complements the bronze flowers of *Hamamelis* × *intermedia* 'Aurora' (4) (Z 5–8) in winter and the orange and gold foliage in fall

107

Castanea sativa • *Pinus sylvestris* • *Populus alba* • *Prunus avium* • *Quercus rubra* • *Sorbus aucuparia* •

Alkaline soils

Alkaline soils are usually thought of as shallow, dry, and lacking in nutrients. However, this is not always the case. Deeper, well-cultivated soil over chalk or limestone deposits will support most trees and shrubs, except for those that specifically require acid or neutral conditions. And there are some trees that are suited to growing on chalk or limestone even where soils are shallow.

Acer campestre 'Streetwise'

Acer platanoides (Zones 3–7), the Norway maple, is a large, handsome, fast-growing tree with big fresh green maple leaves and a broad, rounded head. In mid-spring the branches are graced with clusters of fluffy, greenish yellow flowers, before the leaves unfurl. In fall the leaves usually turn clear bright yellow, sometimes shaded with apricot and orange. An easy tree to grow, it thrives on any soil including shallow chalk or limestone. It can be transplanted as a bare-root tree, even as a larger specimen. *Acer platanoides* 'Globosum' is a smaller, more compact form with a dense, mop-shaped head of short branches. It is useful where space is limited and where a uniform line of trees is needed. It is increasingly used in contemporary planting schemes; the head can be trimmed easily and maintained as a cube or a neat sphere.

The black mulberry, *Morus nigra*, thrives in well-drained soil.

Acer platanoides

Many **acers** grow successfully in alkaline soils. *Acer campestre* (Zones 4–8), the field maple, is a lovely informal tree that fits well in rural settings (see page 100 and Good Companions, page 110). *Acer campestre* 'Streetwise' is a superb selection, with a neat, compact, conical habit suited to a smaller garden or to more formal situations. The leaves turn bright yellow in fall, combining attractively with the red fruits ('keys') that appear in late summer and early fall.

All forms of *Acer negundo* (Zones 2–9), the box elder, thrive in alkaline soil, and are useful, airy trees that suit gardens of all sizes. (See pages 62 and 125.)

Alnus cordata

Acer pseudoplatanus (Zones 4–8), the sycamore, is thought of as an invader because of its ability to establish seedlings that quickly become unwanted trees in unsuitable locations. However, some of the cultivars are

PLANTING ON ALKALINE SOIL

Alkaline soils are usually fast-draining and low in nutrients, so they are improved by adding organic matter in the form of well-rotted manure and garden compost, to increase the humus content of the soil. Humus is the sticky viscous substance that helps to retain water, nutrients, and beneficial micro-organisms in the soil.

When planting trees, add plenty of organic matter and fork it thoroughly into the base of the planting hole. Annual mulching with more manure or compost around the base of the tree will continue to improve the soil and encourages healthy root growth.

Some trees may show yellowing of foliage and a reduction in leaf size when growing on shallow alkaline soils. This may be caused by summer drought, or lack of nitrogen, which is easily washed out of the soil during periods of winter wet. To correct the problem, use slow-release fertilizer—applied across the soil surface above the roots of the tree—and mulch with compost. Thorough watering afterwards carries the nutrients down to the tree's roots.

FLOWERING TREES FOR ALKALINE SOILS

When it comes to selecting a flowering tree for a garden on chalk or limestone, the choice is far from limited. All of the popular flowering cherries (*Prunus*) (**1**) will grow happily, as will most crab apples (*Malus*) (**2**), flowering hawthorns (varieties of *Crataegus laevigata*; Z. 4–7) (**3**) and *Cercis siliquastrum*, the Judas tree (**4**) (Z. 6–9). Where space permits, the horse chestnuts *Aesculus* × *carnea* 'Briotii' (**5**) (Z. 3–7), and *Aesculus hippocastanum* 'Baumannii' (**6**) (Z. 3–7) are magnificent statuesque flowering trees.

better behaved and make attractive foliage trees that grow on any soil including shallow chalk. (See page 112.)

Although often associated with wet conditions, some **alders** tolerate dry soils and are successful on chalk or limestone. *Alnus cordata* (Zones 4–6), the Italian alder, is a medium to large tree with shiny green foliage and attractive tiered branches. In spring, long, ocher-yellow male catkins hang from the branches. The shorter female catkins develop into tiny blackish cones, which persist on the tree through winter. It is attractive, either as a single specimen or in a small group.

Carpinus betulus (Zones 4–8), the hornbeam, is widely used for hedging. Its fresh green foliage looks good all the year and when it is grown as a hedge the leaves—like those on a beech hedge—turn brown in fall and persist into the following spring. If left to its own devices, hornbeam develops into a large tree with a gray

Carpinus betulus 'Fastigiata'

fluted trunk, oval ribbed leaves that turn yellow in fall and a broad, rounded habit. It grows successfully on alkaline soils, but can be difficult to establish in the driest situations. The most widely grown form is *Carpinus betulus* 'Fastigiata'. It has

A L K A L I N E   S O I L S

109

Corylus colurna

Fagus sylvatica 'Dawyck Purple'

Fraxinus excelsior 'Pendula'

upright branches and a more regular habit, excellent for formal effect and for trimming to control its size. (See page 91.)

Corylus colurna (Zones 4–7), the Turkish hazel, deserves wider use in gardens. It grows vigorously into a large pyramidal, symmetrical tree. The leaves are bigger than those of *Corylus avellana*, and turn golden yellow in fall. The bark of the trunk of the Turkish hazel is often creamy white with attractive corrugations, a feature in winter. In early spring, golden yellow catkins adorn the branches. Coping with wet conditions as well as dry chalk or limestone, it is remarkably tolerant. (See Good Companions, right.)

Beech trees predominate in woodland on alkaline soils, and a number of varieties of **Fagus sylvatica** (Zones 4–7) are obvious choices for a big garden with shallow soil over chalk (see page 95). The narrow, compact habit of the purple-leaved **Fagus sylvatica** 'Dawyck Purple' makes it ideal for gardens of all sizes. (See pages 60–61.)

Most **ash** trees (*Fraxinus*), too, thrive on chalk. **Fraxinus angustifolia** 'Raywood'

(Zones 6–9) is a good choice for its light, fernlike foliage and good autumn color. **Fraxinus excelsior** 'Jaspidea' (Zones 5–8) has golden winter twigs and beautiful yellow autumn leaf color. (See page 139.)

In a large space, where a tree can be accommodated as a specimen, **Fraxinus**

excelsior 'Pendula' (Zones 5–8), the weeping ash, makes an interesting choice. A strong-growing tree, it forms a wide-spreading mound clothed in dark green foliage. It is at its most striking in winter, when the silhouette of weeping branches has a dramatic architectural appeal.

GOOD COMPANIONS

The maplelike leaves and white flowers followed by red berries make *Viburnum opulus* (1) (Z. 3–8) a pleasing partner for the field maple, *Acer campestre* (2) (Z. 4–8)—an ideal combination for a country garden on alkaline soil.

The neat, cream-edged foliage of *Buxus sempervirens* 'Elegantissima' (3) (Z. 6–9) is a good combination with the creamy brown, corky bark of *Corylus colurna* (4) (Z. 4–7), the Turkish hazel.

110

OTHER TREES FOR ALKALINE SOILS *Fraxinus ornus* • *Ligustrum lucidum* 'Excelsum Superbum' •

LILACS AS TREES

Sorbus aria 'Lutescens'

The common lilac, *Syringa vulgaris* (Z. 3–7), is usually grown as a large shrub, but mature specimens often grow into small, multi-stemmed trees. They are excellent, easy-to-grow plants for alkaline soils. Good reliable lilacs include *Syringa vulgaris* 'Andenken an Ludwig Späth' (**1**), with single, wine purple flowers; *Syringa vulgaris* 'Charles Joly', with double, dark red-purple flowers; *Syringa vulgaris* 'Katherine Havemeyer', with double lilac-pink flowers; and *Syringa vulgaris* 'Madame Lemoine' (**2**), with double white flowers. The season of interest is spectacular but relatively short. However, it can be prolonged by growing a late-blooming clematis, for example a variety of *Clematis viticella* (**3**) (Z. 5–8), through the branches to add color to the plain green summer foliage.

All **crab apples** grow on chalk or limestone, although *Malus floribunda* (Zones 4–8) can be slower-growing than usual when on shallow alkaline soils. Some crabs are prone to disease, suffering from the same problems as apples grown for fruit, particularly scab and canker. *Malus* 'Rudolph' (Zones 3–7) is a relatively new variety that seems to be hardy and resistant to scab and mildew. It is a small tree of compact, upright habit, with foliage bronze when young, dark green later, and rose red flowers. Small round, orange-red fruits ripen in autumn and persist on twigs after the leaves have fallen. *Malus bhutanica* (Zones 4–7) is disease-resistant and has a more informal, spreading habit. The maplelike leaves color well in fall, and masses of small red and yellow autumn fruits follow the creamy spring flowers.

Morus nigra (Zones 7–9), the black mulberry, has been grown in cultivation since the early 16th century. It is a slow-growing, very long-lived tree that takes years to develop its wide-spreading head and gnarled appearance. It has rough, heart-shaped leaves and red-black edible fruits. Since they fall from the tree when ripe, the tree is best planted in grass rather than alongside paving, where the ripe fruits will stain and make an unsightly mess. Black mulberry is a large tree, to

Malus bhutanica

plant for future generations, and will not make quick impact in a garden.

Where purple foliage is required, *Prunus cerasifera* 'Nigra' (Zones 3–8) is a smaller-leaved, bushier alternative to *Acer platanoides* 'Crimson King' (see pages 58–59). It produces a cloud of pink blossoms in early spring, followed by a dense head of plum-purple summer foliage on dark twigs. (See pages 61 and 120.)

Sorbus aucuparia, the mountain ash, is normally associated with acid soils, whereas the whitebeam *Sorbus aria* 'Lutescens' (Zones 5–6) is an excellent choice for alkaline conditions. Its dark, ascending branches are particularly beautiful in spring, when the silver-gray leaves first emerge (see page 71). It is a good choice for many situations, contrasting well with plain green trees and, being compact, suiting smaller gardens. It can be pruned and trained (see page 91), and looks as much at home in a contemporary design as in a flower-filled country garden.

See also Good Autumn Color on Alkaline Soil, pages 138–39.

Malus 'Evereste' • *Photinia* × *fraseri* 'Red Robin' • *Pinus mugo* • *Populus alba* • *Prunus serrula* • *Rhus typhina* •

Difficult situations

Some situations offer something of a challenge in terms of soil conditions and exposure. Many trees are difficult to establish on poor, dry soil or ground that is wet or waterlogged for part or all of the year. Some trees are easily damaged by winds, so are an unsuitable choice for exposed positions, whereas others withstand gales, even if salt-laden, in a coastal location. For any of these situations, it is important to choose an adaptable subject that will thrive rather than struggle to survive.

Alnus cordata

a medium-sized to large conical tree and will grow on a damp site but does not tolerate waterlogged soil. It will, however, thrive in dry conditions and is one of the most tolerant of alkaline soil. It has bright green, shiny leaves and long golden male catkins in early spring. The small egg-shaped, female catkins develop into tiny woody, dark brown cones that persist on the branches throughout the year.

Alnus glutinosa (Zones 3–7), the common alder, is smaller and bushy in stature. It too has golden yellow catkins

Robinia pseudoacacia is a tolerant tree, thriving on poor soil and in dry conditions.

Alnus incana

The sycamore, *Acer pseudoplatanus* (Zones 4–8), is one of the most adaptable trees, growing on any soil and surviving in very exposed sites. It is a large, spreading, rounded tree, with dark green maple leaves and attractive winged fruits in summer. On some trees these develop a copper-red hue. Sycamore often seeds prolifically, and this is its drawback in gardens. *Acer pseudoplatanus* f. *purpureum* is a lovely form, with purple undersides to the leaves—very effective when ruffled by the breeze.

Most **alders** perform well in wet soil conditions and they are frequently planted in waterside situations, often with willows (*Salix*). However, alders are tolerant plants and many are just as successful on dry soils as they are on wet ones. *Alnus cordata* (Zones 4–6), the Italian alder, is in early spring and dark green foliage. It grows quickly and has an attractive, light habit. It thrives in wet conditions and is a good choice for waterside planting. It also tolerates dry conditions and the salt-laden air of coastal areas. *Alnus incana* (Zones 2–7), the gray alder, is even more tolerant of salt and also thrives on poor, wet soils. It is very noticeable in early spring as the reddish catkins start to develop on the branches just before the leaves unfurl. It is a fast-growing, medium-sized tree with leaves that are gray underneath and less shiny than those of the latter two species. *Alnus* × *spaethii* (Zones 2–7) is one of the most decorative alders, small to medium-sized, with purple-tinged young leaves and pale green, leathery leaves in summer that often color well in fall. The catkins are long and golden (see page 129). This tree grows quickly in any situation and has an elegant conical habit. It succeeds on any soil, wet or dry, and is tolerant of cold, windy situations.

The common ash, *Fraxinus excelsior* (Zones 5–8), is a large, fast-growing tree native to Britain and Europe. It has attractive gray bark and a billowing crown clothed in fine green foliage. Its main drawback is the vast number of seedlings

Alnus × spaethii

Fraxinus excelsior 'Westhof's Glorie'

ESTABLISHING TREES ON EXPOSED SITES

When planting on exposed and windy sites, it is best to start with small specimens; these will adapt to the situation as they grow. Larger transplants need very firm staking to avoid wind rock, which can break developing roots and hinder establishment.

OTHER TREES FOR COLD EXPOSED SITES

Acer platanoides (Z. 3–7), *Betula pendula* (Z. 3–7), *Crataegus monogyna* (Z. 4–7), *Fagus sylvatica* (Z. 4–7), *Laburnum* × *watereri* 'Vossii' (Z. 5–7), *Quercus robur* (Z. 5–8)

---

produced from the annual distribution of ash 'keys' from its branches. *Fraxinus excelsior* 'Westhof's Glorie' is a superb selection of regular habit, with a narrow crown becoming broader with age. It is tough and reliable, succeeding on any soil, and is one of the most wind-tolerant trees, coping even with coastal conditions.

Pinus nigra (Zones 5–8), the Austrian pine, is a large, dense-headed tree with dark green needles. It is easy to grow and tolerates alkaline conditions, dry soils, and salt winds. It is widely used as a landscape plant and is attractive as a young tree, when it is conical in shape with branches to ground level (see page 78).

The British native Scots Pine, *Pinus sylvestris* (Zones 2–8), is adaptable, growing on most soils, including those that are dry, wet, acidic, or alkaline. It is rarely planted as a garden tree but is a good choice in a large space where it can grow to reach its potential. When mature, it is a magnificent tall, columnar tree with reddish bark and dark green foliage carried on horizontal branches way above the ground. (See page 151.)

Most of the **poplars** are large, tough trees that survive wet as well as dry conditions. The white poplar, *Populus*

alba (Zones 3–8), is excellent on the most difficult sites, including exposed coastal areas and permanently waterlogged soils. Its silver-gray leaves and open habit are light and airy, and the tree combines well with the dark green of alder foliage. (See page 70.) *Populus* × *canadensis* 'Aurea' ('Serotina Aurea'; Zones 5–9) is large and fast-growing, often with a broad, tall crown that extends to ground level. The foliage is a pretty copper-gold

Populus × canadensis 'Aurea'

Salix alba var. *sericea*, like all forms of the white willow, is ideal to grow in waterside situations.

Salix alba var. vitellina 'Britzensis'

Salix alba var. vitellina

poor soil and pollution. Mature trees have rugged, furrowed bark and horizontal branches, giving an Asian look. Some trees sucker profusely. Abundant soft green foliage is the backdrop to the white wisteria-like flowers in early summer. These are nectar-laden and attractive to bees and other flying insects. Because of the brittle nature of its branches, robinia is not suited to exposed windy sites. (See page 112.)

Willows are the most obvious choice for wet conditions. Many thrive in permanently waterlogged soils. *Salix alba* (Zones 2–9), the white willow, is a British native found growing by watersides. It is a fast-growing subject, making an effective screening tree and windbreak in a large garden. It will also grow on drier soils, which will restrict its size. Left to grow naturally, it will form a large, conical tree with upward sweeping branches and narrow, silky gray leaves. Greenish yellow catkins appear with the leaves in spring. The varieties with colorful winter twigs are particularly ornamental: *Salix alba* var. *vitellina* 'Britzensis', with scarlet-orange young twigs, and *Salix alba* var. *vitellina*, with deep yellow ones. Both are amenable to pollarding—cutting back to the trunk every year or two to control the size of the tree and bring the colorful growth nearer to the ground. Treated in this way, they will suit almost any size of garden. *Salix alba* var. *sericea* is smaller, with a round head of silvery leaves.

Salix caprea (Zones 4–9), goat willow, is no beauty when it comes to foliage. It has stiff twigs with gray-green oval leaves and grows to form a broad shrub or a small tree. Silky silver female catkins, known as pussy willow, grace some plants in early spring, whereas others are covered in golden fluffy catkins, commonly known as palm. If cut back hard, once the catkins have faded, *Salix caprea* produces long straight wands of deep purple-brown stems, which are not unattractive in winter. It grows anywhere and is useful on inhospitable sites in a rural location.

as it unfurls, becoming clear yellow in spring, greenish yellow through summer and rich gold in fall. A tree in full leaf looks splendid against a clear blue sky. It is a good choice for an open rural situation on wet soil, and copes with strong winds.

Populus tremula (Zones 2–5), aspen, is a lovely medium-sized tree with large leaves on long stalks that move in the slightest wind. Their shiny surfaces reflect the light, and a mature tree on a clear sunny day is a wonderful sight. The leaves are late to appear but they persist in fall, turning clear yellow before they drop. *Populus tremula* suckers profusely so is not a good choice for most gardens. However, in a large, rural garden it is an ideal link with the surrounding countryside.

Robinia pseudoacacia (Zones 3–8), false acacia, is a large tree tolerant of dry,

OTHER TREES FOR DAMP SITES *Amelanchier lamarckii* • *Betula nigra* • *Betula pendula* • *Crataegus laevigata* •

PLANTING WEEPING WILLOWS

The weeping willows, *Salix ×ばつ sepulcralis* var. *chrysocoma* (Z. 2–9) and *Salix ×ばつ pendulina* var. *elegantissima* (right; Z. 6–9) are broad-spreading, medium-sized trees. Although often chosen for waterside planting in smaller gardens, they are far too large and fast-growing for this purpose. They are ruined by hard pruning to control their size, so should only be planted where there is enough space to allow their development. They are best planted as specimens, not crowded by other plantings, which will detract from their beauty and interfere with the long, pendent branches.

For small gardens, choose *Salix purpurea* 'Pendula' (Z. 3–8), trained as a standard. This has long, pendent purple-brown twigs and narrow leaves, blue-green beneath.

Salix daphnoides

The violet willow, **Salix daphnoides** (Zones 2–9), is a fast-growing, small tree with deep violet shoots overlaid with a whitish bloom, attractive in the low light of winter; for best effect hard prune in

Salix ×ばつ sepulcralis var. chrysocoma

early spring. Catkins appear before the leaves in spring.

The **weeping willow** is one of the most beautiful trees. It is medium-sized, with a broad-spreading head and long, pendent, golden yellow twigs. The narrow leaves are at their most beautiful in early spring, when they emerge pale, soft green on the long hanging twigs. Unfortunately, willows are prone to disease, particularly scab and canker, causing disfiguration of the foliage and black lesions and die-back of the twigs and branches. **Salix ×ばつ pendulina var. elegantissima** (Zones

6–9) is very resistant to disease. It is a broadly spreading, medium-sized tree, with long, pendulous branches and narrow leaves that are green above and blue-gray beneath. Catkins appear with the new leaves in spring.

Salix ×ばつ sepulcralis var. chrysocoma (Zones 2–9) is more widely grown and may even become invasive in some areas. It is a hybrid of *Salix babylonica* with *Salix alba* var. *vitellina*, the latter imparting golden yellow twigs. It is a very beautiful tree, with arching branches and long weeping shoots. It is susceptible to disease, which

115

Taxodium distichum

Pinus pinaster thrives on poor sandy soil in coastal situations.

Arbutus unedo

POPLARS, WILLOWS, AND BUILDINGS

Poplars and willows both have extensive root systems that seek out moisture. In doing so, they will invade large areas, entering and blocking drains and potentially damaging buildings and hard surfaces. Poplar roots spread across the soil surface to anchor the trees as they grow, and can easily lift paving and tarmac. A poplar or a willow is not a good choice to plant close to a building, driveway, or paved area, but both are excellent in open, undeveloped locations.

bark and develops a buttressed trunk as it matures. The soft sprays of foliage emerge bright emerald green and turn rich bronze-yellow before falling in autumn. If the tree is grown in wet soil by water, the roots produce curious knobby growths that project above the ground, sometimes 3 ft. (1 m) or more away from the main trunk. *Taxodium distichum* is ultimately a large, conical tree with a fine winter silhouette.

COASTAL SITUATIONS

Coastal gardens usually have the bonus of a mild climate, but salt-laden winds are a challenge, scorching the foliage of many trees and in exposed situations uprooting less sure-footed subjects.

Pines are probably the most widely planted trees in coastal areas. *Pinus pinaster* (Zones 7–9), maritime pine or Bournemouth pine, is an open-branched, medium-sized tree with reddish or purple-

is only controllable on young specimens planted away from water. Avoid spraying with fungicide near ponds or streams because of the risk to aquatic life.

Taxodium distichum (Zones 4–10), swamp cypress, is a beautiful deciduous conifer that thrives on wet soil and by watersides. It has attractive, red-brown

OTHER TREES FOR COASTAL SITES *Acer pseudoplatanus* • *Castanea sativa* • *Crataegus persimilis* 'Prunifolia' •

brown bark and long, gray-green needles. The grayish cones can persist on the branches for years. It thrives on light sandy soils and is frequently planted by the coast, where it develops into a tree of character with a wonderful resinous fragrance.

The strawberry tree, *Arbutus unedo* (Zones 8–10), is a wind-tolerant subject with leathery, dark green leaves that resist the effects of salt spray. It forms a bushy shrub which will develop into a small, dense-headed tree. The cinnamon-colored bark is a feature of mature specimens. *Arbutus* 'Marina' (Zones 7–9) is an attractive hybrid with peeling bark and large, dark green leaves that are bronze when young. The flowers are white flushed pink and appear in fall with the ripening strawberrylike fruits. (See page 72.)

The holm oak, *Quercus ilex* (Zones 7–9), is a large evergreen tree that is widely grown in coastal situations. The dark, olive-green leaves, often with silvery undersides, are remarkably wind- and salt-tolerant. It is a sure-footed tree, often used in shelter belts around exposed gardens. It is well suited to trimming and training so its size can be contained, making it suitable for most gardens. (See pages 77 and 91.)

Of trees with purple foliage, *Prunus cerasifera* 'Nigra' (Zones 3–8) is one of the most resistant to salt-laden air. Although not suited to exposed coastal situations, it does succeed in more sheltered gardens near the sea. (See pages 61 and 120.)

Most trees with silver foliage are successful in coastal gardens. **Eucalyptus** are generally resistant to salt winds; they must be planted as young specimens or they may topple over in gales. (See pages 68–69.) *Hippophae rhamnoides* (Zones 3–7), the sea buckthorn, is often seen as a shrub but can be grown as a small tree. As a mature specimen, it can develop great character, often with a bent, silvery trunk and narrow silver leaves. (See page 69.)

Tamarisk, *Tamarix ramosissima* (Zones 2–8), is also often grown as a shrub, but it can be trained to form a light and

Hippophae rhamnoides

Arbutus 'Marina'

Tamarix ramosissima

airy small tree with feathery, soft green foliage and fluffy pink summer flowers. It responds well to pruning in late winter as the flowers are produced on the new growth that follows. This keeps the head of the tree in shape and removes any dead wood. It is resistant to salt-laden winds and will succeed in exposed situations.

Ilex aquifolium • Laurus nobilis • Populus alba • Quercus petraea • Sorbus aria 'Lutescens' •

SEASONS

Trees capture our attention with an ever-changing picture throughout the year, and set the scene for plants in the lower layers of the planting picture. Dark winter silhouettes break into emerald filigree and frothy blossom in spring; by late spring and summer, the heavy green canopy blends with the bountiful foliage of hedgerow and garden. As days become shorter and light mellows, the landscape is again transformed as the muted shades of fall spread through the branches overhead. Winter reveals hidden assets in the form of shining, colorful bark and twigs.

RIGHT: *Betula pendula.*

Spring

The trees are bursting with frothy clouds of pink and white blossom in spring. Pale fresh leaves unfurl to clothe the bare branches of winter, and golden yellow catkins dance in the breeze. The ornamental cherries are the stars of this season— the first to unfurl their delicate blossoms, becoming braver, bolder, and louder as spring heads towards summer.

Prunus × yedoensis

Prunus cerasifera 'Nigra'

SPRING-FLOWERING CHERRIES

Ornamental cherries tend to predominate throughout the spring season. The winter-flowering cherry, *Prunus × subhirtella* 'Autumnalis' (see page 152), continues to produce its delicate flowers, often in greater abundance as winter melts into spring. *Prunus pendula* 'Pendula Rubra' (*Prunus × subhirtella* 'Rubra'; Zones 6–8) starts to bloom in early spring. It is a lovely form of the weeping spring cherry, medium-sized, with single, deep rose-pink flowers that wreathe the long, pendent branches. *Prunus pendula* 'Pendula Rosea' (Zones 6–8) is small and mushroom-shaped and has paler pink flowers that later fade to blush-pink.

The sugar pink blossom of *Prunus* 'Pink Shell' looks especially vibrant against the watery blue, changing sky of a spring morning.

Perhaps the loveliest and frothiest of the early cherries is *Prunus × yedoensis* (Zones 5–8), the Yoshino cherry. A small- to medium-sized tree, it has arching, spreading branches smothered with blush-white, almond-scented flowers in early spring. The Yoshino cherry is a lovely subject to plant beside a path, where the branches can overhang and be admired against a blue sky. There is a weeping form, *Prunus × yedoensis* 'Shidare-yoshino', which has similar blossoms but a broad, arching habit.

Prunus 'Pandora' (Zones 5–8) is a charming small tree, with some of the characteristics of *Prunus × yedoensis*, one of its parents. Large, pale shell pink blossoms cover the upright branches in early spring, before the leaves emerge; these unfurl bronze-red, become green in summer, and usually turn rich shades in fall. *Prunus* 'Pink Shell' (Zones 5–8) may be a seedling of *Prunus × yedoensis*. It is petite and elegant, with spreading branches, cupped, shell pink blooms, and translucent, pale green new leaves.

Several cherries that have good plum-purple foliage produce clouds of blossoms on their dark twigs before the leaves appear. The pink-flowered *Prunus cerasifera* 'Nigra' (Zones 3–8) and *Prunus cerasifera* 'Pissardii' (Zones 3–8), with pink buds opening to white flowers, are widely grown. They are a glorious sight in full bloom, their small, delicate, single flowers giving them a wonderful lightness. Plant them where they catch the morning or evening sun. *Prunus × blireana* (Zones 5–7) has much larger, double pink flowers that appear with the coppery young leaves in mid-spring. (See also page 61.)

Prunus sargentii (Zones 5–9) is small and round-headed, with several seasons of interest: brilliant autumn color (see page 141) and attractive shiny, dark brown bark that looks best in winter (see page 150). In early spring it produces a display of small, single, sugar-pink flowers that cover the spreading branches just before the young bronze leaves start to unfurl. There is also an upright form, *Prunus sargentii* 'Rancho' (see page 89).

There are several excellent smaller-growing cherries for early flowers. *Prunus* 'Okame' (Zones 6–8) can be very early, producing a mass of deep pink flowers; the small leaves color well in fall. Its relative, *Prunus* 'Kursar' (Zones 6–8), has profuse but small, deep pink flowers that are borne before the bronze young leaves unfurl. An outstanding small cherry is *Prunus* 'Accolade' (Zones 6–8), with upward-reaching, spreading branches and semidouble, sugar pink flowers in clusters along the branches in early to mid-spring. It often colors well in fall, and has a grace and lightness often missing in cherries with larger leaves and flowers.

Prunus cerasifera 'Pissardii'

Prunus sargentii

Prunus 'Kursar'

POSITIONING WEEPING CHERRIES

Weeping cherries, such as *Prunus* 'Kiku-shidare-zakura' (Z. 5–9), *Prunus pendula* 'Pendula Rubra' (left; Z. 6–8) and *Prunus × yedoensis* 'Shidare-yoshino' (Z. 5–8), grow into low, weeping trees that are suitable for island beds. They look good underplanted with evergreen ground cover such as ivies, including *Hedera helix* 'Glacier' (**1**) (Z. 4–9), periwinkles, including *Vinca minor* 'La Grave' ('Bowles' Variety') (**2**) (Z. 5–8), *Rubus tricolor* (Z. 7–9), or *Pachysandra terminalis* (**3**) (Z. 5–8). Weeping cherries are unsuitable as specimens in a lawn, because their trailing branches make mowing difficult.

Prunus 'Pink Perfection'

Prunus 'Ichiyo' is laden with fresh pink blossoms surrounded by unfurling bronze-green leaves.

LARGE-FLOWERED JAPANESE CHERRIES

Of all the spring-flowering trees, the large-flowered Japanese cherries are the most flamboyant. All produce a profusion of blossoms, which usually hangs in bunches from the branches in mid- to late spring. In some cases the display is brief and all too often is shortened by strong winds and heavy rain; however, there is no denying the impact of their spectacle, and several make excellent choices for any garden. For other flowering cherries with good blossoms, see pages 88–89 and 103.

Prunus 'Ichiyo' (Zones 5–9) is a pretty, small tree with spreading, upward-curving branches that carry large, double, shell pink blossoms and bronze-green new leaves. The individual blooms are round and frilled and are carried on long stalks in loose, hanging bunches.

Prunus 'Kanzan'

Prunus 'Kanzan' (Zones 5–8) is a well-known and widely planted Japanese cherry. The large, showy flowers are deep orchid pink, borne in opulent bunches, and the new leaves are copper-red. A vigorous, small to medium-sized tree, it

has an inverted conical head and stiff habit when young, becoming spreading and more graceful with age. It produces a spectacular display in mid-spring, but is ordinary for the rest of the year, so is not a good choice for a small garden, where a tree must earn its keep. For most gardens, *Prunus* 'Pink Perfection' (a hybrid of 'Kanzan' parentage; Zones 5–8) is a better choice. It is smaller and more graceful, with double, bright rose-pink blooms fading to soft pink. These are carried in drooping clusters with the bronze young leaves. It usually flowers later than 'Kanzan'. (See Prunus Planting Partners, page 124.) *Prunus* 'Royal Burgundy' (Zones 5–7) is a less vigorous sort of 'Kanzan', with purple summer foliage and bronze autumn color. (See page 61.)

CHERRY ROOTS

Many flowering cherries produce woody roots very near to the soil surface. These stabilize the tree, but they can cause problems when trees are planted as specimens in lawns or close to the edge of them. In addition, if the roots are damaged by mowing or cultivation close to the trunk, the tree can sucker profusely, sometimes causing even more problems than the presence of roots. The only real solution is to surround a cherry tree with a substantial bed, which can be used for underplanting.

Prunus 'Kiku-shidare-zakura' (often incorrectly called 'Cheal's Weeping'; Zones 5–9) is a popular small weeping tree with early, double, deep pink flowers and bronze young leaves. Although very pretty in flower, this cherry is unattractive for the rest of the year and is difficult to place in the garden. It is particularly awkward when planted as a specimen in a lawn (see Positioning Weeping Cherries, page 121).

Prunus 'Shirotae' ('Mount Fuji'; Zones 6–9) is a deservedly popular semidouble white cherry. It is a small but spreading tree, with horizontal or slightly drooping, arching branches that can reach the ground when mature. The large, fragrant, semidouble flowers are carried in big clusters that hang from the branches. The foliage often colors richly in fall. Where space allows, this attractive cherry looks effective planted in pairs, the spreading branches forming an archway over a path. (See Prunus Planting Partners, page 124.)

Prunus 'Shirofugen' (Zones 5–7) is one of the last of the Japanese cherries to flower but it is relatively long-lasting. The buds are purple-pink, opening to large

Prunus 'Shirotae'

Prunus 'Shirofugen'

double blossoms that are white initially but fade to mauve-pink; the flowers are carried on long stalks in clusters among the young bronze leaves. This is a beautiful, wide-spreading, strong-growing tree that is ideal planted as a single specimen in a large space where it has room to spread.

Prunus 'Taihaku' (Zones 5–8), the great white cherry, is a medium-sized tree that makes a magnificent specimen. The flowers are very large, single, and pure white, shimmering against the copper-red new leaves. It has horizontal branches and a spreading habit.

AVOIDING YELLOW AND PINK

One of the most difficult color combinations to live with in the garden is strong pink and hard yellow; neither color complements the other. With a prevalence of strong yellow spring flowers, such as forsythia and daffodils, it is easy to fall into the trap of introducing bright pink blossom into the garden picture; flowering cherries are often the worst offenders. This combination is best avoided, as these clashing colors will overpower anything else. If plentiful yellow already exists, choose a tree with white flowers, such as *Prunus cerasifera* 'Hessei' (right; Z. 3–8), or perhaps an ornamental crab apple (*Malus*) that flowers after the brash spring yellows have faded.

123

PRUNUS PLANTING PARTNERS

The creamy green flowers of *Prunus* 'Ukon' are enhanced by the bronze new foliage.

Prunus 'Ukon' (Zones 4–7) offers a different flower color—the semidouble blooms are pale yellow, tinged with green, occasionally with a deep pink flush. The new leaves are bronze and look lovely with the flowers and color well in fall. It is a small, robust, spreading tree, but the head is open enough to allow planting below. (See Prunus Planting Partners, left.)

The flowers of *Prunus* 'Ukon' (**1**) (Z. 4–7) open at the same time as the creamy green fragrant flowers of *Skimmia* × *confusa* 'Kew Green' (**2**) (Z. 7–8), which also offers evergreen interest. The sapphire blue grape hyacinths, *Muscari armeniacum* (**3**) (Z. 3–8), give a delightful injection of strong color that looks good with both subjects.

Underplant *Prunus* 'Shirotae' (**4**) (Z. 6–9) with *Euonymus fortunei* 'Emerald Gaiety' (**5**) (Z. 5–8) for year-round interest. The creamy green fragrant flowers of *Narcissus* 'Thalia' (**6**) (Z. 4–9) bloom at the same time as the cherry, extending the color downward.

Beside *Prunus* 'Pink Perfection' (**7**) (Z. 5–8), the purple foliage of *Heuchera* 'Plum Pudding' (**8**) (Z. 4–8) provides year-round color. The dark flowers of *Tulipa* 'Queen of Night' (**9**) (Z. 4–8) complement both the cherry blossoms and the heuchera.

BACTERIAL CANKER

Many deciduous prunus, especially the Japanese cherries, have been prone to bacterial canker in recent years. This manifests itself as wilting of the blossom and new foliage, a general thinning of the mature leaf canopy, and die-back of some of the twigs and branches. Sadly, the symptoms get worse in successive seasons, and there is nothing that can be done to cure the disease. Badly affected specimens should be removed and replaced, ideally with a different type of tree.

OTHER CHERRIES FOR BLOSSOM *Prunus* 'Amanogawa' • *Prunus avium* 'Plena' • *Prunus dulcis* •

OTHER GOOD TREES FOR SPRING

Another small tree that excels in spring is the snowy mespilus, *Amelanchier lamarckii* (Zones 4–8). Its elegant branches are scattered with starry white flowers and copper-red unfurling leaves. It is versatile, and sits as well in a small town garden as it does in a country paddock. (See pages 86 and 136.) *Amelanchier × grandiflora* 'Ballerina' (Zones 4–7) has larger white

Amelanchier × grandiflora 'Ballerina'

Cercis siliquastrum

flowers in profuse sprays; *Amelanchier × grandiflora* 'Robin Hill' (Zones 4–7) bears flowers that are pink in bud, then open pale pink and become white. It has a dense, more upright habit than the other two varieties.

Cercis siliquastrum (Zones 6–9), the Judas tree, is an unusual small tree that produces its rosy-purple, pealike flowers on bare twigs and branches in late spring. It is a good choice for a small garden or to grow against a wall. (See pages 87–88.)

ACERS FOR SPRING FLOWERS

Many acers have delightful flowers in early spring, often before or at the same time as the leaves emerge. Some of the individual flowers are quite insignificant but *en masse* they can be stunning, especially when lit by spring sunshine.

Acer negundo var. **violaceum** (1) (Z. 2–9) is a lovely form of the box elder, with upward-sweeping branches carrying young shoots of purple or violet covered in a fine white bloom. The delicate, red-pink flower tassels that drape this medium to large tree in silky threads emerge at the same time as the new bronze leaves.

Acer platanoides (2) (Z. 3–7), the Norway maple, is a large, vigorous tree with big leaves that turn rich yellow or orange in fall. In early spring, the bare branches are decorated with frothy green flowers. (See also page 95.) In the purple-leaved form, **Acer platanoides** 'Crimson King' (see page 59), they are made all the more striking by the addition of ruby red emerging leaves.

TREES FOR SPRING FOLIAGE

The foliage of all deciduous trees has a sharp, fresh beauty when the new leaves first emerge. However, some trees have particularly exquisite new foliage and are planted specifically for this purpose.

Acer pseudoplatanus 'Brilliantissimum' (1) (Z. 4–8), a small, slow-growing tree with a compact, rounded head, has the most striking new foliage. The young leaves are a glorious shrimp pink color, changing to salmon yellow then yellow-green. It peaks in spring; later in summer and fall it is fairly unattractive, with washed-out, pale yellow-green foliage, and so is best positioned where it can fade into the background, giving the chance for more interesting subjects in the foreground to shine. (See Good Companions, page 128.)

Acer pseudoplatanus 'Prinz Handjéry' (2) (Z. 4–8) is similar but makes a slightly larger tree. The leaves are purple-tinged on the underside and are therefore more of a feature later in the season than the leaves of 'Brilliantissimum'.

Aesculus × neglecta 'Erythroblastos' (3) (Z. 4–9) is a spectacular slow-growing, small tree with brilliant shrimp pink leaves that turn to pale yellow before they fade to green in summer. Pale yellow flowers appear in late spring and early summer.

Prunus padus 'Watereri' • *Prunus persica* 'Clara Meyer' • *Prunus* 'Shôgetsu' • *Prunus* 'Spire' •

Crataegus laevigata 'Paul's Scarlet'

Davidia involucrata

Magnolia × soulangeana

Magnolia × loebneri 'Merrill'

Magnolia × loebneri 'Leonard Messel'

126

The **hawthorns** boast some beautiful cultivars that offer showy, long-lasting late spring blossom. They are easy to grow and suit gardens in almost any situation. *Crataegus laevigata* **'Paul's Scarlet'** (Zones 4–7), a small, round-headed tree, is widely cultivated. It has bright green new foliage, becoming emerald by midsummer, and clusters of double scarlet flowers that smother the elegantly arching branches in late spring. This hawthorn grows on any soil and suits exposed situations, except coastal locations, where it is susceptible to salt damage. *Crataegus laevigata* **'Rosea Flore Pleno'** (Zones 4–7) has a similar flowering habit but the blooms are pink. *Crataegus laevigata* **'Crimson Cloud'** (Zones 4–7) is an attractive alternative, with single scarlet flowers with white eyes. None of these garden trees produces the bright red fruits of hedgerow hawthorns, nor do they color in fall. (See page 138.)

The pocket handkerchief tree, *Davidia involucrata* (Zones 5–8), also known as the dove tree or ghost tree, is an elegant, medium-sized, conical tree that flowers in late spring. The branches are hung with a host of fluttering white blooms, each consisting of a rounded button of tiny dark flowers surrounded by two showy white bracts, the lower one much larger than the upper. Also characteristic are its attractive pleated, heart-shaped leaves that color well in fall. Members of the cornus family, davidias grow on any fertile soil and are extremely hardy. The main drawback is that they take a long time to reach flowering age—if you plant a young pot-grown specimen, expect to wait 10–15 years. *Davidia involucrata* var. *vilmoriniana* is virtually identical, except that the leaves are not hairy beneath and the fruits are slightly more elliptic in shape.

For **lilacs** (*Syringa*), see page 111.

Magnolias are the most extravagant and flamboyant of the spring-flowering trees, hence their popularity. *Magnolia × soulangeana* and its cultivars (Zones 4–9) are favored for their large, tulip-shaped, white, cream, pink, or wine-colored flowers, which smother the branches in mid-spring. These handsome trees grow large and spreading, often with several stems from ground level, and need plenty of space; unfortunately their shape and performance are often ruined by careless pruning to restrict their size in a small garden. These magnolias dislike alkaline soils but are an excellent choice for clay. (See page 106.)

For those gardening on neutral or acid soils, *Magnolia* 'Elizabeth' (Zones 4–9) or *Magnolia* 'Heaven Scent' (Zones 3–8) may be better choices or, if space allows, the magnificent *Magnolia campbellii* (Zones 8–10). (See page 106.)

For any other soil, choose *Magnolia* × *loebneri* (Zones 4–8)—a large shrub or small tree of light habit, with big, starry white flowers borne in early spring. *Magnolia* × *loebneri* 'Leonard Messel' bears lilac-pink flowers; *Magnolia* × *loebneri* 'Merrill' is a vigorous form, with pure white, fragrant flowers, and is the best one to grow as a tree. The flowers of *Magnolia* × *loebneri* and its cultivars are less susceptible to damage from wind and frost than other spring-flowering magnolias with large blooms.

Paulownia tomentosa (Zones 5–9) is an unusual small tree grown for its large, exotic leaves (see page 83). The foliage is even more impressive if the plant is grown as a shrub and pruned close to ground level each year (a process known as stooling—see box, page 69). If left to grow to maturity, this tree produces flower buds in fall that sit like knobby, golden brown candles on the branches until late spring, when they open into foxglovelike blue flowers, before the leaves emerge. It needs a sheltered, sunny site, for in cold areas the buds may be damaged by severe frost. *Paulownia tomentosa* 'Lilacina' grows into a large tree but it flowers earlier in its life and is less susceptible to frost damage than the more delicate *Paulownia tomentosa*.

Paulownia tomentosa

FLOWERING CRABS

Flowering crabs, varieties of *Malus,* are an alternative to ornamental cherries (*Prunus*) for glorious spring blossom. Their season starts in mid-spring, when the cherries are well under way. Many have a strong apple-blossom scent and attractive fruits, which are sometimes even more showy than the blossom (see page 140). The majority are easy to grow and thrive on most soil types, although they can be slow on shallow chalk. They respond better to pruning than cherries and can be pruned in winter, obviously with the loss of some blossom; alternatively, straggly specimens can be cut back and shaped after flowering.

Malus 'Evereste' (Zones 5–9) is one of the finest of all small flowering trees, with a compact, conical habit. The flowers are borne in profusion in mid-spring, red in bud but opening to large white apple blossom, and the leaves are dark green. It is an easy tree to grow and is resistant to fireblight, which can be a problem with crabs of weaker constitution. Orange-yellow fruits are set off by good autumn leaf color.

This *Malus* 'Evereste' has been pruned and trained to form a flat-headed tree, ideal for a small garden.

CRAB APPLE DISEASES
Most of the ornamental crabs are prone to the same diseases that affect fruiting apples: scab, mildew, and canker in particular. Scab disfigures both foliage and fruit with unsightly brown-black spots and patches. Mildew appears as a gray-white bloom on foliage, and eventually causes dead patches and leaf drop; some of the purple-leaved varieties are especially susceptible. Canker affects the wood, appearing as lesions on the bark that spread, causing disfiguration of areas of the branches and their eventual death. If these diseases are already a problem in a garden, choose a variety that is resistant or select a different type of flowering tree.

Malus floribunda

Malus × zumi 'Golden Hornet'

Malus transitoria

Malus 'Directeur Moerlands'

profuse, wonderfully fragrant apple-blossom flowers are pink in bud, opening white. It is a small tree and an excellent pollinator for other crab apples being grown for their fruit. (See page 140.)

There is no lovelier tree than **Malus transitoria** (Zones 4–7) in late spring, when the branches are smothered in creamy white, pink-flushed flowers, heavy with the scent of apple blossom and honey. The small, three-lobed leaves turn yellow in fall and then drop to reveal the tiny, golden yellow fruits hanging on the branches. Although not tall, this tree has very long, horizontally spreading branches, so needs plenty of space to look its best.

The purple-leaved crab apples, with their deep pink to wine-red blossom, are also an impressive sight. Choose a variety that has good disease-resistance, such as **Malus 'Directeur Moerlands'** (Zones 4–8), otherwise the foliage may be poor for the remainder of the season. (See page 61 and Good Companions, below.)

The Japanese crab, **Malus floribunda** (Zones 4–8), is a lovely small tree with spreading branches that in spring are wreathed with crimson buds opening to blush-pink and white flowers. (See page 88 and Good Companions, below.)

Of the crabs primarily grown for their fruit, **Malus × zumi 'Golden Hornet'** (Zones 4–7) has the best blossom. The

GOOD COMPANIONS

Photinia × fraseri 'Red Robin' (1) (Z. 7–9) provides evergreen interest all year and adds color with its bright scarlet new growth—a lively foil for the salmon-colored foliage of *Acer pseudoplatanus* 'Brilliantissimum' (2) (Z. 4–8).

The blush-pink blossom of *Malus floribunda* (3) (Z. 4–8) is lovely with the sapphire flowers of the evergreen *Ceanothus* 'Concha' (4) (Z. 8–10). Both flower profusely and bees and other insects love them.

The wine-red flowers and red-purple new leaves of *Malus* 'Directeur Moerlands' (5) (Z. 4–8) provide a rich contrast to the blue-green foliage and lime flowers of the evergreen *Euphorbia characias* (6) (Z. 8–9).

OTHER GOOD FLOWERING CRABS *Malus hupehensis* • *Malus 'John Downie'* • *Malus × robusta* 'Red Sentinel' •

CATKINS

The catkins of hazel (*Corylus*) and alder (*Alnus*) are usually the first signs of spring, appearing in mild weather from late winter onward. Bare twigs one day are festooned with golden lambs' tails the next. Birch catkins (*Betula*) follow later, at about the same time as the willows (*Salix*), some with rather insignificant catkins, others with the familiar silky pussy willow.

Of the birches, *Betula utilis* var. *jacquemontii* 'Jermyns' (**1**) (Z. 4–7) has the finest catkins. Long and golden, they are up to 7 in. (17 cm) long and dance in the breeze, suspended from the fine, delicate twigs. (See page 148.)

The outstanding ornamental qualities of alders are often overlooked. Usually confined to damp sites and watersides, these trees are rarely considered for more prominent positions in the garden. *Alnus cordata* (Z. 4–6), the Italian alder, will grow on any soil, even dry sites. It is a medium-sized to large tree of elegant shape, with bright ocher-yellow male catkins, about 3 in. (7 cm) long, which festoon the branches in early spring, and bright green glistening foliage. *Alnus glutinosa* (Z. 3–7), the common alder, is smaller in stature with duller foliage. The catkins appear slightly later and are yellowish green in color. It grows on most soils. *Alnus incana* (Z. 2–7), the gray alder, has yellow-red catkins and tolerates most situations, including cold wet sites and coastal conditions.

Alnus incana 'Aurea' (Z. 2–7) is a more attractive small tree with pale yellow leaves, which are very noticeable in spring and early summer. The young shoots are a glowing yellow-orange and rival those of any willow in winter. The superb catkins are 4 in. (10 cm) long and orange-red.

The most outstanding catkins are displayed by *Alnus* × *spaethii* (**2**) (Z. 2–7), a stately medium-sized tree that will succeed in most situations. The reddish-yellow catkins are very long and showy and appear from late winter onward. Decorative cones follow and persist on the tree, still remaining when the next year's catkins appear.

Salix caprea (**3**) (Z. 4–9), the goat willow, is a British native tree, renowned for the silky gray catkins known as pussy willow. The male catkins produce golden stamens later in spring; the catkins are known colloquially as palm. The only variety commonly grown in gardens is the compact, weeping form, *Salix caprea* 'Kilmarnock' (**4**). (See page 87.)

Malus 'Royal Beauty' • *Malus* 'Rudolph' • *Malus* 'Snowcloud' • *Malus* 'Sun Rival' • *Malus* 'Van Eseltine' •

Summer

As spring turns to summer, most of the flower color moves to the lower layers of the planting picture—roses, herbaceous perennials, and annuals tend to steal the show. However, there are still some stunning blooms in the tree canopy, particularly on acid soils. Foliage trees, which are in full leaf by midsummer, come into their own now, displaying the glories of gold, plum, silver, and variegation against billowing greens; a few flamboyant characters produce some of the most extravagant displays of the year.

Aesculus × carnea, the red horse chestnut, is a magnificent sight when in bloom in early summer.

Aesculus indica 'Sydney Pearce'

The **horse chestnuts** are spectacular flowering trees of late spring and early summer. Most, including the following, are too big for the average garden, but make wonderful stately trees for large spaces. (See pages 94–95.) *Aesculus × carnea* 'Briotii' (Zones 3–7) is a more compact form of the red horse chestnut, with deep pink flowers in spikes up to 8 in. (20 cm) long. *Aesculus indica* (Zones 7–9) is more striking in flower, with pink-

Aesculus × carnea 'Briotii'

flushed cream flowers in broad spikes up to 16 in. (40 cm) long; the leaves are dark shining green and color well in fall. *Aesculus indica* 'Sydney Pearce' is more upright and free-flowering, with dark green foliage and large flowers of creamy white marked with yellow and pink.

Albizia julibrissin f. *rosea* (Zones 6–9), the silk tree, is a pretty, small tree with fine, fernlike foliage. The tree is spreading in habit and produces dense heads of fluffy, bright pink flowers on top of the branches in late summer. This is the hardiest form but needs plenty of sunshine to flower well. It is a good choice for sheltered coastal gardens.

Castanea sativa (Zones 4–9) is showy in midsummer, when its dark foliage is lit by profuse creamy green catkins. A large, fast-growing, columnar tree, it is good in a big garden. (See page 95.) Alternatively, if chestnight blight is a problem, choose *Castanea molissima* (Zones 4–8).

The **catalpas**, or Indian bean trees, are at their best in summer, when they produce spikes of creamy, purple- and brown-

Albizia julibrissin f. rosea

spotted foxglovelike flowers, dramatic against the large, soft, velvety leaves. The hybrid × *Chitalpa tashkentensis* **'Summer Bells'** (Zones 5–8) is a small tree with twisted narrow leaves carried on a compact head of upright branches. The pink flowers are beautiful but are produced only in a sunny, sheltered site.

The lovely *Cornus kousa* (Zones 5–8) is a large shrub with spreading branches smothered in creamy white blossoms in early summer. It matures into a beautiful tree with layered branches. The hybrid dogwoods *Cornus* **'Porlock'** (Zones 5–8) and *Cornus* **'Norman Hadden'** (Zones 5–8) are nearly identical. Both grow into graceful, small, spreading trees that retain at least some foliage over winter. The flower heads are freely produced in early summer; like other cornus, these consist of a small, dark sphere of insignificant flowers surrounded by four showy bracts. The bracts are tapered and pointed, starting lime green, turning cream, and then flushing pink, particularly in sunny situations. The flower heads stand along the branches, turning downward when the

Cornus kousa

× *Chitalpa tashkentensis* 'Summer Bells'

Cornus 'Norman Hadden'

Eucryphia 'Penwith'

bracts fall to develop into strawberry-like fruits in fall. Both grow on any deep, fertile soil and are surprisingly tolerant of chalk. They are also suitable for large containers and are an excellent choice for a small garden or confined space.

Eucryphias are spectacular summer-flowering evergreens for acid soils. Their large white flowers with yellow stamens appear in mid- to late summer, smothering the branches of most varieties. The majority are narrow and upright in habit and cast little shade, making them a good choice for mixed plantings (see page 105). *Eucryphia* 'Penwith' (Zones 8–10) makes a vigorous and upright small tree.

Koelreuteria paniculata

Laburnum × watereri 'Vossii'

Robinia × slavinii 'Hillieri'

however, the foliage and form of the tree make it worth growing anyway.

Laburnums, also known as golden rain, are among the showiest flowering trees of early summer, producing hanging chains of yellow, wisterialike flowers on upward-growing, gracefully arching branches. All parts of the plant are poisonous, especially the seeds, which are carried in pealike pods. The best form is *Laburnum × watereri* 'Vossii' (Zones 5–7), with long chains of freely produced flowers and seed pods that fail to develop. It is a small tree, with glossy green leaves and shining green stems that are attractive in winter. Young trees are supple and pliable, making them suitable for training over an arch. Laburnums are a good choice for a small garden, and they are useful to brighten a dark backdrop of heavy evergreens such as laurels or conifers. (See Good Companions, below.)

Robinia × slavinii 'Hillieri' (Zones 5–8) is one of the loveliest flowering trees. It is a good choice in a small, sheltered garden, where it grows quickly into an elegant, vase-shaped tree, the upright branches arching under the weight of plentiful soft foliage. The wisterialike, lilac-pink flowers hang from the branches in early summer; they are so plentiful that they can cause

the delicate twigs to break under their weight. Like most robinias, the wood is brittle, so this tree must have shelter. Pruning in midwinter to cut some of the longer branches back by one-third keeps the tree in shape and helps to prevent damage. It is a good choice where an impressive specimen is needed quickly. The disadvantages are that it is rarely long-lived, it is late to come into leaf, and the winter silhouette is rather dull and bony. (See Good Companions, below.)

The **lindens**, varieties of *Tilia*, are versatile trees that grow on any soil, including heavy clay. They transplant easily and lend themselves to being planted as bare-root specimens in winter. Although most are medium-sized to large trees, they will tolerate hard pruning and are often used for training into formal shapes. Some lindens become infested by aphids in late summer. These produce copious amounts of honeydew, which is a sweet, sticky secretion that drips from the tree.

In summer, lindens produce creamy yellow or green flowers. Although not showy individually, they create a most attractive effect hanging in clusters along the branches. Many are sweetly and heavily scented, especially in the evening. *Tilia cordata* (Zones 3–7), the small-leaved

Koelreuteria paniculata (Zones 5–9), pride of India or golden rain tree, is a beautiful, rounded, medium-sized tree with lovely fernlike foliage and large sprays of small, golden yellow flowers in midsummer. It has a long season of interest—the new leaves are delicate green-yellow, often tinged with pink and apricot; in fall, the foliage turns rich yellow, and conspicuous bladderlike fruits follow the summer flowers. It grows on any reasonable soil but needs a warm, dry summer to flower well;

GOOD COMPANIONS

The light but vigorous *Clematis* 'Purpurea Plena Elegans' (1) (Z. 4–9) will ascend into the canopy of *Robinia × slavinii* 'Hillieri' (2) (Z. 5–8), providing soft, double, plum-purple flowers in late summer after the robinia blooms fade.

The bright golden yellow foliage of *Philadelphus coronarius* 'Aureus' (3) (Z. 4–8) looks striking with the green foliage and golden yellow flowers of *Laburnum watereri* 'Vossii' (4) (Z. 5–7).

OTHER SUMMER-FLOWERING TREES *Catalpa bignonioides* 'Aurea' • *Embothrium coccineum* Lanceolatum Group •

TRAINING LINDENS

Lindens can be pollarded, that is cut back to the main trunk in winter every couple of years. This results in a tree with a rounded head of straight twigs and a curiously architectural form in winter after pruning, when the twigs have been removed and the trimmed, knobby branches remain. They can also be pleached—usually a row of young trees is planted and lateral branches are trained along horizontal wires 12–15 ft. (4–5 m) above ground; all lateral growth is cut back to the main horizontal branches in winter. This method is often used to run along a wall or fence, to add height and color above the structure. Lindens are increasingly used in contemporary urban schemes, trimmed and trained into umbrella or geometric shapes.

Tilia cordata 'Greenspire'

Tilia tomentosa

Tilia 'Petiolaris'

linden, is a medium-sized to large tree that is native to Britain. It has a rounded head of fresh green, heart-shaped leaves and ivory-white flowers, which appear in midsummer and are sweetly fragrant. Varieties of this linden are seed-raised and are therefore variable in habit and flower quality. *Tilia cordata* 'Greenspire' is an American cultivar of similar size but with a broad, conical head. *Tilia cordata* 'Rancho', another American selection, is smaller in stature.

Tilia × *euchlora* (Zones 3–7) is a medium-sized tree that is popular in urban areas. Since it does not suffer from aphid attacks, it doesn't produce the sticky secretion common to many other lindens. The fragrant flowers tend to have a narcotic effect on bees.

Tilia × *europaea* (Zones 4–7), the common linden, and *Tilia platyphyllos* (Zones 5–8), the broad-leaved linden, are the large, commonly planted lindens that are often used for avenues. They suffer from aphid attacks. (See page 98.)

Tilia 'Petiolaris' (Zones 5–8), the weeping silver linden, has graceful, downward-sweeping branches that form a rounded head. The long-stalked leaves are dark green above and silver beneath, and the flowers are richly scented.

Tilia tomentosa (Zones 4–7), the silver linden, is a beautiful large tree with silvery white undersides to the leaves. The creamy yellow flowers are freely produced, and the fragrance on a warm summer's day is the essence of the English garden. The flowers are toxic to bees, but fortunately bees tend to keep away. The tree is aphid-free and therefore not sticky. It is variable in habit but is always majestic. *Tilia tomentosa* 'Chelsea Sentinel' is distinctly columnar in habit and tends to be better for most gardens.

SUMMER FOLIAGE

Trees grown for their colorful leaves are often at their best in early summer, particularly those with purple or variegated foliage. (See pages 58–61 and 62–67.)

Acer platanoides 'Crimson King' (see page 58) and *Acer platanoides* 'Drummondii' (see page 63) are particularly worth a mention. The ruby-purple color of the former and the bright variegation of the latter excel in early summer, vying with the summer flowers for attention. In a large garden, the most dramatic foliage effect of the season belongs to the purple beeches, *Fagus sylvatica* Atropurpurea Group (left; Z. 4–7), the mature trees forming vast domes of splendid, rich wine red leaves that flicker in the sunlight.

Liriodendron tulipifera • *Magnolia grandiflora* • *Stewartia pseudocamellia* • *Styrax japonicus* •

Fall

From late summer to early winter, deciduous trees take their turn to light up the higher layer of the planting picture. Leaves in shades of garnet, scarlet, flame, and gold smolder in the blue-gray light of cloudy days and flicker in the sunshine of brighter ones. As they fall, they create a colorful carpet. A good tree with foliage that develops mellow tints in fall could bring the finest display of color in the gardening year.

nights and bright, still days are the ideal conditions to develop the best autumn color. Plenty of late-summer sunshine also contributes to the best display.

Numerous **acers** provide outstanding autumn color. This large genus includes subjects of all statures, from the diminutive Japanese maples, more often thought of as compact shrubs, to large trees such as the sugar maple and silver maple.

Many of the **snake-bark maples** color well in autumn. *Acer davidii* (Zones 5–8) grows into a small, spreading tree with

Acer davidii 'George Forrest'

Acer rufinerve

Acer rubrum 'Schlesingeri' is one of the earliest trees to color in fall, culminating in a spectacular display of bright, rich scarlet and flame.

Autumn color is a chemical reaction. The parts of the leaf that manufacture food break down as temperatures and light levels fall and the nutrients are reabsorbed into the woody branches and trunk, where they are stored over winter. The tree's growth the following season is dependent on this food store, so the autumn process is an important one.

Various pigments are responsible for different autumn colors: carotenoids cause the bright yellow colors and

anthocyanins are responsible for the red shades. Although changes do occur in some evergreens at this time of year, autumn color is mainly a phenomenon of deciduous trees and shrubs.

Autumn color is usually at its best on moist, acid soil that does not dry out in late summer, although some trees—for instance, certain acers and hawthorns—will still color well on chalk. If planting for autumn color, ensure that the chosen tree will color on that soil type. Cold

attractive green- and silver-striped bark. The oval green leaves turn to shades of orange and red in fall, as do the winged fruits that hang along the branches. *Acer davidii* 'George Forrest' is the most widely grown, with large leaves carried on red stalks. *Acer davidii* 'Serpentine' is more upright, with small leaves turning to orange and gold in fall. (See page 145.) *Acer rufinerve* (Zones 4–8), a spreading, medium-sized maple, is also known for its bright red and yellow autumn colors.

Acer griseum

Acer japonicum 'Aconitifolium'

Acer japonicum 'Vitifolium'

Acer rubrum

Acer griseum (Zones 4–7), the paper-bark maple, is grown primarily for its shining, peeling bark, a great winter asset. However, it also exhibits wonderful glowing red, orange, and scarlet autumn color. (See pages 144 and 145.)

Acer japonicum (Zones 5–8) is a graceful small tree, with soft green leaves that are carried on horizontally inclined branches. It enjoys moist, acid soil and shelter from neighboring trees. *Acer japonicum* 'Aconitifolium' has deeply cut leaves that color rich ruby and scarlet in fall. It will light up a woodland setting and is brilliant against a dark backdrop of coniferous trees. *Acer japonicum* 'Vitifolium' has broader, fan-shaped leaves and equally vibrant autumn color.

A great number of North American maples are renowned for their outstanding contribution to the autumn display. *Acer rubrum* (Zones 3–9), the Canadian maple or red maple, boasts some splendid cultivars that do particularly well on neutral to acid soils. They grow successfully on chalk, but rarely color well and the leaves tend to fall early if the season is dry. *Acer rubrum* 'October Glory' is an American selection, with long-lasting scarlet leaf color. *Acer rubrum* 'Schlesingeri' colors early, the leaves turning rich scarlet. The Canadian maples grow into large trees with splendid cone-shaped crowns. They are ideal for a large garden, against a dark background. Their glowing autumn colors are so intense, the effect is almost unreal

and they have a bewitching luminosity in low light. *Acer × freemanii* (Zones 4–9) is a naturally occurring hybrid of *Acer rubrum* and *Acer saccharinum*. *Acer ×*

freemanii 'Autumn Blaze' (Zones 5–9) is a large, dense, oval-headed tree, with deeply cut, dark green leaves that color orange-red in fall.

JAPANESE MAPLES FOR AUTUMN COLOR

Varieties of the Japanese maple (*Acer palmatum*; Z. 6–8) are well known for their rich colors, and they are ideal in smaller gardens, where space is limited. The lovely *Acer palmatum* 'Sango-kaku' (**1**) is a particularly fine choice—its soft green leaves color to butter-yellow in fall, then drop to reveal glowing scarlet twigs that provide interest throughout the winter. *Acer palmatum* 'Osakazuki' (**2**) is generally regarded as the most outstanding Japanese maple for scarlet autumn color.

135

Acer saccharum 'Newton Sentry'

Acer saccharinum

Aesculus 'Dallimorei'

Acer saccharum (Zones 3–8), the sugar maple, is one of the finest trees for autumn color in North America. It forms a large tree of broad, rounded habit. Autumn color varies from red, through orange and scarlet to yellow. It is worth growing as an ornamental tree, where space allows, in neutral to acid soil. (See Good Companions, right.) The sap of this tree is used to make maple syrup. The sweet quality of the sap was reputedly discovered by children sucking icicles that formed on the branches of the tree in winter. *Acer saccharum* 'Newton Sentry' is a stunning upright form, with ascending branches forming a tall column. It is a useful structure plant in a large space and is spectacular in fall, when it turns into a vibrant pillar of fiery orange.

Acer saccharinum (Zones 3–8), the silver maple, is a large, graceful tree with more delicate autumn color than the sugar maple, in shades of gold, apricot, and soft orange. The undersides of the leaves are silver, creating an attractive subtle effect. This silver color is more evident when the leaves are ruffled by the wind.

The **horse chestnuts** also color in fall, but the leaves often brown and curl at the edges, spoiling the effect. However, there are exceptions. *Aesculus flava* (Zones 3–8), the sweet buckeye, is a medium-sized tree with creamy yellow flowers and

tough, dark green leaves that display good autumn tints of flame, orange, and gold. *Aesculus* 'Dallimorei' (Zones 5–9) is a graft hybrid of *Aesculus flava* on *Aesculus hippocastanum*. It produces large spikes of flowers and an exquisite show of flame-orange autumn color. *Aesculus glabra* (Zones 3–7), the Ohio buckeye, is a smaller tree, coloring orange-yellow in fall. All of the above have a broadly conical habit.

Amelanchier lamarckii (Zones 4–8) is a small tree, with copper-colored new leaves and sprays of starry white flowers in early spring. The small, rounded leaves color pinky orange in fall and create a pleasing effect on the arching branches. (See Good Companions, below.)

GOOD COMPANIONS

The large, brilliant, torchlike flowers of *Kniphofia rooperi* (1) (Z. 6–9) provide strong foreground interest if planted in a bold clump in front of the sugar maple, *Acer saccharum* (2) (Z. 3–8).

Verbena bonariensis (3) (Z. 8–9) blooms into late fall, with vibrant, violet-purple flowers that look wonderful against the pinky-orange autumn leaves of *Amelanchier lamarckii* (4) (Z. 4–8).

Amelanchier lamarckii

OTHER GOOD TREES FOR AUTUMN COLOR *Acer carpinifolium* • *Acer platanoides* • *Davidia involucrata* •

Carya cordiformis

Cercidiphyllum japonicum

Cercis canadensis

Cercis canadensis 'Forest Pansy'

Cornus florida

Amelanchier laevis is similar, and both species are usually recommended for neutral to acid soils, but they seem to succeed in alkaline conditions providing the soil is not too shallow and dry. The autumn color display can be short-lived if the weather has been dry.

Carya cordiformis (Zones 4–9), known as bitternut, is regarded as the best of the hickories for planting in gardens. A large, walnutlike tree, it has brown scaly bark and late leaves, divided into separate leaflets, that turn clear yellow in fall. It does not transplant well as a larger specimen and, like walnut, is best planted as a young container-grown or B&B plant.

Another delight in the autumn garden is *Cercidiphyllum japonicum* (Zones 4–8), the Katsura tree, or candyfloss tree as it is sometimes known. The delicate, heart-shaped leaves have a sweet caramel scent when they fall, and their color changes from soft green to an attractive pale yellow or salmon pink shade. In a moist season, the foliage will fall gradually over a long period; however, late-summer drought causes leaf fall and no color. The

Katsura tree is pretty as a juvenile and is ultimately a broad-spreading, small to medium-sized tree, but casts only light shade. It is suitable for a smaller garden, and will grow on any soil. The new leaves are damaged by hard frost and cold winds, so a sheltered location is advisable.

Cercis canadensis (Zones 5–9), the North American redbud, has heart-shaped leaves carried on dark stems. It is a small tree with a broad, rounded head. The delicate, bright green leaves turn soft yellow in fall. *Cercis canadensis* 'Forest Pansy' has sensational foliage throughout the summer. In fall, the deep wine-purple leaves take on shades of red, and the veins are highlighted with gold.

Cladrastis kentukea (*Cladrastis lutea*; Zones 4–8), the yellowwood, is a broad, medium-sized tree with fragrant white flowers resembling those of *Robinia pseudoacacia* in midsummer. In fall, the leaves turn to clear golden yellow.

Many **flowering dogwoods** are particularly attractive in autumn. The semi-evergreen *Cornus* 'Porlock' (Zones 5–8) displays good flame-colored autumn tints

on some leaves; this color is enhanced by the strawberrylike fruits that hang from the branches. *Cornus florida* (Zones 5–9), the North American flowering dogwood, is very good for autumn color. The leaves are curled, fanning out from a shortened midrib. This effect seems accentuated by late summer, when the reverse of the leaf retains a grayish bloom as the rich autumn tints develop. There are many cultivars, some variegated, and most color well. *Cornus florida* 'Sunset' has gold-edged leaves that are pink when young, turning to pink, red, and purple in autumn.

Euonymus hamiltonianus • *Prunus avium* • *Prunus* 'Spire' • *Sassafras albidum* • *Stewartia pseudocamellia* • *Toona sinensis* •

Crataegus persimilis 'Prunifolia'

Crataegus coccinea

Euonymus phellomanus

they provide the perfect setting for the large, dark red berries, which are carried in clusters at the tips of the branchlets. A healthy small tree will usually be smothered with fruits and a blaze of color in mid-fall, the berries persisting on the branches long after the leaves have fallen. (See also page 88.) *Crataegus coccinea* (Zones 4–7), the native scarlet haw, is similar in habit but it produces fewer, larger fruits and has less shiny leaves.

Some of the larger **euonymus** grow into small trees, providing not only brilliant leaf color but also attractive, colorful fruits. The British native spindle tree, *Euonymus europaeus* (Zones 3–7), has green stems and narrow, dark green leaves that often turn rich scarlet in fall. The curious pinkish red fruits, which are three-lobed, purselike capsules, split to reveal bright orange seeds. *Euonymus europaeus* 'Red Cascade' is the best cultivar, with

AUTUMN BULBS UNDER TREES

Some of the loveliest autumn-flowering bulbs are at home under the dappled shade of trees. They provide additional color and interest at ground level, and their pink and purple flowers form an attractive contrast with the hot autumn shades in the canopy.

Cyclamen hederifolium (**1**) (Z. 7–9) is a particularly successful autumn-flowering bulb, and will eventually colonize an area with its delicate sugar pink, lilac, and white blooms, followed by attractively marbled, ivy-shaped leaves. *Colchicum autumnale* (**2**) (Z. 3–9) produces large, crocuslike blooms that open from slender naked buds; it is especially effective emerging from a carpet of ivy and fallen leaves.

Euonymus europaeus 'Red Cascade'

The hawthorn *Crataegus persimilis* **'Prunifolia'** (Zones 4–7) is the ideal small tree for multiseasonal interest. It is compact in habit, with a rounded head when young, broadening in maturity. The rounded, glossy green leaves turn rich shades of gold, orange, and red in fall, and

138

GOOD AUTUMN COLOR ON CHALK *Acer platanoides* 'Crimson King' • *Crataegus persimilis* 'Prunifolia' •

exceptional color and masses of large fruits. *Euonymus phellomanus* (Zones 4–8) is also free-fruiting, with pink fruits that contain orange seeds; the autumn color is softer, in shades of pink, pale yellow, and mauve.

Fraxinus excelsior (Zones 5–8), the British native ash, usually colors soft yellow in fall but is not particularly noted for its display. However, some of its forms are more striking. *Fraxinus excelsior* **'Jaspidea'** is a vigorous selection that matures into a large, spreading tree with yellow young wood that shines at the branch tips in winter. The autumn color is spectacular, and the fernlike foliage is transformed into a golden yellow cloud.

Fraxinus americana 'Autumn Purple'

Fraxinus angustifolia 'Raywood'

Fraxinus excelsior 'Jaspidea'

is still ablaze with color in late fall. When the final few leaves drop, the curious winged, corky bark that covers trunk and twigs remains a feature throughout winter. The leaves of *Liquidambar styraciflua* **'Worplesdon'** (Zones 5–9) are particularly elegant; they are divided into long, narrow lobes and color orange and yellow as well as scarlet in fall. *Liquidambar styraciflua* **'Lane Roberts'** (Zones 5–9) is regarded as one of the best liquidambars for autumn color. The leaves turn dramatically to very dark crimson-purple shades with deep red highlights.

Liquidambar styraciflua 'Worplesdon'

Fraxinus angustifolia **'Raywood'** (Zones 6–9) is smaller and has finer, shinier, deep green foliage. In fall its light and airy, rounded canopy gradually turns to rich plum-purple, often streaked with garnet and amber. It is relatively compact in habit, so is often used as a street tree; an added bonus is that its fine leaves will not block drains or gutters when they fall.

Fraxinus americana **'Autumn Purple'** (Zones 3–9) is a lovely form of the white

ash, with a conical habit and dark green leaves that turn reddish purple in fall.

If space allows for a large tree, and the soil is not shallow chalk, **liquidambar** is an excellent choice for autumn color. Often mistaken for a maple (*Acer*), but more closely related to witch hazel (*Hamamelis*), liquidambar produces the most amazing, long-lasting autumnal displays. The first signs of rich wine shades in the foliage canopy appear in late summer, and the tree

Euonymus europaeus 'Red Cascade' • *Fraxinus excelsior* 'Jaspidea' • *Malus tschonoskii* • *Parrotia persica* • *Prunus sargentii* •

CRAB APPLES (MALUS)

The fruiting crab apples, *Malus*, are well known for their beautiful apple blossom in late spring. (See pages 127–28.) Often fragrant, some varieties also work as effective pollinators for apples grown for their fruit. Several varieties have attractive purple- or red-tinged foliage, and many have showy fruits that often persist on the branches after the leaves have fallen. The fruits of some varieties are large and succulent and can be used to make preserves; they are also popular with birds and wildlife.

Malus 'John Downie' (Z. 4–8) is the best crab for edible fruits. It is a small tree of conical habit, with white apple-blossom flowers in spring, followed by conical, bright orange and red fruits, which make delicious crabapple jelly. It is an excellent pollinator for apples, so is well worth growing in any productive garden.

Malus 'Neville Copeman' (1) (Z. 4–8) is a small, spreading tree with light purple flowers and purple-tinted green leaves. The orange-red fruits, which are conical and rounded, have a waxy bloom and hang from slender branches.

Malus × *robusta* (Z. 4–7) is a vigorous, medium-sized, spreading, disease-resistant tree that is often referred to and sold incorrectly as the Siberian crab. White or blush-pink flowers are followed by cherrylike fruits that vary in color from yellow to red. *Malus* × *robusta* 'Red Sentinel' (2) is often regarded as the best fruiting crab. Single white flowers in spring are followed by clusters of shiny, deep red fruits that last well into winter.

Malus 'Sun Rival' (3) (Z. 4–8) is a disease-resistant improvement on the popular variety *Malus* × *scheideckeri* 'Red Jade'. A small weeping tree with dark stems, it has pink buds that open to white flowers, followed by small red fruits that last well.

Malus 'White Star' (Z. 4–8) is a compact and disease-resistant small tree of strong constitution. Starry white flowers are followed by golden yellow fruits, which persist after the leaves have fallen and last until midwinter.

Malus × *zumi* 'Golden Hornet' (4) (Z. 4–7) is an attractive small, pyramidal tree with profuse apple-blossom flowers that open pink from white buds in spring. The large crop of miniature, applelike fruits starts to ripen in early fall, becoming rich golden yellow. The fruits may last into winter if the birds do not take them. If left on the tree they decay on the branches, leaving messy brown fruits that may persist throughout winter—the main disadvantage of growing this otherwise lovely variety.

Nyssa sylvatica

Parrotia persica

Native to North America, **Nyssa sylvatica** (Zones 3–9), the tupelo or sour gum, is renowned for the brilliance of its scarlet, orange, and yellow autumn color. A specimen in full color is a magnificent sight and provides a strong focal point in the autumn landscape. Broadly columnar in shape, it is slow-growing, but even a young specimen has presence. This species likes a rich, moist, acid soil and is often chosen for a waterside location. There are a number of exceptional named clones; the best-known, **Nyssa sylvatica 'Sheffield Park'**, which was raised at the garden of the same name in Sussex, England, starts to turn brilliant orange-red earlier than other tupelos. All tupelos resent disturbance and must be planted as young container-grown plants.

While most trees produce richer autumn color on acidic or neutral soils, **Parrotia persica** (Zones 4–8), the Persian ironwood, is an exception, being equally happy on alkaline soil. The leaves of the

OTHER GOOD MALUS FOR FRUIT   *Malus* × *atrosanguinea* 'Gorgeous' • *Malus bhutanica* • *Malus* 'Butterball'

ironwood change from deep green to rich mahogany, red, and orange, and persist on the tree. As this parrotia matures, it forms a spreading, open bowl-shaped small tree of great beauty; it is perfect as a specimen or as the centerpiece in a large bed. (See Good Companions, below.)

The majority of **ornamental cherries** are grown for their spring blossom. Few have remarkable summer foliage, but some have stunning autumn color. *Prunus sargentii* (Zones 5–9) has attractive chestnut-brown bark and bronze new leaves in spring, as well as single pink flowers, which smother the branches

Prunus 'Shirotae'

Prunus sargentii

in early spring. The best feature of the tree, however, is its autumn color, which develops in early fall, when the leaves turn luminous shades of orange and pinkish red. It is a lovely round-headed tree, reaching 30 ft (10 m) or so. (See Good Companions, right, and page 121.) The upright cultivar *Prunus sargentii* **'Rancho'** also colors well in fall and is ideal for smaller spaces. (See page 89.)

Many of the large-flowered Japanese cherries develop good autumn color. The lovely semidouble, white-flowered *Prunus* **'Shirotae'** (Zones 6–9) is no exception. The leaves, which are carried elegantly on horizontally spreading branches, turn golden orange. (See also page 123.)

GOOD COMPANIONS

The orange lanterns of *Physalis alkekengi* var. *franchetii* (Z. 4–7) make interesting ground cover beneath the shiny brown bark and warm, glowing autumn tints of *Prunus sargentii* (1) (Z. 5–9).

The deep rich shades of *Parrotia persica* (2) (Z. 4–8) complement the stunning sapphire blue flowers and ruby brown autumn foliage of *Ceratostigma willmottianum* (3) (Z. 8).

141

Malus 'Evereste' • *Malus hupehensis* • *Malus transitoria* • *Malus tschonoskii* • *Malus yunnanensis* •

SORBUS

There are many excellent varieties of sorbus. Most have white flowers in spring, berries in fall, and occasionally fantastic autumn leaf color. With more than one season of interest, they are a good choice for the garden, particularly as they are tolerant and easy to grow on most soils. As members of the rose family, some individuals can be prone to fireblight, a disease that causes sudden death of the tree. However, sorbus are quick to reward from an early age, so the slight risk of failure is always worth taking.

Rowan and other sorbus classified as Aucuparia Section have leaves consisting of many small leaflets arranged along a central stalk, giving a fernlike effect. In small gardens, trees with smaller leaves are an advantage at leaf fall—underlying plants are less smothered, the leaves are less visible, and they break down more quickly, reducing the need for raking. The berries appear in late summer and fall, and some remain on the branches after the leaves have fallen (provided the birds do not get there first). Generally, the yellow and white berries tend to last longer on the tree than red or orange fruits.

Sorbus aucuparia var. *edulis* (**1**) (Z. 3–7) is a vigorous form of the British native mountain ash or rowan, with larger leaves and big, edible red berries that are good for making rowan jelly. It survives in cold, exposed sites.

Sorbus aucuparia var. *xanthocarpa* (**2**) (Z. 3–7) has a spreading habit and large bunches of amber-yellow berries. It may produce fruit in alternate years.

Sorbus cashmiriana (**3**) (Z. 4–7) will suit any garden. Small and open in habit, it has delicate foliage and pink spring flowers. The berries are large and pure white, carried in loose clusters; they remain on the branches in winter, after the leaves have fallen.

Sorbus commixta 'Embley' (**4**) (Z. 6–8) is an excellent small, broadly conical tree. The leaves turn glowing red in fall, at the same time as bunches of orange-red fruits appear.

Sorbus 'Eastern Promise' (**5**) (Z. 4–7) is a small, oval-headed tree with dark green leaves that turn rich purple and orange in fall. The berries are deep salmon pink and weigh down the branches.

Sorbus 'Joseph Rock' (**6**) (Z. 7–8) is an outstanding small tree with a compact head, upright-branching when young, spreading with age. The leaves color in shades of deep amber-red flushed with ruby—the perfect setting for large bunches of rich yellow berries.

OTHER GOOD SORBUS FOR AUTUMN *Sorbus aucuparia* 'Sheerwater Seedling' • *Sorbus* 'Chinese Lace' •

Quercus rubra

Quercus coccinea 'Splendens'

Rhus typhina

Sorbus 'Sunshine' (**7**) (Z. 5–7) makes a good alternative to 'Joseph Rock'. It is small and upright, with dark glossy green leaves, and the attractive large, golden yellow fruits are freely produced.

Sorbus hupehensis (**8**) (Z. 6–8) is a small, vigorous tree of compact habit, with upright branches and distinctive blue-green leaves. The pink-tinged white berries are freely produced in large, loose clusters and remain after the leaves have turned red and fallen in autumn.

Sorbus vilmorinii (**9**) (Z. 6–8) is another good choice for a small garden. A tree of petite, spreading habit, it has clusters of fine, fernlike leaves that turn red and purple in fall. The small berries are carried in loose clusters, pinkish red at first, then pink, and finally white flushed pink.

OTHER GOOD SORBUS

Sorbus aucuparia 'Cardinal Royal' (Z. 3–7) is a small tree, upright in form, with good green foliage and plentiful bunches of bright red berries.

Sorbus aucuparia 'Streetwise' (Z. 3–7) is a vigorous but compact form of ash selected by Hillier Nurseries. It has large bunches of bright orange fruits and good foliage. Its neat habit makes it ideal for the smaller garden.

Many deciduous **oaks** retain their leaves into early winter. Generally, autumn color consists of shades of russet and gold; however, some species color more richly. *Quercus rubra* (Zones 4–8), the red oak, has large, oval, lobed leaves, matte green above and blue-green underneath. These turn red in fall, progressing to red-brown before they drop. It is a large, broad-headed, vigorous tree that will grow on any soil and tolerates air pollution. It is easier to establish and grow than the more refined *Quercus coccinea* 'Splendens' (Zones 4–8), the scarlet oak, which needs acid soil to thrive. It has shinier leaves that turn rich scarlet, the color spreading slowly through the leaf canopy and lasting into winter. *Quercus palustris* (Zones 5–8), the pin oak, also prefers neutral to acid soil but is a better garden tree. It has an elegant, conical habit when young, with horizontal branches that droop gracefully. The shiny green leaves are smaller than those of the previous two oaks, but they color just as beautifully in late autumn.

Rhus typhina (Zones 3–8), the stag's horn sumach, produces an architectural frame of irregular brown, downy branches topped with bold, fernlike foliage and dense, conelike clusters of red-brown furry fruits later in the year. In fall, the leaves reliably turn brilliant shades of scarlet, orange, and gold. Although this small plant has many good characteristics, it is often cursed by gardeners for its suckering habit and tendency to be invasive. *Rhus typhina* 'Dissecta' has deeply cut leaflets, giving it a lighter, prettier foliage effect.

143

Winter

Deciduous trees become more dominant in winter—stripped of their heavy foliage mantle, they reveal their underlying form—a delicate tracery of twigs and branches. Attractive bark is also on display now. Evergreens and conifers defy the col der weather, retaining their foliage and, in some cases, their fruits and cones. A few brave plants even manage delicate flowers, their blooms being all the more noticeable without competition from the more flamboyant characters of the spring and summer garden.

The filigree framework of deciduous trees is revealed in winter as the mantle of leaves slips away.

TREES WITH LOVELY BARK

The snake-bark maples are wonderful small to medium-sized trees that deserve wider planting in gardens. In addition to beautiful bark, reminiscent of the skin of a snake, they have good, healthy foliage and an attractive shape (most are spreading), and the majority display stunning autumn color (see page 134). *Acer capillipes* (Zones 5–7) is a small tree that has bright green bark with gray-white striations. The three-lobed leaves are coral red as they emerge and turn orange and red before they fall. *Acer davidii* 'Serpentine' (Zones 5–8) is a small, more upright tree with striking, striped bark and small leaves turning orange in fall. *Acer davidii* 'George Forrest' (Zones 5–8) is a popular snake-bark maple with glorious, heavily striated green and white bark. *Acer grosseri* var. *hersii* (Zones 4–8) differs in the marbled patterning of its bark. As well as good autumn leaf color, it has long clusters of winged fruits. *Acer rufinerve* (Zones 4–8) is a larger tree with blue-green young shoots, a green trunk, and branches conspicuously marked with white vertical lines. (See also page 134.)

Acer griseum (Zones 4–7), the paper-bark maple, is the best-known tree for spectacular bark. Small, spreading, and slow-growing, it also has pretty, divided leaves that color well in fall. The older bark on the trunk and branches peels in flakes and curls to reveal shiny, cinnamon-colored bark beneath. Usually raised from seed, *Acer griseum* varies both in the character of the bark and the length of time it takes for the bark to acquire its interesting color and peeling characteristics. (See box and Good Companions, opposite.)

Acer pensylvanicum 'Erythrocladum' (Zones 3–8) is more fussy—it prefers neutral to acid, fertile soil and resents disturbance. The young shoots are brilliant salmon pink with white striations, and the older bark is ocher-yellow. This broadly upright maple is usually grown as a multi-

GROWING ACER GRISEUM

Acer griseum (**1**) (Z. 4–7) is a superb small tree that contributes year-round interest and will grow on most soils. It is ideal in a small space, and will stand as a specimen tree as well as associating effectively with ground-cover perennials and grasses. This tree does not transplant easily when mature, and is therefore usually offered as a small container-grown plant. Patience is needed to see it reach maturity; if faster results are required in a planting scheme, choose **Prunus serrula** (**2**) (see page 150).

Acer davidii 'Serpentine'

Acer grosseri var. *hersii*

Acer pensylvanicum 'Erythrocladum'

stemmed specimen, branching from just above ground level—this brings the showier young shoots closer to eye-level and increases the tree's vigor. It is always planted as a young pot-grown specimen, and needs cutting back when young to encourage growth. **Acer × conspicuum**

'Phoenix' (Zones 6–9) is similar but the color is stronger. The young shoots are bright red, finely streaked with white. It also needs acid conditions and is seen at its best with witch hazels and other subjects grown for their winter stems. (See Good Companions, below.)

GOOD COMPANIONS

The brilliant, upright coral shoots of *Acer × conspicuum* 'Phoenix' (1) (Z. 6–9) contrast with the horizontal branches and soft yellow flowers of the witch hazel *Hamamelis × intermedia* 'Pallida' (2) (Z. 5–8).

The peeling cinnamon bark of *Acer griseum* (3) (Z. 4–7) complements the flame-colored twigs of *Cornus sanguinea* 'Winter Beauty' (4) (Z. 5–8) in winter, and the cornus' yellow-green foliage in summer.

The dark twigs and white stems of this stand of *Betula pendula*, the silver birch, are well displayed against a blue winter sky.

Betula nigra

Birches are the ultimate trees for winter. Their delicate, elegant silhouettes are unique, and their bark—in shades of white, salmon, tan, and cream—is unsurpassable. Birches have the advantage of a light canopy and often a narrow spread, making them ideal for gardens of all sizes, and allowing cultivation of other plants beneath them. The color and character of their bark presents many possibilities for exciting planting combinations.

One of the most exquisite birches, native to China, is ***Betula albosinensis*** var. ***septentrionalis*** (Zones 5–6). A medium-sized tree, it has matte green leaves and

Betula ermanii

Betula albosinensis 'Bowling Green'

gray-pink bark, coppery pink on the branches. ***Betula albosinensis*** 'Bowling Green' (Zones 5–6) is a lovely form, with distinctive honey-brown peeling bark.

The beautiful ***Betula ermanii*** (Zones 5–6) is a large, conical tree distinguished from other birches by its silky smooth, creamy white or pinkish bark, which is marked with pale coffee-colored lenticels. These are corky, slightly raised areas that run softly across the trunk and protect the breathing pores of the bark. It has one of the most tactile trunks of any tree, with the feel of fine, soft leather. The leaves are large, bright green, and almost heart-shaped. (See Good Companions, opposite.)

Betula ermanii 'Grayswood Hill' v selected for its outstanding creamy wh bark. It is often offered as a substitute the rare and choice ***Betula costata*** (Zo 5–8), which it closely resembles.

Betula maximowicziana (Zones 4– the monarch birch, is a giant amc birches, reaching 70 ft. (20 m) in gc growing conditions. It is a vigorous, bro growing tree with large, heart-shap green leaves that turn clear yellow fall. The trunk is orange-brown, eventu becoming gray and pink; it peels in narr strips, giving a ringed appearance. branches are copper-brown.

Betula nigra (Zones 4–9), the ri birch, is rugged and spreading, a medi to large tree with bigger leaves than m birches and pink and orange, shaggy b that flutters in the wind and catches the l winter light. On older specimens, the tru becomes brown and ridged. It is ideal damp and waterside locations, but also grow on dry soils. The larger lea and heavy canopy cast more shade th other birches. ***Betula nigra*** 'Herita is an outstanding selection, with ligh orange-brown bark.

Betula pendula

Betula pendula 'Tristis'

Betula pendula 'Youngii'

The British native common silver birch, or lady of the woods, **Betula pendula** (Zones 3–7), is a medium-sized tree with dark, rough, warty twigs and small, diamond-shaped leaves with serrated edges. Forms vary in habit and in the whiteness of the trunk, but the species is easily distinguished from other birches by its more craggy bark with vertical charcoal fissures. *Betula pendula* grows in most soils, acid and chalky, but it is sensitive to salt spray, so is unsuitable for coastal gardens. There are many forms and cultivars; their advantage over other birches is their small leaves, which cast less shade and are also less of a problem at leaf fall.

Betula pendula 'Tristis' is the most graceful silver birch—tall and slim with slender, hanging branches. Its silhouette is unmistakable, and it is one of the best garden trees for adding height without weight. The leaves turn yellow in fall. **Betula pendula** 'Laciniata', the Swedish birch, is often sold, incorrectly, as *Betula pendula* 'Dalecarlica'. It is tall and elegant, with drooping branchlets and prettily cut leaves. Unfortunately it can be affected by rust, which causes the leaves to discolor and drop. **Betula pendula** 'Youngii', Young's weeping birch, is a much smaller tree, forming a dense, domed, twiggy head. Although small in stature, it is spreading and needs space, so is not the best choice for a small garden, even

Betula utilis

though it is often recommended for this purpose. It can be striking in shape when mature, but can also look awkward and ungainly, and is often ruined by poor pruning in an attempt to control its size.

Betula utilis (Zones 4–7), the Himalayan birch, is a beautiful light tree. It is best known for its forms with white bark, but the bark of the species itself varies, often being coppery pink and peeling with a

GOOD COMPANIONS

The white flowers of the winter-flowering heath *Erica* × *darleyensis* 'White Perfection' (1) (Z. 4–7) look superb surrounding the chalk white bark of *Betula utilis* var. *jacquemontii* 'Grayswood Ghost' (2) (Z. 4–7).

The fine, coppery foliage of the sedge *Carex comans* bronze-leaved (3) (Z. 7–9) continues the pinkish color of the bark of *Betula ermanii* (4) (Z. 5–6) on to the ground, beneath the light canopy of the tree.

THE WHITE-BARKED HIMALAYAN BIRCHES

There are numerous named selections of *Betula utilis* var. *jacquemontii* (Z. 4–7), each differing slightly in the whiteness of their bark, their ultimate size, and the color and texture of their leaves. They are extremely similar, and are easily confused by the gardener and nurseryman. A good specimen of any of the following will make a magnificent tree in any garden.

Betula utilis var. *jacquemontii* 'Doorenbos' ('Snow Queen') has striking white, peeling bark from an early age; it is apricot when it is first exposed.

Betula utilis var. *jacquemontii* 'Grayswood Ghost' (1) has bright, white bark and glossy green leaves. (See Good Companions, page 147.)

Betula utilis var. *jacquemontii* 'Jermyns' (2) is large and vigorous, retaining its fine white bark into maturity. The catkins are long and showy, and the foliage is healthy and free from rust.

Betula utilis var. *jacquemontii* 'Silver Shadow' (3) is smaller, with a dazzling white trunk and drooping dark green leaves.

GETTING THE BEST FROM BIRCH STEMS

As birches mature, some selective thinning of the lower branches is desirable, to expose the bark of the mature branches and trunk and show it to its best advantage. This should be done in early winter, after the leaves have fallen. A sharp pruning saw is the best tool to remove some of the small side-shoots, cutting them off close to the main branches. Thinning the canopy in this way will allow more light and rain to pass through to plants beneath when the tree is in leaf. Green algae and dirt often detract from the whiteness of white-barked birches. This is easily removed with clean water and a soft scrubbing brush; the improved brilliance of the stems is well worth the effort.

Betula szechuanica

gray-pink bloom. The shape is broadly conical, the leaves are relatively large and diamond-shaped, and in spring the twigs carry long, greenish yellow catkins that dance in the breeze. The naturally occurring form with white bark is **Betula utilis var. jacquemontii** (Zones 4–7), which is widely grown as a single-stemmed tree or as a multi-stemmed specimen, both on its own and in groups. There are numerous cultivars (see box, left.) All forms of the Himalayan birch grow on most soils, and will tolerate exposed positions.

The recently selected **Betula utilis 'Fascination'** (sometimes known as *Betula albosinensis* 'Fascination'; Zones 4–7) is an outstanding medium-sized to large tree with an oval or a conical habit. It has large, dark green leaves and showy yellow catkins in spring. The bark color is quite spectacular: orange peeling to peach-pink and cream. It is an easy cultivar to grow, thriving on most soils.

Betula szechuanica (Zones 4–7) is a good alternative to the *Betula utilis* var. *jacquemontii* cultivars. A vigorous tree of medium size and conical in shape, it has glossy blue-green leaves and dazzling white bark that looks stunning in the low light of winter.

GOOD PLANTING PARTNERS

White-barked birches and eucalyptus make stunning planting partners, provided you have the space. At Marwood Hill, Devon, in England, they are planted as a naturalistic grove in grass. This is a scheme that would work well in a large garden or paddock, where the white stems of both trees would make a dramatic focal point in winter.

Like birches, **eucalyptus** are renowned for their beautiful bark. They are at their best in winter, when the outer layer of many species falls away in long, curling strips.

Eucalyptus dalrympleana (Zones 9–11) is a superb medium-sized, broadly columnar tree, and may be grown as a single or multi-stemmed specimen. The patchwork bark of summer becomes silver-white in winter on mature trees. *Eucalyptus pauciflora* ssp. *niphophila* (Zones 8–10) is more suitable for small gardens and has snakeskinlike bark in shades of soft green, gray, and cream. (See pages 68–69.)

The golden ash, *Fraxinus excelsior* 'Jaspidea' (Zones 5–8), is striking in winter, with golden yellow young shoots and black

Eucalyptus dalrympleana

Fraxinus excelsior 'Jaspidea'

buds. The older branches are yellowish, but the bark of the main trunk matures to the characteristic smooth gray of the common ash (*Fraxinus excelsior*). A large, spreading tree, it is at its best while young, when its regular branching habit makes it look like an ornate golden candelabra. However, young trees can suffer from frost damage. *Fraxinus excelsior* 'Allgold' is similar, but it is tougher and better for cold areas. Both have beautiful clear yellow autumn leaf color (see page 139); this display makes up for some of the loss of stem color in mature trees.

Certain **cherries** are grown more for their bark than for their flowers or foliage. *Prunus maackii* 'Amber Beauty' (Zones 2–6), a form of the Manchurian cherry, is a delightful small tree with shining, smooth, amber-colored bark that glows in the winter sun. It has a narrow, conical head of upward-sweeping branches and attractive green leaves. The flowers are more like those of the cherry laurel (*Prunus laurocerasus*) than those of the larger-flowered cherries. 'Amber Beauty' is a versatile tree that mixes well with shrubs and perennials in mixed plantings. It is a good choice to give height to any planting of shrubs grown for their winter stems. (See Good Companions, left.)

GOOD COMPANIONS

The spidery orange flowers of the witch hazel *Hamamelis* × *intermedia* 'Orange Peel' (1) (Z. 5–8) form a striking contrast with the smooth, polished amber bark of the cherry *Prunus maackii* 'Amber Beauty' (2) (Z. 2–6).

The blue-green foliage and lime green flowers of *Euphorbia characias* (3) (Z. 8–9) complement the polished mahogany bark of the Tibetan cherry, *Prunus serrula* (Z. 5–8) or *Prunus* × *schmittii* (4) (Z. 5–8).

WINTER

149

Prunus serrula

Prunus × schmittii

Salix alba var. vitellina 'Britzensis'

Prunus sargentii (Zones 5–9) has shiny, deep chestnut-brown bark banded with rougher, darker areas. The head has a spreading habit and produces a cloud of single, sugar pink early flowers, before the relatively large, new coppery leaves appear. The foliage colors early in fall in a magnificent cocktail of orange, red, and flame. (See pages 121 and 141.) *Prunus serrula* (Zones 5–8), the Tibetan cherry,

tree if three young specimens are planted together in the same hole. Where a taller tree is needed, *Prunus × schmittii* (Zones 5–8) is a good alternative. A fast-growing, upright, medium-sized tree, it has shiny, dark mahogany bark ringed with darker brown streaks and small pink flowers in spring. The foliage is usually better than that of *Prunus serrula*. (See Good Companions, page 149.)

as shrubs (see box, below.) Where space permits, *Salix daphnoides* (Zones 2–9), the violet willow, works well in naturalistic plantings on wet soil—it has long, violet-purple shoots that are overlaid with a fine white bloom. (See pages 114–15.)

Salix alba var. vitellina

is a lovely small tree with glistening red-brown bark, like polished mahogany. The rounded head of dark twigs produces an early display of small, single white flowers followed by green, willowlike leaves. Neither leaves nor flowers are remarkable, but the bark is spectacular throughout the year, particularly in the low light of winter. It is a good alternative to *Acer griseum*, as it is faster and easier to grow and can be planted as a more mature specimen. It also makes an attractive multi-stemmed

Some **willows** have brightly colored young stems that will rival the brilliance of any dogwoods (*Cornus*) in winter. *Salix alba* var. *vitellina* 'Britzensis' ('Chermesina'; Zones 2–9), the scarlet willow, is a vigorous large tree with young branches of vivid scarlet-orange that look striking against a blue winter sky. *Salix alba* var. *vitellina* is less vigorous, with young shoots of bright egg-yolk yellow. Both enjoy wet soil conditions and respond well to hard pruning, pollarding or stooling

BRIGHTER WINTER STEMS

Salix alba varieties (Z. 2–9) and *Salix daphnoides* (Z. 2–9), which are grown for their colorful winter stems, need hard pruning every few years in early spring to promote long, straight, vigorous stems of strong color. If they are grown as shrubs, they can be stooled, which means cut right down to ground level. As trees, they are usually pollarded, which involves cutting back to the same point each time, to create a thick trunk crowned with a head of long, straight, colored stems. The stems can be used for floral decorations.

CONIFERS FOR WINTER FOLIAGE

All conifers look good in winter; their foliage responds to the wetter conditions and colder temperatures. Some change or intensify their color as the season progresses, making a dramatic impact in the winter garden.

Cryptomeria japonica Elegans Group (1) (Z. 6–8), a lovely form of the Japanese cedar, has a tall, bushy habit, eventually developing into a narrow, fluffy tree. Soft, feathery, evergreen foliage of deep sea green turns red-brown in fall and winter.

Picea pungens 'Koster' (2) (Z. 2–7) is the finest form of the blue spruce, growing to form a small, conical, evergreen 'Christmas' tree with intensely silver-blue needles, especially brilliant at the tips of the branches. The color is best on acid soil and in areas with clean air.

Pinus sylvestris Aurea Group (3) (Z. 2–8) is a slow-growing form of the Scots pine, making a small, columnar, evergreen tree with bristling needles of yellowish green. In winter, the color intensifies to golden yellow. (See also page 57.)

Salix babylonica var. pekinensis 'Tortuosa'

Pinus sylvestris

Metasequoia glyptostroboides

Salix babylonica var. *pekinensis* 'Tortuosa' (Zones 6–9), the dragon's-claw willow, is a small upright tree with twisted and contorted branches that are particularly effective in winter, when they contrast strongly with the straight wands of shrubs grown for their winter stems. *Salix* 'Erythroflexuosa' (Zones 5–9) is a small, weeping tree with similarly contorted shoots that are pendulous in habit and an attractive yellow-orange color.

CONIFERS WITH BEAUTIFUL BARK

Some mature conifers have spectacular bark, which seems to come alive in the low winter sun. The British native Scots pine, *Pinus sylvestris* (Zones 2–8), is usually seen as a large, tall, columnar tree of great character, with dark grayish brown, furrowed older bark and characteristic reddish brown younger bark on the branches. It grows on all soil types, but it is often found in larger gardens, underplanted with flowering shrubs.

Pinus bungeana (Zones 4–8), the lace-bark pine, has the most beautiful bark of all the pines. Smooth and gray-green, it flakes and falls away, creating a beautiful patchwork of white, yellow, purple, green, and brown. A small tree or large shrub, it is better than many pines for cultivation in the average garden, and is particularly useful for Asian planting schemes.

The handsome, large deciduous conifer *Metasequoia glyptostroboides* (Zones 4–8), the dawn redwood, has shaggy, cinnamon-brown bark on a tapering trunk that supports an elegant conical head of horizontal branches. It is beautiful in winter, with colorful stems and trunk and a striking silhouette. For wet soil, the swamp cypress, *Taxodium distichum* (Zones 4–10), has similar characteristics. (See page 116.)

Acacia dealbata

and *Prunus × subhirtella* 'Autumnalis Rosea' (Zones 5–8), with pink blossoms. These small trees have a light habit and pale brown twigs and branches that usually spread horizontally on mature specimens. The delicate, small, semidouble flowers are produced intermittently from late fall to early spring in spells of mild weather. In recent years, many varieties of *Prunus × subhirtella* have become infected by bacterial canker, causing wilting of the blossoms and later the leaves. Usually, trees recover only to produce a thinner canopy of leaves and suffer further problems the following winter. This condition is exacerbated by mild, damp winters and makes the long-term value of these lovely trees questionable in gardens.

THE GLASTONBURY THORN

Crataegus monogyna 'Biflora' (Z. 4–7), the Glastonbury hawthorn, is a curiosity rather than a good garden tree. A variety of the British native hawthorn, it produces its leaves early and occasionally has a small crop of flowers in mid- to late winter. Legend has it that after the death of Christ, Joseph of Arimathea came to Britain to spread the message of Christianity. He lay down to rest at Glastonbury, England, plunging the staff that he had brought from the Holy Land into the ground by his side. The next morning, he found that it had taken root and produced leaves and flowers. The tree and its offspring still bloom every winter and spring to this day, and a branch is sent to the British monarch every year, shortly after Christmas.

WINTER-FLOWERING TREES

The showiest of the winter-flowering trees is the florist's mimosa or silver wattle, *Acacia dealbata* (Zones 10–11). A fast-growing tree, it will quickly grow to 30 ft. (10 m) high, with a light, feathery form and very fine, fernlike foliage. In early winter, sprays of tiny round, light green buds appear; these open in late winter into frothy bouquets of bright yellow, fluffy flowers with a sweet marzipan fragrance. A native of Australia, this acacia needs a fairly mild climate; in colder zones, the frost can cause the leaves to drop. It also needs some shelter, as the branches become heavy when the flowers open and are liable to break, especially under the weight of heavy rain or snow. It is often grown as a wall shrub against a high, sunny wall. *Acacia dealbata* can be pruned to control size, but this may result in the production of a mass of suckers from the base of the plant. Light pruning after flowering to control size and promote bushiness is the best approach.

Most winter-flowering trees are varieties of prunus, the best known and most widely planted of which are the pretty, white-flowered ornamental cherry *Prunus × subhirtella* 'Autumnalis' (Zones 5–8)

OTHER TREES WITH ATTRACTIVE BARK *Acer × conspicuum* 'Silver Vein' • *Alnus incana* 'Aurea' •

Prunus × subhirtella 'Autumnalis Rosea'

Prunus incisa 'February Pink'

Prunus incisa 'Kojo-no-mai'

Prunus incisa (Zones 5–7), the Fuji cherry, has been cultivated by the Japanese for centuries for bonsai. A lovely light, dainty tree, it has the advantage of small, neat leaves and excellent autumn color as well as a mass of delicate early flowers. *Prunus incisa* 'February Pink' bears small, pale pink flowers in profusion in late winter. *Prunus incisa* 'Praecox' can bloom even earlier, with pink buds opening to pretty white flowers. The shrubby, dwarf cultivar, *Prunus incisa* 'Kojo-no-mai', flowers later, usually in early spring, with a mass of delicate white, pink-tinged blooms on fine, zigzag twigs. It makes an excellent subject for a pot and can be easily pruned and trained to create a garden 'bonsai' (see pages 92–93).

Prunus mume (Zones 6–8), Japanese apricot, is a lovely small, spreading tree with single pink, almond-blossom flowers on bare branches. It normally flowers in early spring, but in mild weather will often open its blooms in late winter. *Prunus mume* 'Alboplena' has semidouble white flowers. *Prunus mume* 'Beni-chidori' produces fragrant, semidouble flowers in clear rose-pink, with cream stamens. *Prunus mume* is unremarkable for the rest of the year, so is not a good tree for a prominent position. Stems in bud can be cut and brought into the house, where the blossoms will open in water.

Prunus mume 'Beni-chidori'

153

Arbutus × andrachnoides • *Carpinus betulus* • *Luma apiculata* • *Pinus pinaster* • *Tilia cordata* 'Winter Orange' •

Authors' choice:
some of the best trees for general planting

Here is a selection of trees that have proved to be reliable performers in the majority of situations and soil conditions. All give a long season of interest with their form and foliage, sometimes with the added bonus of blossom, catkins, or attractive bark. A tree is chosen for its shape or ultimate size, or perhaps for its speed of growth or habit. In this selection there is a tree for any garden, however small or large.

SMALL ULTIMATE SIZE 15–30 FT. (5–10 M)   **MEDIUM-SIZED** ULTIMATE SIZE 30–60 FT. (10–20 M)   **LARGE** ULTIMATE SIZE OVER 60 FT. (20 M)

SMALL ROUND-HEADED TREES

Prunus cerasifera 'Nigra' (Z. 3–8; pages 60, 61, 120) Perhaps the best purple-foliage tree, with a dense rounded head and clouds of delicate pink blossoms in early spring.

Also…

Acer platanoides 'Globosum' (Z. 3–7; p108)
Crataegus laevigata 'Paul's Scarlet' (Z. 4–7; p126)
Sorbus 'Joseph Rock' (Z. 7–8; p142)

MEDIUM-SIZED ROUND-HEADED TREES

Acer platanoides 'Drummondii' (Z. 3–7; page 63) Excellent variegated tree with large maple leaves broadly edged with cream. Light but bold rounded form.

Also…

Fraxinus angustifolia 'Raywood' (Z. 6–9; p139)
Malus hupehensis (Z. 4–8; p102)
Sorbus aria 'Lutescens' (Z. 5–6; p71)

LARGE ROUND-HEADED TREES

Fagus sylvatica Atropurpurea Group (Z. 4–7; page 95) Magnificent copper beech; young leaves turn deep purple in summer; golden brown autumn foliage hangs on in winter.

Also…

Aesculus hippocastanum 'Baumannii' (Z. 3–7; p95)
Juglans regia (Z. 4–9; p102)
Quercus ilex (Z. 7–9; p77, 97)

SMALL TO MEDIUM-SIZED CONICAL TREES

Pyrus calleryana 'Chanticleer' (Z. 4–8; page 89) Elegant upright tree with white flowers in early spring and good foliage color in fall; the leaves persist on the tree well into winter.

Also…

Acer campestre 'Streetwise' (Z. 4–8; p108)
Alnus × *spaethii* (Z. 2–7; p113, 129)
Carpinus betulus 'Fastigiata' (Z. 4–8; p91, 109)

MEDIUM-SIZED AND LARGE BROADLY CONICAL TREES

Betula utilis var. *jacquemontii* 'Jermyns' (Z. 4–7; pages 129, 148) Tall and vigorous but light and airy tree with striking white bark and long, showy golden catkins borne in early spring.

Also…

Corylus colurna (Z. 4–7; p110)
Metasequoia glyptostroboides (Z. 4–8; p151)
Quercus palustris (Z. 5–8; p143)

SMALL TO MEDIUM-SIZED COLUMNAR TREES

Prunus 'Amanogawa' (Z. 6–9; pages 88–89) Slim tree with fragrant, semidouble pink blossoms in mid-spring. Ideal in a confined space. Branches from near ground level.

Also…

Fagus sylvatica 'Dawyck Purple' (Z. 4–7; p60–61, 110)
Prunus sargentii 'Rancho' (Z. 5–9; p89)
Taxus baccata 'Fastigiata' (Z. 6–7; p90)

SMALL TO MEDIUM-SIZED BROADLY COLUMNAR TREES

Sorbus hupehensis (Z. 6–8; page 143) Compact, vigorous tree with bluish green foliage. White flowers in spring are followed by clusters of pink-tinged white berries that hang on after the leaves have fallen.

Also...

Alnus incana 'Aurea' (Z. 2–7; p129)
Robinia pseudoacacia 'Frisia' (Z. 3–8; p57)
Sorbus aucuparia 'Cardinal Royal' (Z. 3–7; p143)

LARGE BROADLY COLUMNAR TO OVAL TREES

Liriodendron tulipifera (Z. 4–9; page 96) Fine specimen tree for a big space; distinctive leaves with concave tips turn butter yellow in fall; mature trees flower in summer.

Also...

Quercus frainetto 'Hungarian Crown' (Z. 6–8; p97)
Salix alba var. *vitellina* 'Britzensis' (Z. 2–9; p114)
Tilia tomentosa (Z. 4–7; p133)

SMALL SPREADING TREES

Crataegus persimilis 'Prunifolia' (Z. 4–7; pages 88, 138) Small hawthorn with a compact but spreading head. White flowers in spring are followed by large red berries in fall, when the glossy leaves turn red and yellow.

Also...

Malus transitoria (Z. 4–7; p103, 128)
Parrotia persica (Z. 4–8; p140)
Prunus 'Shirotae' (Z. 6–9; p123)

SMALL WEEPING TREES

Pyrus salicifolia 'Pendula' (Z. 4–7; pages 70, 89) Gracefully weeping tree with narrow, silver, willowlike leaves and white flowers in spring. Adds height to a mixed border.

Also...

Betula pendula 'Youngii' (Z. 3–7; p147)
Cotoneaster 'Hybridus Pendulus' (Z. 6–9; p73, 87)
Malus 'Royal Beauty' (Z. 3–7; p88)

LIGHT AND AIRY TREES

Betula pendula 'Tristis' (Z. 3–7; page 147) Tall, slim birch with white, fissured stems and hanging branches. Small leaves and a light canopy make this an ideal subject to provide height in a small space.

Also...

Alnus glutinosa 'Imperialis' (Z. 3–7; p100)
Eucalyptus pauciflora ssp. *niphophila* (Z. 8–10; p69)
Gleditsia triacanthos 'Sunburst' (Z. 3–9; p56)

LARGE FAST-GROWING TREES

Eucalyptus dalrympleana (Z. 9–11; pages 68, 149) Evergreen gray-green leaves and patchwork bark that whitens as the tree matures. Copes well with exposed situations.

Also...

Acer platanoides 'Crimson King' (Z. 3–7; p58, 59, 60)
Alnus cordata (Z. 4–6; p109)
Salix alba var. *vitellina* 'Britzensis' (Z. 2–9; p114)

SMALLER FAST-GROWING TREES

Robinia pseudoacacia 'Frisia' (Z. 3–8; page 57) Golden yellow, pinnate leaves from spring to fall, with color richest in late summer. Striking from an early age; a good subject for new gardens.

Also...

Cotoneaster frigidus 'Cornubia' (Z. 7–9; p73, 75)
Malus 'Directeur Moerlands' (Z. 4–8; p61)
Sorbus hupehensis (Z. 6–8; p143)

TREES TO PLANT FOR THE FUTURE

Liquidambar styraciflua (Z. 5–9; pages 65, 139) Long-lived and ultimately large tree with spectacular long-lasting autumn foliage color. It is attractive from an early age, giving joy today and tomorrow.

Also...

Cedrus libani (Z. 6–9; p94, 99)
Cercis siliquastrum (Z. 6–9; p87)
Quercus rubra (Z. 4–8; p143)

Index

Suffix 'i' in page references indicates an illustration. Page references with suffix 'b' refer to bottom strip only. The letter 'z.' refers to USDA zones.

INDEX

PICTURE CREDITS

The publishers would like to
acknowledge with thanks all
those whose gardens are
pictured in this book.

All photography by Andrew McIndoe
and John Hillier except:

Pip Bensley 44(10), 49GC4, 70e,
71GC2, 80b, 102(3)
Sue Gordon 64(1)

Kevin Hobbs 33d, 34(5), 43g, 44(9),
57(1), 66a, 67(6), 79(7), 96b, 131e,
137a, 138(1)
Julian Holland 152b
Jane Sterndale-Bennett 153b
Robin Whitecross 40(1).